BeagleBone Black Cookbook

Over 60 recipes and solutions for inventors, makers, and budding engineers to create projects using the BeagleBone Black

Charles A. Hamilton

BIRMINGHAM – MUMBAI

BeagleBone Black Cookbook

Copyright © 2015 Packt Publishing

First published: November 2015

Production reference: 1121115

Published by Packt Publishing Ltd.
Livery Place
35 Livery Street
Birmingham B3 2PB, UK.

ISBN 978-1-78398-292-9

www.packtpub.com

Credits

Author
Charles A. Hamilton

Reviewers
Nathan Burles
Anuj Deshpande
Deepak Karki
Agrima Seth

Commissioning Editor
Edward Gordon

Acquisition Editor
Richard Brookes-Bland

Content Development Editor
Rohit Kumar Singh

Technical Editor
Vijin Boricha

Copy Editor
Shruti Iyer

Project Coordinator
Mary Alex

Proofreader
Safis Editing

Indexer
Monica Ajmera Mehta

Production Coordinator
Conidon Miranda

Cover Work
Conidon Miranda

About the Author

Charles A. Hamilton is the owner of HudsonWerks, a New York City-based DIY hardware and development shop for new products. Passionate about emerging technologies, open source hardware, and the maker movement, his background as a "technology creative", entrepreneur, and maker provides readers with a unique perspective.

Besides BeagleBone Black, Charles works frequently with other hardware platforms, including the Raspberry Pi, Arduino, and UDOO development boards, open source board architecture and PCB design, micromechatronics, and sensors. He is also an advocate and keen user of emerging low-cost manufacturing and design tools such as 3-D printers and laser cutters. Among other subjects, Charles keenly follows advances and design challenges in the arenas of IoT, space technologies, and next-generation health and wellness devices. He writes and blogs at `http://www.hudsonwerks.com`.

He is a former creative director at AT&T and product developer at a New York City-based new product development agency. Charles' development expertise spans devices in the consumer electronics, digital media, display, voice recognition, and telecommunication markets. He is also a proud papa to his 4-year-old son, Hudson.

I would first like to acknowledge the support of Jason Kridner, the Texas Instruments embedded applications Evangelist and founder of `Beagleboard.org`, without whom this book would never have achieved liftoff. Additionally, immeasurable thanks need to go to John Reaves of Learning Worlds and Masuo Kitano of Seiko Epson Corporation, who ignited the prototyping-and-build-something-crazy spark in me. Jonathan Hirschman of PCB:NG gave it a further push by showing us the way to cook up PCBs from scratch, literally. Finally, more than thanks are necessary to the two people that showed the greatest forbearance in seeing this project to its conclusion: my wife, Mary, and little boy, Hudson. Without their encouragement, patience, and love, this book would never have happened. For this, I am humbled and grateful.

About the Reviewers

Nathan Burles is a postdoctoral researcher with a PhD in computer science. He is currently working for University of York on subjects as diverse as artificial neural networks, automated programming / software improvement, and optimization for power consumption.

In his free time, Nathan enjoys tinkering with embedded systems and electronics ranging from full systems, such as Raspberry Pi and BeagleBone Black, to simple microcontrollers, such as Arduino, adding circuitry to communicate using 433MHz RF and infrared.

He blogs about his projects and topics such as website development, Android, and dancing at `http://www.nburles.co.uk`.

Anuj Deshpande is a fan of BeagleBone Black and all things embedded. He dabbles in embedded Linux and loves to prototype ideas and build interactive installations.

Some of the projects that Anuj has been a part of are Userspace Arduino and Tah. He completed his bachelor's degree in computer science from PICT, Pune.

Anuj currently runs his own development and consulting firm called Makerville Solutions (`http://makerville.io`).

Deepak Karki is a software developer and open source Evangelist based in Bangalore, India. He enjoys working with like-minded hackers and is often a participant in hackathons in and around the city. During the day, Deepak works on challenging hyperconvergence problems with Nutanix, and in the night, he keeps busy pushing code onto GitHub.

He was a Google Summer of Code (GSoC) student for `beagleboard.org` in 2014 and, consequently, a mentor for the same organization during GSoC 2015. Deepak's main areas of interest include SaaS application development, embedded systems, parallel computing, networks, and security.

Lately, he has been heavily involved in IoT projects and is working with World Wide Web Consortium (W3C) to help standardize Internet of Things by contributing to their WoT platform.

Apart from writing code, Deepak loves teaching and working out. You can catch him at `github.com/deepakkarki` or on `#beagle` freenode IRC as `nick: karki_`.

Agrima Seth is currently a senior year student pursuing a bachelor's degree of engineering in information technology at University of Pune, India. Her research interests include machine learning and information retrieval systems. She is currently an intern with the SIG (Generalized Information Systems) research team under Professor Josiane Mothe at IRIT, France. Here, Agrima is working on performing effective data indexing and query reformulation on TREC datasets to study and create better information retrieval systems. She has been the recipient of Sir Ratan Tata Memorial Scholarship and other merit scholarships.

Apart from machine learning, Agrima has also worked on computer graphics and computer vision at Indian Institute of Space Science and Technology, India. Her work is published at arXiv (`http://arxiv.org/abs/1409.5024`). Agrima has worked on a project for Thermax India on making a mini solar tracker using MSP430. She has been involved in the creation of a machine learning group at her institute where she trained undergraduate students on various machine learning techniques and computer graphics. Agrima is a voracious reader and a trained Indian Classical dancer who enjoys participating in public speaking events.

A complete list of her work is available at `http://agrimaseth.github.io`, and the latest happenings can be read at `https://agrimaseth.wordpress.com`.

I would like to thank my parents and my HoD, Dr Sangeeta Jadhav, for constantly encouraging me to pursue my dreams and work towards achieving excellence.

www.PacktPub.com

Support files, eBooks, discount offers, and more

For support files and downloads related to your book, please visit www.PacktPub.com.

Did you know that Packt offers eBook versions of every book published, with PDF and ePub files available? You can upgrade to the eBook version at www.PacktPub.com and as a print book customer, you are entitled to a discount on the eBook copy. Get in touch with us at service@packtpub.com for more details.

At www.PacktPub.com, you can also read a collection of free technical articles, sign up for a range of free newsletters and receive exclusive discounts and offers on Packt books and eBooks.

https://www2.packtpub.com/books/subscription/packtlib

Do you need instant solutions to your IT questions? PacktLib is Packt's online digital book library. Here, you can search, access, and read Packt's entire library of books.

Why Subscribe?

- ▸ Fully searchable across every book published by Packt
- ▸ Copy and paste, print, and bookmark content
- ▸ On demand and accessible via a web browser

Free Access for Packt account holders

If you have an account with Packt at www.PacktPub.com, you can use this to access PacktLib today and view 9 entirely free books. Simply use your login credentials for immediate access.

Table of Contents

Preface

It's maker madness out there! SBCs, MCUs, FPGAs, PCBs, GPIOs, BeagleBone Black and Whites, Raspberry and Banana Pis, Odroids, Udoos, Arduinos, MCUduinos, TinyDuinos...

What does this impossible stew of acronyms and techno arcana mean? How do we make sense of it all, especially if all you want to do is make, invent, and design great whizzy things that go beep and bump and flash brightly or just grab hot data from temperature sensors? Most importantly, what to do if you are not a specialist, an engineer, or a hard-core software programmer?

This is a book precisely for those of you who want to know about BeagleBone Black but are afraid to ask, overwhelmed by its complexity, or underwhelmed by the dearth of understandable, timely information about this tiny but powerful microcomputer.

Why BeagleBone Black?

Although many of the competing small board computers (or SBCs) have their strengths, the virtues of BeagleBone Black are significant:

▸ **Physical computing options**: With its huge array of pins, you can wire up far more—be it sensors, motors, displays, or other hardware—than almost any other board on the market, even RPi.

▸ **Out-of-the-box simplicity**: As the BBB comes preloaded with a Linux OS (Debian), all you need to get going quickly is a mini USB cable to power up the board. There is no futzing around with installing software or adding peripherals to operate it.

▸ **Internal drive**: While other small board computers of this ilk can only run from an SD or microSD boot, BeagleBone Black comes with an internal solid-state drive, referred to as eMMC, to run the OS.

- ▶ **Open source design**: If you want to knock it off for a custom project, you can do it; all board designs and schematics are freely available.

- ▶ **Real-time applications**: Unlike other boards, such as Raspberry Pi, BeagleBone Black has a set of separate processors that can ensure that your code runs rock-solid and according to your expectations, which is an extremely unique feature for a computer at such a low price point.

As you begin tasting the various recipes throughout this book, perhaps a key difference worth keeping in mind is that the designers of BeagleBone Black regard the board as a prototyping platform to build embedded applications and products. An embedded computing device is typically part of a larger electronics system. This is quite unlike the design strategy of other boards, such as Raspberry Pi, which is a device specifically created as a full-blown desktop system and targeted at the grade school market.

What this book covers

This book explores a range of recipes for the novice user, gaining in complexity as the material progresses. In a nutshell, these are the chapters and their topics:

Chapter 1, *Setting Up for the First Time*, starts by booting up your board out of the box, getting it connected online, teaching how to control it remotely, and then diving into the essential Linux command-line commands.

Chapter 2, *Basic Programming Recipes*, moves briskly along to scenarios using several flavors of programming ingredients on BeagleBone Black, including BoneScript (an easy JavaScript variant for BeagleBone), Node.js, Python, and Johnny Five.

Chapter 3, *Physical Computing Recipes Using JavaScript, the BoneScript Library, and Python*, tells it like it is as we will take the recipes discussed in *Chapter 2*, *Basic Programming Recipes* and apply them to the use of buttons, sensors, LEDs, and motors.

Chapter 4, *Exploring GNU/Linux Recipes Using Bash, Autotools, Debugger, and systemd*, looks at some foundational Linux tools that you will need to bend the board to your will, tools that come in handy for a wide variety of use cases.

Chapter 5, *Basic Programming Recipes with the Linux Kernel*, helps you start putting your arms around the system kernel by installing the latest version and then building a custom kernel. We will also will cook up some mischief with one of the hallmarks of all ARM devices, Device Tree, which makes it easier to add peripherals and daughterboards to your system. We will finish using the universal cape overlay, a toolset that makes manipulating GPIO pins and Device Tree infinitely simpler.

Chapter 6, Run Faster, Run Real Time, enables you to get more advanced in your skills; you will learn how to modify the Linux kernel (yikes!) and then dive into the realm of real-time computing, looking at recipes to use the RT-PREEMPT patch, Xenomai, and the unique subsystem features of BeagleBone Black—the programmable real-time units (PRUs).

Chapter 7, Applied Recipes – Sound, Picture, and Video, looks at some ways to use sound, display, and video in your projects. We will begin by wiring up a mini sound amplifier and speakers and then take this lesson to creating a high-quality audio platform using the open source music platform, Volumio. Then, we will cook up a variety of recipes to utilize video and different types of displays in projects, including an OLED and a mini LCD. This chapter ends by building a video chat client from source.

Chapter 8, The Internet of Things, plunges into a sampling of things for the Internet of Things; things such as looking at ways to use sensors with middleware systems, setting up location-based devices to interact with BeagleBone Black, and mix a recipe for making a smarter object, specifically a cloud-driven digital picture frame.

Chapter 9, The Black in Outer Space, concludes the book by heading into more distant regions: outer space (or near space, to be more exact), delving into recipes to track satellites and craft, such as the International Space Station. We will discuss how to use the very low-cost but powerful and exciting Software Define Radio chip RTL-SDR.

What you need for this book

Describing every permutation and combination to set up BeagleBone Black is beyond the scope of this book. Although every recipe starts by describing your hardware requirements, we will suggest a baseline setup here that can be assumed for nearly all chapters.

There will be a number of recipes scattered throughout the book that require additional hardware, such as sensors, jumper wires, resistors, breadboards, and so on. Never fear! The vast majority of these parts is very low cost and typically already a part of your physical computing and electronic kits. There are a few examples, however, where you might need to spend a little more money on daughterboards (called capes) and some other peripherals, such as powered USB hubs.

The hardware requirements are as follows:

> ▶ **BeagleBone Black Revision C**: Typically referred to as Rev C, the version of the board we will use is the most current one available on the market at the time of writing. Earlier versions should work with the vast majority of the recipes in this book; however, we cannot guarantee their reliability in all cases.

▶ **MicroSD card (minimum 8 GB)**: Even though the board has an internal solid-state drive (eMMC) to run the OS, we often need to test recipes and different flavors of the kernel. So, being able to quickly swap out the operating system on a MicroSD card is an enormous timesaver. In fact, you will see us more commonly booting from the MicroSD than the internal drive.

▶ **Power supply**: You have more than one option to power up, though the recipe will recommend specifically which of these to use:

  ◦ **5V power**: This is a 5V 2A (2000mA) switching power supply.

  ◦ **A mini-B USB cable**: A great many of the recipes allow you to power the board with nothing more than the USB cable that should have come with your board when you purchased it. The standard USB connector goes into the USB port on your desktop client, which becomes the power source for BeagleBone Black.

▶ **Display**: There are basically three options to get a display going on your board:

  ◦ **An HDMI screen**: This out-of-the box approach assumes that you will connect your board to an HDMI monitor. Compatible hardware is listed at `http://elinux.org/Beagleboard:BeagleBoneBlack_HDMI`. If you do use this option, you will need a micro HDMI to standard HDMI cable.

  ◦ **A mini LCD or "cape"**: We will learn how to connect a small LCD to the board's header pins. As this is somewhat of a custom solution, we do not assume that you will typically use this method except in relevant use cases.

  ◦ **A remote session**: As we will see in an early chapter, much of your work on BeagleBone Black can be done via remote sessions using Secure Shell (SSH) on a client desktop machine, such as a Mac or Windows box. Note that this will be our favored approach and recommendation because it obviates the need for a keyboard, monitor, and mouse.

▶ **A USB hub**: We frequently recommend a powered hub, otherwise, the board's power draw will cause some peripherals, such as Bluetooth dongles, to underperform or not perform at all. Note that this must be a powered USB hub.

▶ **A client machine**: Interacting and controlling BeagleBone Black is often greatly simplified by connecting it to a client desktop machine running Windows, Mac OS, or even Linux. We are biased toward the Mac OS, so most of the recipes assume that you are using a Macintosh box. However, if you are not on Mac, the recipes are essentially the same and the principal steps and code are not affected.

▶ **A board enclosure**: This is not actually a requirement but a highly recommended "nice-to-have" tool. Besides protecting the board from damage, enclosing it in some kind of small box makes it much more manageable, especially when you have multiple wires snaking all over the place. You can find a variety of enclosures at `http://bit.ly/1KTNPbF` and on our site at `http://bit.ly/1WrBqrv`.

The software requirements are as follows:

- **Debian Linux**: If you purchased your board directly from a well-established distributor, it should have come preloaded with Debian 7 Wheezy (kernel 3.8.x-bone kernel), which will be our principal assumption for the OS. We will also be referencing Debian 8 Jessie (kernel 3.14.x).

  You will learn to load other versions of the software as we proceed through the book. *Note that prior versions of the board were shipped with Angstrom Linux. However, this book will not run recipes using this distribution.*

- **Homebrew**: If you are using a Mac box, adding Homebrew to Mac gives you Linux-savvy tools on your desktop. It includes a basket of Linux utilities so that you don't always have to fire up the board to run a test. For a "how-to" on installing Homebrew, refer to the developers' website at `http://brew.sh/`.

- **Drivers**: If on Mac, install the latest versions of developer Joshua Wise's HoRNDIS drivers for USB tethering to BeagleBone Black, which you can find at `http://joshuawise.com/horndis#available_versions`. We will provide more details on this step in *Chapter 1, Setting Up for the First Time*.

Who this book is for

This is a book primarily for those of you who are new to microcontrollers, small board computing, and physical computing. Although we will get into some relatively advanced examples, the vast majority of our book's recipes are for the aspiring maker, casual programmer, and budding engineer or tinkerer who has wondered how to get started on a full-blown microcomputing Linux system.

You might find some things in here that you could have found in some form on the Web. As we are dealing with open source tools and technology, this is inevitable. However, what we found when trying to learn about using BeagleBone Black for the first time was that although we could find some answers, it is always a struggle to get to an answer quickly.

As we proceed, our intention is to do our best to give you clear and simple introductions to concepts. So, for example, if you already know your way around things such as i2c, sysfs, and GPIO pins and know how to write custom functions in Python, you may find this book a bit too slow.

Given the speed of changes in the small board computing sector, many online tutorials are quickly aging out or just too advanced for a beginner. Thus, we believe that there is a dearth on the market of good, "easy-to-succeed" introductory books and material on BeagleBone Black.

Furthermore, unlike Raspberry Pi, which is surrounded by warm and fuzzy support forums, the BeagleBone community forum is comparatively sparse. Worse, it is often intimidating and unwelcoming to a new user. Our intention is to be light-hearted, fun, and inviting for a first-time user.

Sections

In this book, you will find several headings that appear frequently (Getting ready, How to do it, How it works, There's more, and See also).

To give clear instructions on how to complete a recipe, we use these sections as follows:

Getting ready

This section tells you what to expect in the recipe, and describes how to set up any software or any preliminary settings required for the recipe.

How to do it...

This section contains the steps required to follow the recipe.

How it works...

This section usually consists of a detailed explanation of what happened in the previous section.

There's more...

This section consists of additional information about the recipe in order to make the reader more knowledgeable about the recipe.

See also

This section provides helpful links to other useful information for the recipe.

Conventions

In this book, you will find a number of text styles that distinguish between different kinds of information. Here are some examples of these styles and an explanation of their meaning.

Code words in text, database table names, folder names, filenames, file extensions, pathnames, dummy URLs, user input, and Twitter handles are shown as follows: "There is no reason to recapitulate all the material covered in the `START.htm` presentation."

A block of code is set as follows:

```
function updateDuty() {
    // compute and adjust duty_cycle based on
    // desired position in range 0..1
    var duty_cycle = (position*0.115) + duty_min;
    b.analogWrite(SERVO, duty_cycle, 60,
    scheduleNextUpdate);
    console.log("Duty Cycle: " +
        parseFloat(duty_cycle*100).toFixed(1) + " %");
}
```

Any command-line input or output is written as follows:

```
$ sudo apt-get update
$ sudo apt-get upgrade
$ sudo apt-get install gdb
```

New terms and **important words** are shown in bold. Words that you see on the screen, for example, in menus or dialog boxes, appear in the text like this: "From your BBB's desktop, open up **LXTerminal**."

 Warnings or important notes appear in a box like this.

 Tips and tricks appear like this.

A few words about nomenclature

BBB: One thing that gets tiresome to repeat is the darned name of the board—BeagleBone Black. Too many syllables! So, instead of spelling it out every time, we will often just refer to the board as the BBB or the Black.

 There are other versions of the BeagleBone out in the wild, including BeagleBone XM, BeagleBoard (white), and the new super-charged (and much pricier) BeagleBoard-X15.

Desktop: Even though your BeagleBone Black has a desktop if you're running it on an external monitor or via an x11 (xwindows) session, we'll use the term *desktop* to refer to the client PC or Mac or Linux box that you're running as part of the development environment for the BBB.

Say hello to Major Tom

Ubiquitous and nearly inevitable in the world of computer programming is the typical beginner's example code "Hello World". Although we certainly use simple use cases to get you started, we don't use the Hello World rubric. Instead, because we're space geeks, we use "Major Tom" as a touchstone, evoking the astronaut from David Bowie's iconic *Ziggy Stardust*. To that end, we round out the book with an assortment of recipes using your BBB for tracking space stuff, satellites and the International Space Station, specifically. Geeks, indeed.

Reader feedback

Feedback from our readers is always welcome. Let us know what you think about this book—what you liked or disliked. Reader feedback is important for us as it helps us develop titles that you will really get the most out of.

To send us general feedback, simply e-mail `feedback@packtpub.com`, and mention the book's title in the subject of your message.

If there is a topic that you have expertise in and you are interested in either writing or contributing to a book, see our author guide at `www.packtpub.com/authors`.

Customer support

Now that you are the proud owner of a Packt book, we have a number of things to help you to get the most from your purchase.

Downloading the example code

You can download the example code files from your account at `http://www.packtpub.com` for all the Packt Publishing books you have purchased. If you purchased this book elsewhere, you can visit `http://www.packtpub.com/support` and register to have the files e-mailed directly to you.

In many cases, you will also be downloading code from the author's github site at `https://github.com/HudsonWerks`.

Downloading the color images of this book

We also provide you with a PDF file that has color images of the screenshots/diagrams used in this book. The color images will help you better understand the changes in the output. You can download this file from `https://www.packtpub.com/sites/default/files/downloads/2929OS_GraphicBundle.pdf`. Where noted, you may also download some of the images and diagrams from the author's website at `http://www.hudsonwerks.com/beaglebone-black-recipe-book/images/`

Errata

Although we have taken every care to ensure the accuracy of our content, mistakes do happen. If you find a mistake in one of our books—maybe a mistake in the text or the code—we would be grateful if you could report this to us. By doing so, you can save other readers from frustration and help us improve subsequent versions of this book. If you find any errata, please report them by visiting `http://www.packtpub.com/submit-errata`, selecting your book, clicking on the **Errata Submission Form** link, and entering the details of your errata. Once your errata are verified, your submission will be accepted and the errata will be uploaded to our website or added to any list of existing errata under the Errata section of that title.

To view the previously submitted errata, go to `https://www.packtpub.com/books/content/support` and enter the name of the book in the search field. The required information will appear under the **Errata** section.

Piracy

Piracy of copyrighted material on the Internet is an ongoing problem across all media. At Packt, we take the protection of our copyright and licenses very seriously. If you come across any illegal copies of our works in any form on the Internet, please provide us with the location address or website name immediately so that we can pursue a remedy.

Please contact us at `copyright@packtpub.com` with a link to the suspected pirated material.

We appreciate your help in protecting our authors and our ability to bring you valuable content.

Questions

If you have a problem with any aspect of this book, you can contact us at `questions@packtpub.com`, and we will do our best to address the problem.

1
Setting Up for the First Time

In this chapter, we will focus on the following topics:

- ▶ First boot up
- ▶ Power requirements – basic guidelines
- ▶ Display
- ▶ Essential GNU/Linux commands – the command shell
- ▶ Essential GNU/Linux commands – typical commands
- ▶ Edit a text file from the command shell
- ▶ Connectivity
- ▶ Package management – Installing packages using apt-get
- ▶ SSH / Remote access
- ▶ System images

Introduction

Getting off to a running start with your BeagleBone Black requires diving into a number of fundamental recipes first. After all, you have to learn to chop and dice before making a proper soup.

As you probably already know, creating the right development environment saves time, reduces errors, and creates a good workflow. To this end, after we get our display hardware hooked up, it's critical to learn a bit about the Linux commands that power our projects. Then, we will move on to getting your board both connected online and controlled remotely over a network. Next, we will learn the basics of installing and managing applications (packages). Finally, we will explore how to get an OS onto your board, whether it's with the internal solid-state drive (eMMC) or via an SD card.

First boot up

BeagleBone Black (BBB) designers have worked hard to simplify the user's first out-of-the-box experience. Although things get more challenging later, which is natural, it is pretty close to Plug and Play at the outset.

You do not even need to load any software as the platform arrives preloaded with a custom distribution of Linux Debian on the internal solid-state drive (eMMC).

Getting ready

Here's what you need:

 ▶ **Desktop client PC**: As noted in the introduction, we will principally be using a Mac box as our client machine. However, the following steps apply equally to a Windows or Linux machine.
 ▶ **USB cable**: A mini USB-B to USB cable is required, which is typically supplied with your board.
 ▶ **BeagleBone Black Rev. C**: To reiterate a point from this book's introduction, our recipes use Rev. C, which is the currently shipping version of the board. If you have an earlier board, you may run into occasional conflicts with the recipes.

How to do it...

Perform the following steps:

1. To power up, plug the USB cable into the BBB and your client box.

2. Wait for the three blue LEDs to light up; each of them functions as a useful indicator of the board's health:

   ❑ **Power**: Once power is supplied to the board, the LED next to the 5V barrel jack will remain on without flashing

   ❑ **USR0**: Next to the tiny reset button (S1), this light maintains a continuous, solid "heartbeat" blink when powered

   ❑ **USR2**: Two down from the Ethernet jack, this LED flutters subtly during CPU access

 Unless otherwise noted, all images are copyright Charles A. Hamilton.

3. Within a few moments on your client machine, the BEAGLE_BONE drive should appear as a visible volume on your desktop. Browse the folder and open up the START.htm file.

4. Once opened, you will find a clear set of quick start steps, including how to install drivers (if needed).

5. Browse your board—BeagleBone Black's boot system includes a handy web server that allows immediate connectivity. Clicking on the link will take you to the local IP address of the board at `192.168.7.2`. Once there, you will find a very helpful presentation on the board.

   There is no reason to recapitulate all the material covered in the `START.htm` presentation. Instead, review it as a good jumping off point for the upcoming recipes in this chapter.

Getting ready

Power down: Before proceeding, remove all cables and power (USB, Ethernet, DC cord, HDMI, and so on).

How to do it...

Perform the following steps:

1. **Connect the USB cable**: With a USB 2.0 A to Mini-B cable, connect the BBB to a USB port on your desktop PC.

2. **Look for status lights**: After plugging in the USB cable, you will see the board's first LED light up, followed subsequently by the three other LEDs. If all goes well, the `BEAGLE_BONE` device will appear on your desktop.

3. **Install drivers**: I won't belabor this step. It suffices to say that your desktop—whether it's a Windows, Mac, or Linux machine—requires certain drivers to recognize and run the BBB via USB properly. If your desktop OS doesn't come with the drivers already installed (as some do), install them via the link, `http://beagleboard.org/Getting-Started`.

4. Once your drivers are installed, browse to the `BASIC_START.htm` file on the `BEAGLE_BONE` device and open it.

If the planets are aligned and the drivers are installed properly, you will see the following at the top of the browser window:

Your board is connected! BeagleBone Black rev 0A5C S/N xxxxxxxxxxxx running BoneScript 1.2.3 at 192.168.7.2.

At this point, you're ready to fly; at least at low altitude. With a co-pilot...on an emulator.

Power requirements – basic guidelines

Giving your BBB the proper amount of love and power is crucial to having a happy board. Following these basic guidelines will ensure that your BBB operates reliably and predictably.

The board's user manual recommends that you supply current to at least 1.2A (or 6W). However, if you connect up anything over the USB, at least 2A (or 10W) is recommended. Here are some additional rules of thumb:

- You can power the BBB via the USB tether. However, if you attach additional USB devices, such as webcams, Wi-Fi or Bluetooth dongles, keyboards and mice, and then power them through the USB tether, it may lead to unreliable connections and power fluctuations. We were successful in powering some USB dongles directly via the BBB's USB port, whereas some devices, such as USB webcams, were not reliably powered.

- If you connect USB devices, it is best to power them from a powered USB hub and then supply power to the BBB via a 5 VDC power supply of at least 1A.

- 5V DC power—most users of the board will invariably recommend that you always power your board using a 5V DC supply.

- You can also use a 5V wall charger power adapter with a USB port on it as long as it can deliver 1A.

Downloading the example code

You can download the example code files from your account at `http://www.packtpub.com` for all the Packt Publishing books you have purchased. If you purchased this book elsewhere, you can visit `http://www.packtpub.com/support` and register to have the files e-mailed directly to you.

In many cases, you will also be downloading code from the author's github site at `https://github.com/HudsonWerks`.

Display

The BBB's on board micro HDMI port provides a relatively easy way to attach a display device. With the new Debian distribution, compatibility, and ease of installation, the process is greatly simplified. We will take a look at two types of devices you may be using: an HDMI monitor and a small form-factor LCD (without HDMI).

Using a display is not a requirement to operate the board and is merely optional. You will learn how to control the BBB without a display later in this chapter.

Connecting an HDMI LCD

Running your board with an HDMI monitor is the default method to use your BBB.

How to do it...

1. Check the compatibility list for your HDMI LCD monitor at `http://elinux. org/Beagleboard:BeagleBone_Black_Accessories#Monitors_and_ Resolutions`.

   Given the large universe of LCDs out there, this is not a definitive list. However, it does lend guidance on displays that will work with the BBB. You will also be pleasantly surprised that most consumer-grade HDTVs work pretty well out of the box with your board.

2. Check your resolution at `http://elinux.org/Beagleboard:BeagleBoneBlack_ HDMI`.

3. Plug in one end of your HDMI cable to your monitor and the other end, which is the micro HDMI end, into your powered-down BBB.

4. Fulfill the power requirements; power up your board with a 5V adapter.

    Since HDMI displays can draw a lot of power, don't try to run off your desktop's USB slot. Otherwise, you will get flaky results at best and, more likely, no picture at all.

5. You should get a straightforward boot up into the default desktop "beagle" screen.

Connecting a non-HDMI LCD or cape

There's no obligation to use only an HDMI display on BeagleBone Black. For example, with the right HDMI to VGA converter cable, you can actually attach a standard VGA monitor to the BBB. Compatible converters can be found at `http://elinux.org/ Beagleboard:BeagleBone_Black_Accessories#HDMI_Adapters`.

You may also develop an embedded prototype device that only needs a small LCD and no HDMI. Here's one recipe for a scenario using a 3.5-inch screen from Circuitco (`http://elinux.org/CircuitCo:BeagleBone_LCD3`) that I've used in my own projects. The display is in the category of add-ons to the BBB called **capes**, which are akin to the shields on an Arduino board. Capes are typically robust daughterboards and, unfortunately, tend to be much more expensive than Arduino add-ons.

CircuitCo LCD3 cape

How to do it...

Perform the following steps:

1. Power down your board.

2. Examine the header pins at the bottom of the LCD3 and note the pin layout: one short row and one longer row. Also, note the Power (**PWR**) button at one end.

The pin line up at the bottom of the **PCB** (printed circuit board)

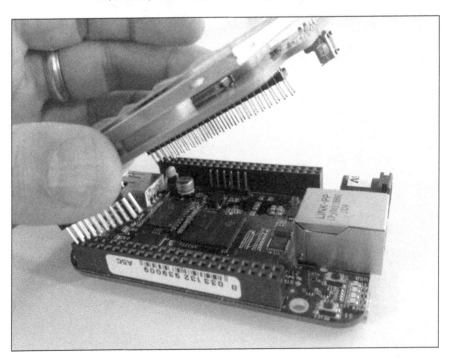

3. Position the long row of pins on the LCD on top of the **P9** pin slots on the BBB and the short pin row on the **P8** row. Don't push the pins in yet. The **PWR** button should rest between the Ethernet port and the 5V barrel jack, as in the following image:

4. Next, slowly push the pins into the BBB headers. All pins should go in more or less simultaneously. It's a little tricky as you also have to squish the **PWR** button in place at the same time so that it lodges snugly between the 5V barrel and the Ethernet jack, as in the following image:

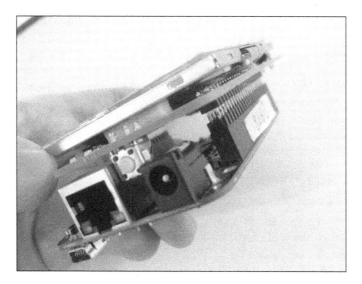

5. All pins on both sides of the LCD should be firmly pushed into place on the board, and the **PWR** button should be securely squeezed in place.

6. Power up your board. Most distributions—including the Debian firmware, of course—have compatible drivers for the display, so you should boot right into your desktop within a few moments.

There's more...

For more information on the following topics, refer to the respective websites:

- ▸ HDMI Troubleshooting: `http://elinux.org/Beagleboard:BeagleBoneBlack_ HDMI`

- ▸ Other LCD cape options: `http://elinux.org/Beagleboard:BeagleBone_ Capesux driver`

Essential GNU/Linux commands – the command shell

Fancy GUIs are nice, but on BeagleBone Black, you will be mainly working with the command shell and its accompanying command-line tools to provide access to the operating system. First, let's take a look at some terminology: *command shell*, *command-line shell*, *command line*, or simply *shell* will all be used somewhat interchangeably as they all basically refer to the same thing—a means to provide access to the operating system with the command line and without a GUI. Bash is the default shell on Linux.

Terminal is yet another typical way to refer to the shell. The term is derived from its preceding technologies where any interaction with a computer required using a text-based terminal interface.

Often intimidating to new users, command shell is the starting point for any serious embedded system project. The Debian distribution for BeagleBone Black comes preloaded with two command-line tools to use a command shell: **LXTerminal** and **Root Terminal**. Although there are others with more robust and colorful interfaces that you can install, such as **xterm** and **eterm**, for simplicity's sake, we will use **LXTerminal**. In the next section, you will learn about the command syntax required within the tool. Finally, we will create, edit, and save a text file from the command line.

Getting ready

Ensure that your BeagleBone Black is set up and running in the manner described in the *Introduction* section. (Note that here, we will show the two different methods of running the board: powered via USB and powered via 5V).

How to do it...

1. Begin by opening up **LXTerminal**, which you will find in the **Accessories** application on the lower left-hand side of the screen:

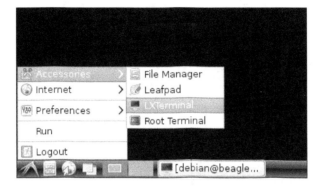

2. You will now see a command prompt that looks similar to this on your screen:

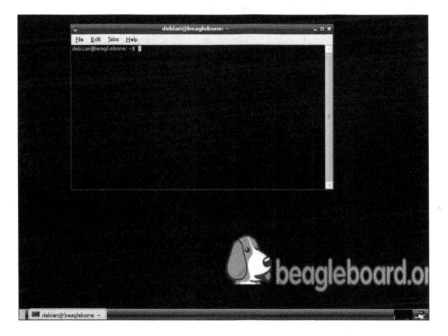

3. Just for fun, let's type in the following at the command prompt:

```
debian@beaglebone:~$   echo Can you hear me Major Tom?
```

This will show the following output:

Congratulations! You've just sent your first command to BeagleBone Black (and it wasn't `Hello World`). But we're getting ahead of ourselves. Commands are for the next section.

How it works...

Let's take a quick look at the various parts of what LXTerminal shows us. Firstly, we know that Linux likes to keep the current user name at the front and center, in this case `debian`. This way, you always have a quick reference point to know whether you are a root user, which gives you total control over the system, or just another user with limited privileges.

Then comes the address of the device you're working on: `beaglebone`. You can actually customize the name, but we will save that for the appendix. Lastly, consider the $ sign, which denotes that you're logged in as a regular user. If you were a root user, the symbol would be the # sign. You will learn more about users and root users in a later section.

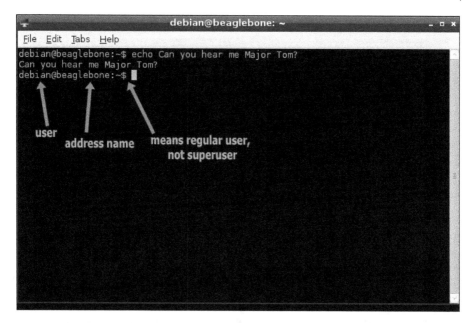

Essential GNU/Linux commands – typical commands

The command line is your friend.

For advanced users, this is an obvious statement; for the beginner, not so friendly. Where do you start with that darn blinking cursor?

How many Linux commands are there? A whole bunch. Thousands. Tens of thousands depending on dependencies and packages. But don't worry, you don't have to learn them all.

Saying or writing something original about Linux commands is a bit difficult: far smarter, folks than I have written about, compiled, and battle-tested the multiple combinations of commands available to the Linux user. And this book is not intended to be about Linux commands. So instead, I will give you a handful of basic commands that I find myself consistently using on the BBB and also provide you with some of my favorite reference materials and cheat sheets that will give you a more comprehensive list of important commands.

Getting ready

Of course, we assume that if you intend to use some **command line interface** (**CLI**) commands, you have to have your command shell window open and gain root access:

`sudo`

Using `sudo` as part of your command syntax is a requirement that often bedevils new Linux users. It is important to understand that many Linux commands demand what are known as "superuser" privileges, which grant you total control over the board and its software. Having full admin rights within a command prevents any casual user from coming along and destroying your hard work, by design or accident.

The "open sesame" of Debian Linux, the magic `sudo` command (pronounced "soo-doo"), means "Super User do x-command" when dissected. If you don't append your command at the beginning with `sudo`, your `mkdir` command, for example, will return a "bad command" error.

`sudo -i and root`

Adding the `-i` option (the `sudo -i` command) provides even more control over the environment: the root user access. When running commands as a root user, there are ample opportunities to completely mangle your system, so exercise extreme caution in its use.

However, not all commands require superuser privileges. For instance, when you're really just poking around the system and not modifying files, directories, or the system itself, `sudo` isn't necessary.

You should keep in mind several things when working with the command line:

- **Lowercase**: Using lowercase syntax is the shell's required expectation, with the exception of some options and arguments that are uppercase.

- **Arguments and options**: Most commands have multiple options or arguments that can be used to fine-tune your command. We will only be able to touch on a few instances of how and when these options are used.

- **Help**:
    - **Help (no hyphens)**: Typing `help` before a command outputs information about this command. An example of this is `$ help cd`.
    - **Help (hyphens)**: Many executable commands have more help and information about their options or arguments. An example of this is `$ mkdir --help`.
    - **Man pages**: Short for "manual pages", adding `man` to the beginning of many Linux commands opens up a manual for these commands. It can often yield too much information, but it can be helpful if you're looking for a deeper understanding of a command. An example of this is `$ man chmod`.

▶ **Tab command**: This lists recent commands. In order to use this, you need to do the following:

- Type a letter (or a string of letters) and then press the *Tab* button. All commands that begin with this letter or string will be shown. This will prevent a vast majority of typing mistakes.
- Press *Tab* twice quickly, and it will show all the commands that are currently in your path.

Conventions

Early in the book, we will frequently use the entire line from the command line, including the user name, address, symbols connoting user type, directory, and so on. So, for example, you will see a line that looks similar to the following:

```
debian@beagle_bone:~$ mkdir
```

However, as we become more familiar with the shell, we will mostly shorten the command instruction to only include the command itself:

```
~$ mkdir
```

Alternatively, you will see a slight variation on the preceding command when we refer to a root user. Note the # sign in place of the $ sign in the following command:

```
~# mkdir
```

Now, let's move on to the commands. A super-duper subset of commands, anyway. We've organized them into *System navigational commands*, *Device and system insight*, and *Modify content/data commands*.

System navigational command – change your directory – cd

To move from one directory to another, there are numerous variations on how to do it.

How to do it...

Perform the following steps:

1. To change from your current default directory to the Desktop directory, type in these commands:

   ```
   debian@beaglebone:~$ cd Desktop
   debian@beaglebone:~/Desktop$
   ```

2. To go back one directory level, use the following command lines:

```
debian@beaglebone:~/Desktop$ cd ..
debian@beaglebone:~$
```

3. Go to the Home directory using the following command:

```
debian@beaglebone:~/Desktop$ cd ~
debian@beaglebone:~$
```

4. Go back to the previous directory you were in by typing in the following commands:

```
debian@beaglebone:~$ cd -
/home/debian/Desktop
debian@beaglebone:~/Desktop$
```

There's more...

In addition to the preceding commands, you should be familiar with the four special directory symbols:

- ▸ The current directory (.)
- ▸ The parent directory (. .)
- ▸ The root directory (/)
- ▸ The home directory (~)

System navigational command – show your current directory – pwd

This stands for print working directory, a means to show the user where in the system they are currently working or the absolute path relative to the current directory.

How to do it...

Use the following command to show your current directory:

```
debian@beaglebone:~$ pwd
/home/Debian
```

System navigational command – find a file – find

Looking for a file? One way to search for it is with the find function. Just be sure to add the `-name` option so that the output shows the directory location. Add `sudo` as well so that you do not get directory access errors.

How to do it...

Use the following command to find a file:

```
$ sudo find / -name <filename>
```

Device and system insight – shows what's inside a directory – ls

The `ls` command lists the contents of your current directory.

How to do it...

Use the following command to see the list of contents in the current directory:

```
debian@beaglebone:~$ ls
Desktop
```

At the moment, the only thing you will see is the `Desktop` directory. As we continue adding content in subsequent chapters, there will be more that would be seen upon using `ls`.

Adding the `-lah` option at the end of the command gives more detailed information on the files, as follows:

```
debian@beaglebone:~$ ls -lah
total 112K
drwxr-xr-x 19 debian debian 4.0K May  4 23:37 .
drwxr-xr-x  3 root   root   4.0K May  5 00:05 ..
-rw-------  1 debian debian   55 May  4 23:37 .Xauthority
-rw-------  1 debian debian 2.4K May  5 01:41 .bash_history
-rw-r--r--  1 debian debian  220 Jan  1  2015 .bash_logout
-rw-r--r--  1 debian debian 3.4K Jan  1  2015 .bashrc
drwxr-xr-x  6 debian debian 4.0K Mar  8  2015 .cache
```

```
drwxr-xr-x  9 debian debian 4.0K Mar  4 23:51 .config
drwx------  3 debian debian 4.0K Mar  4 23:37 .dbus
-rw-r--r--  1 debian debian   35 Mar  4 23:37 .dmrc
drwxr-xr-x  2 debian debian 4.0K Mar  8 2015 .fontconfig
drwxr-xr-x 24 debian debian 4.0K Mar  8 2015 .gimp-2.8
drwx------  3 debian debian 4.0K Mar  8 2015 .local
```

The options in the command now reveal a variety of things about the file: their permission status (column 1), owner and group (columns 3 and 4), file sizes (column 5) , and modification date (column 6). The `l` option outputs in the list form, adding the `a` forces the command to show any hidden files, and the `h` option turns it all into a human readable format.

Device and system insight – find out what USB devices are connected – lsusb

This captures and lists all USB devices currently connected to the BBB while showing basic information about the device.

How to do it...

Use the following command to find out about the USB devices connected:

```
debian@beaglebone:~$ lsusb
Bus 001 Device 002: ID 0d8c:013c C-Media Electronics, Inc. CM108 Audio
Controller
Bus 001 Device 001: ID 1d6b:0002 Linux Foundation 2.0 root hub
Bus 002 Device 001: ID 1d6b:0002 Linux Foundation 2.0 root hub
```

 Note that the first device here shows a connected USB audio dongle.

Device and system insight – get information about connected devices – cat/proc/bus/input/devices

Where `lusb` leaves off, this command lists more detailed information about any device connected to the BBB. Note the difference in output for the same USB audio device (C-media) shown in our preceding recipe using `lsusb`.

How to do it...

Use the following command to get information about connected devices:

```
debian@beaglebone:~$ cat /proc/bus/input/devices


I: Bus=0000 Vendor=0000 Product=0000 Version=0000
N: Name="tps65217_pwr_but"
P: Phys=
S: Sysfs=/devices/ocp.3/44e0b000.i2c/i2c-0/0-0024/input/input0
U: Uniq=
H: Handlers=kbd event0
B: PROP=0
B: EV=3
B: KEY=100000 0 0 0


I: Bus=0003 Vendor=0d8c Product=013c Version=0100
N: Name="C-Media Electronics Inc.      USB PnP Sound Device"
P: Phys=usb-musb-hdrc.1.auto-1/input3
S: Sysfs=/devices/ocp.3/47400000.usb/musb-hdrc.1.auto/usb1/1-1/1-1:1.3/
input/input1
U: Uniq=
H: Handlers=kbd event1
B: PROP=0
B: EV=13
B: KEY=78 0 e0000 0 0 0
B: MSC=10
```

There's more...

The stem of this command is `cat`, which is one of the most popular commands to quickly read files without writing or modifying them:

```
$  cat file4
```

You can try it with any file to see how the screen output looks.

Device and system insight – get your version of Linux

You can find out which version and distribution of Linux you are running through several methods.

How to do it...

To find out your version of Linux, use the following command:

```
debian@beaglebone:~$ lsb_release -a
```

The screen output will look similar to this:

```
No LSB modules are available.
Distributor ID: Debian
Description: Debian GNU/Linux 7.6 (wheezy)
Release: 7.6
Codename: wheezy
```

The preceding command is a good complement to the more typical way we determine the actual kernel version, which is as follows:

```
$ uname -r
3.8.13-boneXX
```

Device and system insight – find out running processes – ps

In Linux, applications are referred to as processes, and each is given a unique ID number or PID. The ps (that is, process status) command provides information about the currently running tasks or processes. The output includes the PIDs.

How to do it...

This command takes a snapshot of your board. You can run the command unadulterated and with no options, as follows:

```
$ ps
```

But the output is a thin gruel:

```
debian@beaglebone:~$ ps
PID     TTY       TIME      CMD
1623    pts/0     00:00:00      bash
2035    pts/0     00:00:00      ps
```

So, it is often better to modify the output in order to get more insight into the running processes and display this information in a more orderly fashion, as in the following command:

```
$ ps aux
```

The following is the output:

```
debian@beaglebone:~$ ps aux
USER      PID %CPU %MEM     VSZ    RSS TTY       STAT START    TIME COMMAND
root        1  0.0  0.5    4468   2652 ?         Ss   14:41    0:01 /lib/systemd/systemd
root        2  0.0  0.0       0      0 ?         S    14:41    0:00 [kthreadd]
root        3  0.0  0.0       0      0 ?         S    14:41    0:02 [ksoftirqd/0]
root        5  0.0  0.0       0      0 ?         S<   14:41    0:00 [kworker/0:0H]
root        7  0.0  0.0       0      0 ?         S<   14:41    0:00 [kworker/u:0H]
root        8  0.0  0.0       0      0 ?         S    14:41    0:00 [watchdog/0]
root        9  0.0  0.0       0      0 ?         S<   14:41    0:00 [khelper]
root       10  0.0  0.0       0      0 ?         S    14:41    0:00 [kdevtmpfs]
root       11  0.0  0.0       0      0 ?         S<   14:41    0:00 [netns]
root       12  0.0  0.0       0      0 ?         S    14:41    0:00 [bdi-default]
root       14  0.0  0.0       0      0 ?         S<   14:41    0:00 [kintegrityd]
root       15  0.0  0.0       0      0 ?         S<   14:41    0:00 [kblockd]
root       16  0.0  0.0       0      0 ?         S    14:41    0:00 [khubd]
root       17  0.0  0.0       0      0 ?         S    14:41    0:00 [irq/70-44e0b000]
root       18  0.0  0.0       0      0 ?         S    14:41    0:00 [kworker/u:1]
root       21  0.0  0.0       0      0 ?         S    14:41    0:00 [irq/7-tps65217]
root       24  0.0  0.0       0      0 ?         S    14:41    0:00 [irq/30-4819c000]
root       33  0.0  0.0       0      0 ?         S<   14:41    0:00 [rpciod]
root       35  0.0  0.0       0      0 ?         S    14:41    0:00 [khungtaskd]
root       36  0.0  0.0       0      0 ?         S    14:41    0:00 [gatekeeper/0]
```

The `aux` series of options complement the basic command by doing the following:

- The `a` option shows the processes for all users. Historically, `ps` requires different syntax depending on our flavor of Linux or Unix. This option simplifies the method required to add options.

- Using the `u` option tells the command to display the user or owner of the process in the output. The reason you want to do this is that there are processes typically running at the root level and other processes running at a non-root-user level. However, we frequently want to see all processes running regardless of user, so this option is important.

- The `x` option ensures that processes that are not currently running in a terminal window—which form the majority of running processes—are also in the output that we want to see.

Device and system insight – find out the resources used by running processes – top and htop

This command takes it a bit further than the `ps` command as it dynamically updates not only the processes running but also the CPU resources used by the processes. The status is continuous and in real time.

How to do it...

Use this command line:

```
$ top
```

The output is as follows:

PID	USER	PR	NI	VIRT	RES	SHR	S	%CPU	%MEM	TIME+	COMMAND
549	messageb	20	0	2736	1424	1008	S	0.3	0.3	0:12.02	dbus-daemon
1086	root	20	0	3160	696	572	S	0.3	0.1	0:32.40	agetty
1087	root	20	0	23884	7004	1824	S	0.3	1.4	0:28.78	wicd
1107	root	20	0	14708	7596	3456	S	0.3	1.5	0:13.48	wicd-monitor
1393	root	20	0	4448	1400	832	S	0.3	0.3	0:24.32	tmux
1784	root	20	0	0	0	0	S	0.3	0.0	0:04.39	kworker/0:0
4298	debian	20	0	15152	10m	2436	S	0.3	2.2	0:02.92	Xtightvnc
5202	**debian**	**20**	**0**	**2668**	**1148**	**792**	**R**	**0.3**	**0.2**	**0:00.48**	**top**
1	root	20	0	4468	2652	1416	S	0.0	0.5	0:01.11	systemd
2	root	20	0	0	0	0	S	0.0	0.0	0:00.00	kthreadd
3	root	20	0	0	0	0	S	0.0	0.0	0:02.34	ksoftirqd/0
5	root	0	-20	0	0	0	S	0.0	0.0	0:00.00	kworker/0:0H
7	root	0	-20	0	0	0	S	0.0	0.0	0:00.00	kworker/u:0H
8	root	rt	0	0	0	0	S	0.0	0.0	0:00.09	watchdog/0
9	root	0	-20	0	0	0	S	0.0	0.0	0:00.00	khelper
10	root	20	0	0	0	0	S	0.0	0.0	0:00.00	kdevtmpfs
11	root	0	-20	0	0	0	S	0.0	0.0	0:00.00	netns
12	root	20	0	0	0	0	S	0.0	0.0	0:00.00	bdi-default

The `top` command is adequate and one that you will hear most Linux users call upon, but there is now a much lovelier, easier way to read a package—htop. Let's install it and compare it to top with the following command:

```
$ sudo apt-get install htop
```

Now, the output will be as follows:

```
 CPU[|||                                    5.1%]    Tasks: 68, 152 thr; 1 running
 Mem[|||||||||||||||||||||||||||||||||||162/495MB]   Load average: 0.31 0.20 0.11
 Swp[                                     0/0MB]     Uptime: 03:45:58

   PID USER      PRI  NI   VIRT    RES    SHR S  CPU% MEM%    TIME+  Command
  6064 debian     20   0   3148   1508    968 R   4.0  0.3  0:01.34 htop
  1087 root       20   0  23884   7004   1824 S   0.0  1.4  0:32.91 /usr/bin/python -O /usr/s
     1 root       20   0   4468   2652   1416 S   0.0  0.5  0:01.11 /lib/systemd/systemd
   205 root       20   0   4256   1308   1028 S   0.0  0.3  0:03.67 /lib/systemd/systemd-jour
   226 root       20   0   2492   1360    720 S   0.0  0.3  0:00.41 /sbin/udevd
   539 avahi      20   0   2760   1408   1148 S   0.0  0.3  0:00.18 avahi-daemon: running [be
   549 messagebu  20   0   2736   1424   1008 S   0.0  0.3  0:13.78 /usr/bin/dbus-daemon --sy
   552 root       20   0   1332    688    580 S   0.0  0.1  0:00.00 /usr/sbin/acpid
   555 root       20   0   4604   1552   1268 S   0.0  0.3  0:00.01 /sbin/wpa_supplicant -u -
   679 root       20   0  36984  23400   2872 S   0.0  4.6  0:00.00 /usr/bin/ruby1.9.1 /usr/l
  1234 root       20   0  36984  23400   2872 S   0.0  4.6  0:00.00 /usr/bin/ruby1.9.1 /usr/l
  1235 root       20   0  36984  23400   2872 S   0.0  4.6  0:00.00 /usr/bin/ruby1.9.1 /usr/l
  1236 root       20   0  36984  23400   2872 S   0.0  4.6  0:01.09 /usr/bin/ruby1.9.1 /usr/l
  1237 root       20   0  36984  23400   2872 S   0.0  4.6  0:00.09 /usr/bin/ruby1.9.1 /usr/l
  1238 root       20   0  36984  23400   2872 S   0.0  4.6  0:00.02 /usr/bin/ruby1.9.1 /usr/l
  1239 root       20   0  36984  23400   2872 S   0.0  4.6  0:00.02 /usr/bin/ruby1.9.1 /usr/l
  1240 root       20   0  36984  23400   2872 S   0.0  4.6  0:00.67 /usr/bin/ruby1.9.1 /usr/l
  1243 root       20   0  36984  23400   2872 S   0.0  4.6  0:00.11 /usr/bin/ruby1.9.1 /usr/l
   556 root       20   0  36984  23400   2872 S   0.0  4.6  0:13.62 /usr/bin/ruby1.9.1 /usr/l
   689 root       20   0  86136  25656   4656 S   0.0  5.1  0:00.28 /usr/bin/node autorun.js
  1111 root       20   0  86136  25656   4656 S   0.0  5.1  0:00.00 /usr/bin/node autorun.js
  1114 root       20   0  86136  25656   4656 S   0.0  5.1  0:00.00 /usr/bin/node autorun.js
```

As you can see, it has an output that is much cleaner and easier to read.

Device and system insight – quitting processes – kill

The typical way to force quit—or kill—an application is to use the `kill` command and combine it with the process ID (PID), which you can derive from any of the preceding recipes to capture process information. Let's take a look at the basic method.

How to do it...

Use the following command to kill processes:

```
$ kill <process_id>
```

Here's a real example, which would force quit the top process shown in our prior recipe:

```
$ kill 4569
```

When you know the name of a process, you can use the `pkill` command, which operates on the process name instead, as follows:

```
$ pkill -9 gdb
```

Naturally, there is yet another way to skin the cat while killing a process. For example, you may discover that there are several processes associated with one application, and killing them one by one gets a bit slippery. Instead, use `killall` and kiss them goodbye:

```
$ killall chromium
```

Device and system insight – message reports – dmesg

As you already know, every time you boot up your device, a ton of messages quickly scrolls past on the screen. Unless you wear a blue leotard with a red cape and possess exceptionally fast eyes, you likely will not catch all these pearls of ASCII wisdom. Yet, these messages can be extremely useful at times, particularly when you need to troubleshoot a system problem.

How to do it...

The `dmesg` command is used as follows:

```
$ dmesg
```

Typically, the output looks similar to this:

```
[    0.000000] Booting Linux on physical CPU 0x0

[    0.000000] Initializing cgroup subsys cpu

[    0.000000] Linux version 3.8.13-bone47 (root@imx6q-wandboard-2gb-0)
(gcc version 4.6.3 (Debian 4.6.3-14) ) #1 SMP Fri Apr 11 01:36:09 UTC
2014

[    0.000000] CPU: ARMv7 Processor [413fc082] revision 2 (ARMv7),
cr=50c5387d

[    0.000000] CPU: PIPT / VIPT nonaliasing data cache, VIPT aliasing
instruction cache

[    0.000000] Machine: Generic AM33XX (Flattened Device Tree), model: TI
AM335x BeagleBone

[    0.000000] Memory policy: ECC disabled, Data cache writeback

[    0.000000] On node 0 totalpages: 130816

[    0.000000] free_area_init_node: node 0, pgdat c0824280, node_mem_map
c089f000
```

The list goes on and on as your machine is full of activity! So, limiting `dmesg` to output smaller chunks of information with a command option is primarily the course followed. In this case, we want to show the last ten events on the system, so we will use the following:

```
$ dmesg | tail
```

Alternatively, we can use the `less` option, which allows us to advance forward in the list more methodically, as follows:

```
$ dmesg | less
```

Device and system insight – shows disk space – df -h

This command outputs information on your board's available disk space and displays it in human readable format.

How to do it...

Use the following command to find out the disk space:

```
debian@beaglebone:~$ df -h
Filesystem        Size  Used Avail Use% Mounted on
rootfs            7.2G  1.6G  5.4G  22% /
udev              10M      0   10M   0% /dev
tmpfs             100M  824K   99M   1% /run
/dev/mmcblk0p2    7.2G  1.6G  5.4G  22% /
tmpfs             249M     0  249M   0% /dev/shm
tmpfs             249M     0  249M   0% /sys/fs/cgroup
tmpfs             100M     0  100M   0% /run/user
tmpfs             5.0M     0  5.0M   0% /run/lock
/dev/mmcblk0p1     96M   71M   25M  75% /boot/uboot
/dev/mmcblk1p2    1.7G  1.7G      0 100% /media/rootfs
/dev/mmcblk1p1     96M   11M   86M  11% /media/boot
```

Device and system insight – explore network – Ifconfig

This lists all the network devices with network information. You will commonly find yourself using this command on the BBB when you need to troubleshoot a problem or set up network connections.

How to do it...

Use the following command to explore network configuration:

```
$ ifconfig
```

The output is as follows:

```
debian@beaglebone:~$ ifconfig
eth0      Link encap:Ethernet  HWaddr 90:59:af:65:5b:ba
          inet addr:192.168.15.100  Bcast:192.168.15.255  Mask:255.255.255.0
          inet6 addr: fe80::9259:afff:fe65:5bba/64 Scope:Link
          UP BROADCAST RUNNING MULTICAST  MTU:1500  Metric:1
          RX packets:34715 errors:0 dropped:0 overruns:0 frame:0
          TX packets:19912 errors:0 dropped:0 overruns:0 carrier:0
          collisions:0 txqueuelen:1000
          RX bytes:6195835 (5.9 MiB)  TX bytes:7328600 (6.9 MiB)
          Interrupt:40

lo        Link encap:Local Loopback
          inet addr:127.0.0.1  Mask:255.0.0.0
          inet6 addr: ::1/128 Scope:Host
          UP LOOPBACK RUNNING  MTU:65536  Metric:1
          RX packets:11284 errors:0 dropped:0 overruns:0 frame:0
          TX packets:11284 errors:0 dropped:0 overruns:0 carrier:0
          collisions:0 txqueuelen:0
          RX bytes:1429208 (1.3 MiB)  TX bytes:1429208 (1.3 MiB)

usb0      Link encap:Ethernet  HWaddr ce:eb:cb:d1:4a:c3
          inet addr:192.168.7.2  Bcast:192.168.7.3  Mask:255.255.255.252
          UP BROADCAST MULTICAST  MTU:1500  Metric:1
          RX packets:0 errors:0 dropped:0 overruns:0 frame:0
          TX packets:0 errors:0 dropped:0 overruns:0 carrier:0
          collisions:0 txqueuelen:1000
          RX bytes:0 (0.0 B)  TX bytes:0 (0.0 B)
```

Modify content / data commands – make a new directory – mkdir

This command helps you create a directory (folder) where you want to work or place files.

How to do it...

Use the following command to make a new directory:

```
debian@beaglebone:~$ mkdir test
```

Now is a good time to check your work with the `ls` command, as follows:

```
debian@beaglebone:~$ ls
Desktop   test
```

Modify content/data commands – remove a file or directory – rm

As the name implies, this command removes a file or directory that you designate.

How to do it...

Removing a file is very simple. You just need to type out the following:

```
$ rm file1
```

Adding the `-i` option is good practice, especially for beginners, as it prompts you to confirm the file's removal as follows:

```
$ rm -ir file1
rm: remove regular file `file1'?
```

To remove directories, there are principally two commands you can use. Firstly, when you have an empty directory, the command is similar to the following:

```
$ rmdir dir1
```

However, `rmdir` works only if the directory is empty. If you want to remove a directory with all its contents, you can use `rm` with the `-r` option. This option tells `rm` to remove a directory recursively, as in the following command:

```
$ rmdir -r dir1
```

Red Alert!

Obviously, `rm -r` can wreak havoc on your system and delete files and directories that you may actually need. To be cautious, the first few times you use this command, you might want to include the `-i` option. This way, each time you delete a directory and its contents, you will get a prompt before each file is deleted.

Modify content / data commands – download files – wget

Running this command gives you control over grabbing and downloading files from web servers via HTTP, HTTPS, and FTP. Unlike the experience of downloading a file in a web browser, `wget` is noninteractive. This means that you don't have to be logged on for the command to complete its task, which is potentially a great time-saver with large file downloads.

How to do it...

In order to download files, you can use a command such as the following:

```
$ wget http://
```

This will download the Major Tom page at www.hudsonwerks.com into your current directory and create a file named `index.html`. Next, perform the following steps:

1. Check your work using the following command:

   ```
   $ ls

   Desktop     test     index.html
   ```

2. Now, perform another `wget`; this time, download via `ftp`. Here, we will grab `wget` source code from the GNU site as follows:

   ```
   wget ftp://ftp.gnu.org/pub/gnu/wget/wget-1.15.tar.xz
   ```

3. Check your work again, using the following command this time:

   ```
   $ ls

   Desktop     test     index.html     wget-1.15.tar.xz
   ```

There's more...

Where do we put the new tarballs, packages, and so on? It is good practice to create a directory called /home/username/Packages/. This is where you can put tarballs, their extracted files, compiled code, backups of replaced files, and installation scripts. For this, you can use the following command:

```
$ mkdir /home/username/Packages/
$ wget -P /home/debian/packages <download-url>
```

Modify content / data commands – open a tar file – tar [options]

Working with files in the .tar (tarball) format, a type of archived file, is common in Linux. The various options that come with the tar command will considerably ease your management of the files that are not archived.

How to do it...

Use the following command to open a tar file:

```
$ tar -zxvf file_name.tar.gz
```

Before actually running the command, let's understand a bit about the options:

- -z: This is used to uncompress the resulting archive with the gzip command
- -x: This is used to extract to disk from the archive
- -v: This produces a verbose output, which means that it shows progress and file names while extracting files
- -f document.tar.gz: This reads the archive from the file called document.tar.gz

Other file types include .xz, which is the actual file type we downloaded previously using wget—wget-1.15.tar.xz. So, here are the essential recipe steps:

1. By default, files are extracted into your current directory. However, you can simultaneously extract your files and put them in a different directory with the -C option. Using the following command, we will extract files and put them in the /test directory:

```
$ wget-1.15.tar.xz -C test
```

2. Check your work by navigating to the new directory created and running the following command:

```
$ cd /test/ wget-1.15
```

You should see all the unarchived `wget` source files with their accompanying directories.

The flip side of unarchiving is archiving. Here's how you can create a `tar` file:

```
$ tar -cvf file.tar inputfile1 inputfile2
```

Replace `inputfile1` and `inputfile2` with the files and/or directories that you want to combine. You can use any name in the place of `file.tar`; you should keep the `.tar` extension, though.

There's more...

You may occasionally run into errors while opening tarballs (or other `gzip` files). If so, one troubleshooting tip is to ensure that the file is actually a zipped archive with the following command:

```
$ file filename
```

This will show the file type and size; if it's not an archive, you can't run the `tar` command on it.

Modify content / data commands – clean up files – autoclean

This command removes partial packages from the system.

How to do it...

Use the following command to clean up files:

```
$ sudo apt-get autoclean
```

Modify content / data commands – purge a package – apt-get purge, apt-get remove --purge

These commands completely get rid of packages and dependencies.

How to do it...

Use the following command to get rid of packages and dependencies:

```
$ sudo apt-get purge packagename
```

Alternatively, you can use the following command:

```
$ sudo apt-get remove  --purge packagename
```

Modify content/data commands – shutdown the system – [options]

It is a bad idea to pull the plug on your board to turn it off. Doing so can often lead to a corrupted SD card or mangled files. Instead, here's how you power down your board gracefully.

How to do it...

If you want to shut down the BBB and reboot it, the following command will be useful:

```
sudo shutdown -r now
```

However, if you simply want to shut down the system and power down completely, then either of the following two options will do the trick:

```
sudo shutdown -h now
```

You can alternatively use the following command:

```
sudo poweroff
```

See also

▶ **Linux in A Nutshell**: The online version of this book delivers an abbreviated list of 687 commands (`http://www.linuxdevcenter.com/cmd/`)

▶ **Working with commands**: You can work with commands at `http://linuxcommand.org/lc3_lts0060.php`

You will find some of the best one-page cheat sheet references for Linux commands. Print them out and post them in an honored place!

▶ **The table from Make use of**: `http://www.makeuseof.com/pages/linux-commands-reference-pdf`

▶ **Free electrons' command memento**: This is well designed and comprehensive and can be found at `http://free-electrons.com/doc/training/linux-kernel/command_memento.pdf`

▶ An excellent cheat sheet that comes in different languages and printable PDFs can be found at `http://fosswire.com/post/2007/08/unixlinux-command-cheat-sheet/`

▶ You can read up more on cleaning up packages at `http://www.stchman.com/cleanup.html`

Edit a text file from the command shell

There is nothing pretty about the text editing tools in Linux. After all, it is a command shell environment; how pretty can it be? But if you are a minimalist at heart, you will feel right at home.

Two editors mostly dominate Developerland: `nano` and `vim`. The latter is the most powerful and fully featured. However, the `vim` command is not a good starting point for neophytes as it is more complex. Instead, our text editing tool of choice for the rest of this book will be `nano`. In this section, you will learn your way around the editor and then create and edit a text file.

How it works...

When you're using `nano`, take note of all the options at the bottom of the screen: `Exit`, `Get Help`, `Read File`, and so on. You access these functions with the keyboard shortcuts shown next to each option. Beware that these shortcuts actually may change their function or mode when you navigate to another screen or choose an option. So, remember what the bottom menu says before assuming that the shortcut you just used remains in the same mode.

In the main (default) window, here's a quick rundown on the most commonly used functions and their shortcuts:

- *Ctrl + X*: Closes the file.
- *Ctrl + V*: Takes you to the next page.
- *Ctrl + Y*: Takes you back to the previous page.
- *Ctrl + K*: Cuts text (deletes the line of text where your cursor is).
- *Ctrl + U*: Uncuts text (undoes the line deletion from the last line that you cut. Repeating this command will keep adding the same line of text that you cut).
- *Ctrl + G*: Help menu.
- *Ctrl + C*: Shows the current position (gives you line, column, and character coordinates).
- *Ctrl + R*: Inserts a file into the file you have open. Now that's a time saver, huh?

I recommend using *Ctrl + G* periodically when you're just beginning as a reminder for the additional functions available, many of which are powerful and useful. Overall, you will find that even a simple Linux-based text editor such as nano comes loaded with features that most Wintel/Mac desktop versions don't typically include.

How to do it...

This function can be performed through the following steps:

1. Let's begin by opening nano and simultaneously creating a file named major_tom:

```
~$ nano major_tom
```

   Pow! A window opens. That's the nano interface in all its glory. All right, not so sexy. But very functional, as you can see in the following image:

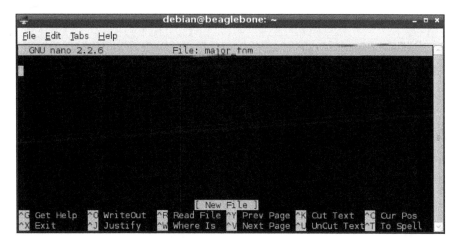

2. On the first line, which is where your cursor should be by default, type (or paste) the following:

   ```
   I love my Beaglebone Black so much I want to send it into orbit
   with Major Tom.
   ```

   Quickly looking around the window, you will notice the following:

   > At the top of the window, you will see the version of `nano` that you're using and the file name, `major_tom`.
   >
   > At the bottom of the window is an assortment of options.

   If you've played around with any of the options in the menu, ensure that you're back in the main screen where we began with our typed line about `Major Tom`.

3. Next, save the file by pressing *Ctrl + x*; when prompted, type `y` for yes:

   Error! What a bummer that we couldn't save our work. This is because we didn't first execute `nano` with the right user privileges. So, try again by closing the file by pressing *Ctrl + x*; when prompted, type `n` for no.

We lost our work, but it was only one line of text. We would now have popped back into the command line, and we will have another go; this time, we need a few more steps:

1. Let's make a custom directory; run this command:

   ```
   mkdir bbb_recipe_book
   ```

2. Go into this new directory and make a subdirectory; then, make a subdirectory of this one. This may sound overly complicated, but we're just trying to set up some files and directories by organizing principles early. Use the following commands for this:

   ```
   cd bbb_recipe_book
   mkdir projects
   cd projects
   ```

3. Check your work to ensure that you've set up the directory structure properly. Use the following command:

   ```
   pwd
   ```

4. Now, let's type `sudo nano major_tom.txt`. This time, we appended the filename with a text file type. If you don't do this, `nano`—and Linux—won't know with which application type to associate the file.

5. In the nano window again, type I love my Beaglebone Black so much I want to send it into orbit with Major Tom., as shown in this image:

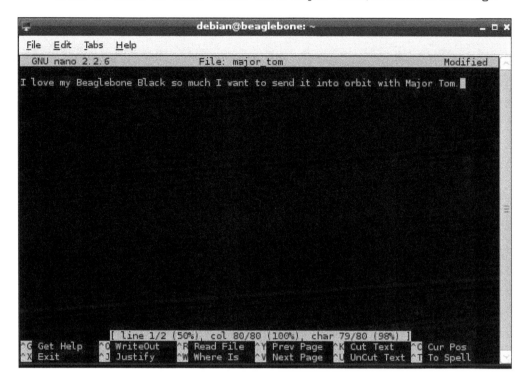

6. Then, press *Ctrl + x*; when prompted type y for yes.

7. Now you will see that the bottom menu has a new prompt, which reads as follows:

    File name to write: major_tom.txt

8. Hit return (*Enter*) on your keyboard. The file is saved to the new directory we're working in (/home/debian/bbb_recipe_book) and closed simultaneously.

You've now made a very exciting .txt file that you can go back and read whenever you want. Okay, that wasn't terribly challenging. But don't worry; we will be adding more complexity as we proceed in upcoming chapters.

See also

For those who find nano a bit Spartan in functionality and prefer a more powerful editor, vim is a popular choice. Although challenging to learn at first, you may find it to be a more rewarding and flexible choice as a tool. Learn how to use it at http://www.openvim.com/tutorial.html.

Connectivity

We will show you the two principal recipes to get your BeagleBone Black connected:

- ▸ Ethernet
- ▸ Wi-Fi

Beware that there is a third way to get the BBB online, which is by tethering your board to your desktop machine and piggybacking on its network connection. This is a highly useful but occasionally tricky option.

Connectivity – Ethernet

If you have direct access to your network's router, using the Ethernet connection is pretty much Plug and Play on the BBB.

Getting ready

Here's what you need for this recipe:

- ▸ 5V DC power supply
- ▸ An Ethernet cable
- ▸ A BBB connected to an HDMI monitor. For ease of use and first time connectivity, we suggest that you have your board connected to a monitor for this recipe. After you gain confidence and learn more about connectivity methods, you will be able to dispense with using an external monitor.

How to do it...

Perform the following steps for Ethernet connectivity:

1. With your BBB powered down, plug in one end of an Ethernet cable to the BBB and the other end to your router.
2. Power up your board via the 5V power supply.
3. The connection should occur seamlessly, assuming your Ethernet cable is sound, your internet connection is reliable, and the BBB has no defects.
4. At your screen's login prompts, enter your login name and password. You will be taken to the desktop.

5. Next, we will check our connection via a terminal session. In the lower left-hand corner of your screen, click on the bird-like icon and then navigate to **Accessories | LXTerminal**.

6. In the open terminal window, type the following:

```
$ ping www.google.com
```

You should be getting ping responses back that look similar to the following output:

```
debian@beaglebone: ~                                          _ □ ✗

File   Edit   Tabs   Help

debian@beaglebone:~$ sudo ping www.google.com
PING www.google.com (74.125.21.104) 56(84) bytes of data.
64 bytes from yv-in-f104.1e100.net (74.125.21.104): icmp_req=1 ttl=41 time=91.4
ms
64 bytes from yv-in-f104.1e100.net (74.125.21.104): icmp_req=2 ttl=41 time=90.6
ms
64 bytes from yv-in-f104.1e100.net (74.125.21.104): icmp_req=3 ttl=41 time=89.3
ms
64 bytes from yv-in-f104.1e100.net (74.125.21.104): icmp_req=4 ttl=41 time=93.1
ms
64 bytes from yv-in-f104.1e100.net (74.125.21.104): icmp_req=5 ttl=41 time=98.2
ms
64 bytes from yv-in-f104.1e100.net (74.125.21.104): icmp_req=6 ttl=41 time=106 m
s
64 bytes from yv-in-f104.1e100.net (74.125.21.104): icmp_req=7 ttl=41 time=105 m
s
64 bytes from yv-in-f104.1e100.net (74.125.21.104): icmp_req=8 ttl=41 time=88.8
```

Connectivity – Wi-Fi

Since its original release in the spring of 2013, Wi-Fi on the BBB has been a bit of an Achilles Heel for the platform. Compared to the typical experience with Raspberry Pi, you could pull out your hair getting Wi-Fi to work on the BBB. If you were happy using Angstrom only for your projects, you were in luck as this distribution was (mostly) solid, given that several USB minidongles on the market worked well.

However, on Debian and Ubuntu, unless you did not mind using larger dongles with protruding antennae, connections were flaky. Alternatively, you could invest a chunk of time writing custom drivers. So much for out-of-the-box portability.

Fast forward to the (mostly) good news. With the three different Wi-Fi dongles that we tested on the current shipping version of Debian 7 Wheezy for the BBB (using 3.8.13-bone71) and on Debian 8 Jessie, we largely got positive results. The bad news? With the exception of using Debian Jessie, not all dongles were recognized by the BBB without some configuration. However, it is fairly easy to set up the hardware, and you also may get lucky with the dongle you have in your kit and get immediate connectivity.

[If you are using Debian 8 Jessie, skip immediately to **Method Four: Debian Jessie**.]

Getting ready

The following are the prerequisites for Wi-Fi connectivity:

- DC power to the BBB—the board should be powered from a 5V DC 1A minimum supply and not via USB.
- A connected HDMI monitor.
- Wired or wireless keyboard and mouse connected to the USB hub.
- A powered USB hub—the Wi-Fi dongle draws more power than the BBB can deliver if you only power the board via the USB port on your client box. Instead, you need a powered hub to do the job. If you don't use a powered hub, you may be able to get away with decent stability, but you are just as likely to get poor results.
- Wi-Fi dongle—refer to tables to test compatible versions.

We will divide this recipe into three different setup methods as some dongles are happy with one method while others prefer the second one. We will also include the setup for Debian 8.0 (Jessie) as this distribution has greatly improved and simplified the process.

Some of the setup instructions are derived from `http://elinux.org/BBBWiFiConfigs`.

The micro USB dongle models

The universe of low-cost Wi-Fi dongles available on the market is fairly large, the following table being a very small subset. The mini dongles we used in these recipes have been historically problematic with the BBB but are now more reliable with the current Debian distribution. Your best results, however, may be with a standard-sized (nonmicro) dongle that also comes accompanied by an antenna.

The following table shows the tested and working models of micro USB dongles for our recipes. Note that the first three models use **Method Two** for setup and the last two use **Method Three**. All dongles are priced around USD $10.00-12.00:

Method Two					
Product Name	**Supplier**	**Manufacturer**	**Chipset**	**Power requirements**	**NOTES**
Ourlink	Adafruit	Realtek	RTL8188CUS	powered USB	This is the same product as #2

Method Two					
Product Name	**Supplier**	**Manufacturer**	**Chipset**	**Power requirements**	**NOTES**
802.11b	Adafruit	Realtek	RTL8188CUS	none	This is sold by Adafruit as the same product as #1; however, there seems to be some difference since a powered USB is not required.
Trendnet TEW648UBM	B&H	Realtek	RTL8188CUS	powered USB	The board may freeze up without using a powered USB. May also need to reboot and run. Use the reset (S1) button to get a connection.
Method Three					
UWN100	Logic Supply	Ralink/ MediaTek	MT7601	powered USB	
UWN200	Logic Supply	Ralink/ MediaTek	MT7601	powered USB	This uses antennae.

 UWN200 is not tested by the author but cited by the BBB Google forum posters as a compatible dongle with possibly superior performance given the antenna addition.

How to do it...

Method one: Graphical desktop application

In lieu of the command line, the current distribution of Debian 7 (3.8.13-bone71, Wheezy) includes a handy graphical tool—Wicd Network Manager—to set up Wi-Fi. This recipe is quite simple:

1. Power up your BBB via 5V DC.

2. Log in to a desktop session.

3. In the lower left-hand corner of your screen, click on the bird-like icon and then navigate to **Internet | Wicd Network Manager**.

4. In the newly opened window of the application, click on the **Switch On Wi-Fi** button. The dongle will now begin scanning for accessible networks.

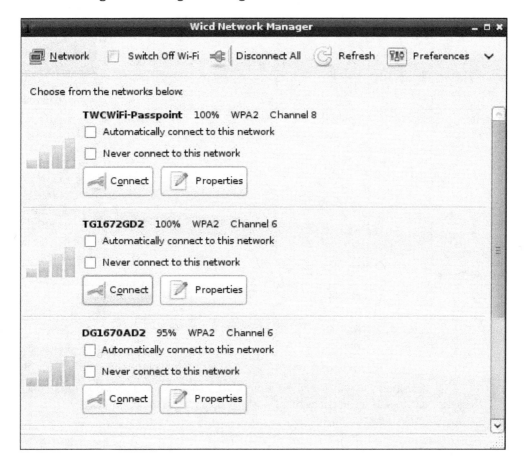

5. Choose your local network. Enter your password in the popup window according to the type of encryption your network uses. Then, click on **OK**. After a few moments, your dongle will be connected.

6. Check the connection with the ping command:

```
$ ping www.google.com
```

If all is well, you will be getting solid pingback messages.

Although the preceding steps are straightforward, you might find that your dongle will not work with this recipe or that you are using a different version of the kernel and easy connectivity eludes you. If so, here are other recipes to get connected.

Method Two: command line option 1

Consult the table at the beginning of this section for the tested models that use **Method Two**. Note that they all use the same RTL8188CUS chipset. This means that you will likely be able to use other dongles with the following steps as long as they use the aforementioned chipset. Now to the steps:

1. From your BBB's desktop, open up **LXTerminal**.

2. In the command prompt window, open the file in the directory specified in the following path:

   ```
   $ sudo nano /etc/network/interfaces
   ```

   Among other settings, you should see the following lines in the file's open window:

   ```
   ## WiFi Example
   #auto wlan0
   #iface wlan0 inet dhcp
   #    wpa-ssid "mynetworkname"
   #    wpa-psk  "mypassphrase"
   ```

3. With the exception of the first explanatory line, uncomment (which means remove) the # sign at the beginning of each line. To clarify, it should look similar to this:

   ```
   ## WiFi Example
   auto wlan0
   iface wlan0 inet dhcp
       wpa-ssid "mynetworkname"
       wpa-psk  "mypassphrase"
   ```

4. Change `mynetworkname` to your Wi-Fi network's name, and `mypassphrase` to your Wi-Fi password.

If your network name uses spaces or other odd characters, some dongles may not recognize the name and establish a connection.

5. Close the file by pressing *Ctrl + x*; when prompted, type `y` for yes and then press the return (*Enter*) key.

6. Power down the BBB in the terminal window with the following command:

    ```
    $ sudo poweroff
    ```

7. Power up the board again and log in to your BBB desktop.

8. You will now get a solid Wi-Fi connection. Test it via the command shell with this command:

    ```
    $ ping www.google.com
    ```

    If all went well, you should see a steady screen output from the ping.

Method Three: command line option 2

Consult the table for the tested models that use the following steps. The main difference between these steps and the previous recipe is that the drivers in these dongles require a different interface—a wireless supplicant—with the BBB to function properly. Before starting the steps, be sure to remove any Wi-Fi dongles you may have inserted into the USB hub:

1. We need to create a `.conf` file for `wpa_supplicant`, a tool that comes preloaded on the current Debian distribution. The following command line will be useful for this:

    ```
    $ sudo nano /etc/wpa_supplicant/wpa_supplicant.conf
    ```

2. Paste in the open file the following information:

    ```
    ctrl_interface=DIR=/var/run/wpa_supplicant GROUP=netdev
    update_config=1
    network={
      ssid="my-ssid"
      scan_ssid=1
      psk="my-psk"
      proto=RSN
      key_mgmt=WPA-PSK
      pairwise=CCMP
      auth_alg=OPEN
    }
    ```

3. Two things need to be modified (just as in **Method Two**): `my-ssid`, which you will replace with your network's name, and `my-psk`, which will be your network's password.

4. We now need to figure out the Wi-Fi dongle's interface name. To do this, we will first examine which interfaces are present using the following command:

   ```
   $ ifconfig -a
   ```

   This command outputs the currently active interfaces, which may include `eth0`, `lo`, and `usb0`.

5. Reboot your board.

6. Plug in your dongle and run the same command again:

   ```
   $ ifconfig -a
   ```

   The output should now show the new device's interface name, which could be `ra0`, `wlan0`, or so on.

7. Open the file in the directory specified in the following path:

   ```
   $ sudo nano /etc/network/interfaces
   ```

8. At the top of the file, paste the following code, replacing `interfacename` with the name that appeared in Step 6:

   ```
   allow-hotplug ra0
   iface interfacename inet manual
     wpa-roam /etc/wpa_supplicant/wpa_supplicant.conf
   iface default inet dhcp
   ```

9. Close the file by pressing *Ctrl + x*; when prompted, type `y` for yes, then press the return (*Enter*) key.

10. Assuming your dongle is still plugged in, run a command that brings up the interface:

    ```
    $ ifup interfacename
    ```

11. Power down the BBB by running this:

    ```
    $ sudo poweroff
    ```

12. Make sure your Wi-Fi dongle is plugged into a powered USB hub with the hub's USB cable inserted into the BDB's USB port.

13. Restart the board; this time, plug into the DC power supply.

14. You will now get a solid Wi-Fi connection. Test it via the command shell using the following command:

    ```
    $ ping www.google.com
    ```

    If all went well, you should see a steady screen output from the ping.

Sometimes you may need to power off, unplug the 5V input, and then plug in again as the dongle isn't always recognized through the S1 (Reset) or the S3 (Power) buttons.

Method Four: Debian Jessie

Using Jessie is the easiest and fastest route to a reliable Wi-Fi connection. Here is how to do this:

1. Plug an Ethernet cable connected to your router into the BBB's Ethernet port.

2. Boot up and log in to your BBB connected to a monitor.

3. Open a terminal window and log in as root with the following command:

   ```
   $sudo -i
   #
   ```

4. Install the package network manager. Before installing a new package, always begin by updating your repositories as follows:

   ```
   # apt-get update
   # apt-get install network-manager
   ```

5. Now, open up the new package with this command:

   ```
   # nmtui
   ```

   A rudimentary interface should open up in the terminal window, similar to the following image:

6. Select **Activate a connection**.

7. In the next window, select your network, and you will be prompted for the password.

8. Quit the network manager screen after putting in your password. Then, check to verify that your dongle now has an IP address in the wlanX interface with this command:

```
# ifconfig -a
```

9. Now, power down, remove the Ethernet cable, and reboot using this command:

```
# reboot
```

10. Run the magical ping command to check how we did:

```
$ ping www.google.com
```

Voila! Your BBB should now be connected wirelessly.

There's more...

Some users report that the board can interfere with a Wi-Fi dongle's USB signal. So, if you do not get a reliable connection, position your powered USB device containing the Wi-Fi dongle a few feet away from the BBB.

See also

Take a look at a list of other compatible dongles here at `http://elinux.org/Beagleboar d:BeagleBoneBlack#WIFI_Adapters`.

Package management – Installing packages using apt-get

If you are a newcomer on Linux, you will find that managing software on your BBB is a very different experience from the one on your Windows or Mac box. Linux distributions have a very different sensibility when it comes to installing and supervising your software.

In some ways, it is akin to what your smart phone universe is like: you go to a centralized place (Google Play, App Store, and so on) and download a vetted application.

Of course, there are huge differences in Land o' Linux. Firstly, everything is free. Secondly, everything is (mostly) open source. Thirdly, pieces of your package—dependencies, libraries, and so on—that evolve and improve are treated as separate entities that only need to be conjoined when you are ready to actually install a piece of software.

This means that you're always getting the freshest, most stable build. Whereas in Closed Source Land, executables are built to be self-contained. Any new module or better library that is built after the binary was compiled....well, too bad. You will have to wait for the next release, whenever that might be. And then you have to pay for the upgrade.

Software applications for Linux are referred to as packages. Henceforth, we will mainly use the term package in lieu of application. In this section, we will learn the basics of package management through the following topics:

- ▸ Updating packages
- ▸ Upgrading packages
- ▸ Installing packages

 These recipes assume that you have internet connectivity working via any of the methods explained in the earlier *Connectivity* section.

For our recipes throughout this book, we will principally use the apt-get command for package management. Although there are other methods, apt-get is the easiest and most common way to handle packages for a beginner.

Getting ready

Use the following steps to install packages:

1. **Updating packages**: Before actually installing new software in Linux, it's best practice to ensure that you have downloaded the most current versions of your local package lists along with information about their dependencies. You execute one of the most common commands in the Linux repertoire:

   ```
   $ sudo apt-get update
   ```

   As a result of this command, we get a resynchronized package index file that is targeted not only at your specific Linux distributions, but your hardware environment as well. For the BBB, this means that your package manager knows to only grab packages that are Debian-savvy and compatible with the Arm board architecture.

2. **Upgrading packages**: Next, you want to grab and upgrade to new versions of the packages already installed on your BBB, which the apt-get update will presumably have chronicled, through the following command:

   ```
   $ sudo apt-get upgrade
   ```

3. Finally, you get to install your new whizzy tool or app! Use this command:

```
$ sudo apt-get install pkg_name
```

How to do it...

Let's do a real package, though, one that we will be using in a later chapter. For our recipes focused on debugging in *Chapter 3, Physical Computing Recipes Using JavaScript, the BoneScript Library, and Python*, we will use a tool called gdb, also known as GNU Debugger, which is a standard tool in the Linux arsenal thus:

```
$ sudo apt-get update
$ sudo apt-get upgrade
$ sudo apt-get install gdb
```

Once you've installed the pretty package on your BBB, it's useful—and often interesting—to take a peek inside. So, another apt-get variant gives you some interesting insight:

```
$ sudo apt-cache show package-name
```

In our case, this would be as follows:

```
$ sudo apt-cache show gdb
Package: gdb
Version: 7.4.1+dfsg-0.1
Installed-Size: 5192
Maintainer: Hector Oron <zumbi@debian.org>
Architecture: armhf
Depends: libc6 (>= 2.13-28), libexpat1 (>= 2.0.1), libgcc1 (>= 1:4.4.0),
libncurses5 (>= 5.5-5~), libpython2.7 (>= 2.7), libreadline6 (>= 6.0),
libtinfo5, zlib1g (>= 1:1.2.0), gdbserver
Suggests: gdb-doc
Description-en: The GNU Debugger
 GDB is a source-level debugger, capable of breaking programs at
 any specific line, displaying variable values, and determining
 where errors occurred. Currently, gdb supports C, C++, D,
 Objective-C, Fortran, Java, OpenCL C, Pascal, assembly, Modula-2,
 and Ada. A must-have for any serious programmer.
Homepage: http://www.gnu.org/s/gdb/
Description-md5: 8132571fab028a898d029eecd88e571e
```

See also

To list all installed packages, enter:

```
dpkg --list
```

Alternatively, you can use this command:

```
dpkg --list | less
```

You can also run the following command:

```
dpkg --list | grep -i 'http'
```

Note the `grep` option as part of the command string. One of the most popular commands on Linux, `grep` is a powerful search mechanism to find a particular file, a directory, a pattern or chunk of code.

SSH / Remote access

Local control of your BBB should always be supplemented with the ability to control it remotely. There are a variety of reasons you may want to do this. For example, you may want to operate the device from one location while you are in another location.

The primary and most typical reason for remote access, however, is to run the board headlessly. This means running it without a display, keyboard, or mouse. Headless control is, in fact, the way I operate the board about 99 percent of the time. I rarely even use an external monitor with the BBB since it requires fewer pieces of hardware and reduces headache.

There are two basic recipe types for remote usage:

1. Command line via SSH
2. GUI-centric via VNC

Using SSH to control your BBB

Using SSH (secure shell) on a desktop PC or other client will give you control over your BBB across a network. Here is the recipe.

How to do it...

On your BBB:

1. Open **LXTerminal**.
2. Now, enter the following command:

    ```
    ~$ sudo ifconfig
    ```

3. In the onscreen text, get the IP address of your BBB. Under eth0O, look for inet addr: xxx.xxx.xxx.xxx.

On your PC/Mac/Linux box:

1. Open your preferred terminal app. On the Mac, it's just called **Terminal**.
2. At the command prompt, type the following:

    ```
    ~$ ssh-keygen -R <your_ip_address>
    ```

3. You should then get the following:

    ```
    /Users/username/.ssh/known_hosts updated.
    ```

    ```
    Original contents retained as /Users/ username/.ssh/known_hosts.old
    ```

    ```
    username@hrh:~$
    ```

4. Next, type the following:

    ```
    username@devicename:~$ ssh debian@<your_ip_address>
    ```

5. Now, you will see the following on screen:

    ```
    The authenticity of host '<your_ip_address> (<your_ip_address>)' can't be established.
    ```

    ```
    RSA key fingerprint is 97:b4:04:f5:24:f3:75:f9:90:3c:cc:ff:78:36:f3:d9.
    ```

    ```
    Are you sure you want to continue connecting (yes/no)?
    ```

6. Type yes (no quotes, all lowercase).
7. You will then see the following with a new prompt:

    ```
    Warning: Permanently added '<your_ip_address>' (RSA) to the list of known hosts.
    ```

    ```
    debian@<your_ip_address>'s password:
    ```

8. Type the password of your BBB login (the default is `temppwd`).

9. If you typed in your password correctly, you will end up back here:

   debian@beaglebone:~$

Congratulations! You've now gained control over your BBB using the command line from another box.

Using VNC to control your BBB

So, are you still not entirely comfortable with the command line and want access to some of the GUI-based tools? Or, do you need to test and control using an actual GUI? Or, perhaps, is your app not running properly from only the command line? Then, it's time for VNC.

Virtual Network Computing (**VNC**) allows remote access to a device that's running an X session or windows/GUI-based system from a remote device or client machine. With the current Debian distribution, running VNC is easier than ever as the BBB arrives preloaded with the relevant package, the TightVNC server. On your client box, you need to install a remote viewer.

Getting ready...

For your client box, download and install one of the following remote viewer applications:

▶ The Windows, Mac, and Linux boxes: `http://www.tightvnc.com/`

▶ VNC Viewer: `http://www.realvnc.com/download/viewer/`

Once again, we're cooking up a recipe from a Mac perspective, so VNC Viewer it will be.

How to do it...

As noted, the BBB now comes with the remote server installed, so the only new installation required is the one for your client box. For this, perform the following steps:

1. Install the client app on your desktop box.

2. From the terminal window, run the VNC server on the BBB through the following command:

   ```
   $ vncserver
   ```

3. Next, you will need your BBB's port address. You will find it in the status message now running in the CLI window:

```
New 'X' desktop is beaglebone:1
```

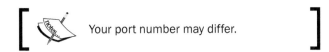

Your port number may differ.

4. On your desktop box:
    ❑   Open up VNC viewer (or whichever client app you're using)
    ❑   Type in the IP address of your BBB and the port number at the end of the VNC server field: 123.456.78.9:1. The default my be "beaglebone:1.

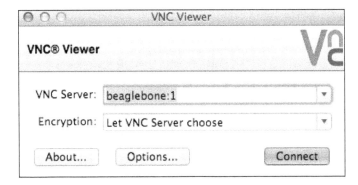

5. You will then have a window pop up **Unencrypted Connection**.
6. Click **Continue**.
7. Select **Connect**.

You will now be logged in to your BBB, be able to see the desktop, and have full control over the device using the mouse on your client box.

There's more...

▶   **Security**: Using the default or basic settings in VNC is not secure. Unless you're familiar with doing so, the sessions are not encrypted. One quick, though imperfect, measure is to change from the default server port 5900 to a spare, randomly chosen port.

▶ **Getting the IP address on a headless BBB**: From another computer on the network, use the following steps to list a network's basket of IP addresses:

```
ifconfig | grep inet
```

- ❑ Note that this will show the IP address range and only name specific host devices but not other addresses.

- ❑ This method may only be feasible in a smaller network, where the number of addresses is more limited and you do not have to look for a needle in a haystack.

- ❑ You will likely need to install the NMap security scanner (`http://nmap.org/`). Check whether it's installed first.

- ❑ Then, type in `sudo nmap -sn -PE 192.168.1.0/24` (with the IP address of the host machine and then /xxx from the end range shown in Step 1).

▶ **Browse to the local router admin address**: Find the configuration options that show all computers/devices on the network with their IP addresses.

▶ **Set a static IP address**: This takes several steps, but one of the best tutorials is Derek Molloy's at `http://derekmolloy.ie/set-ip-address-to-be-static-on-the-beaglebone-black/`.

System images

In this section, we will give you the recipes to download, install, and update the Debian distribution firmware and software kernel that comes preloaded on your board. Finally, we will walk you through changing over from the currently shipping Debian 7.0 (Wheezy) to the newer Debian 8.0 (Jessie).

There are two basic methods to install and update your board's software: install the OS onto the eMMC solid-state internal drive or a compatible SD card (refer to the compatibility list in further chapters). In either case, the process is commonly called flashing the image, which is how we will refer to it.

One of the signature features of the BBB is its ability to use many different flavors of Linux to run the board. In the further chapters, you will find references and material to install various versions of Linux, including Ubuntu, ArchLinux, and Android.

OS image flashing – internal drive boot

Although your board comes preloaded with a shipping version of Debian 7, you certainly want to understand how to replace it or update it when necessary. Here, we will discuss the recipe to flash the OS to your internal solid-state drive along with how to update to Debian 8.

As of the writing of this book, Debian 8 (Jessie) is still considered a testing option, whereas Debian 7 (Wheezy) is the official shipping firmware OS for the BBB. Additionally, you will notice "LXQt" as part of the URL download link. LXQt is a lightweight Qt variant of LXDE, the Lightweight Desktop Environment. Qt is a toolset to build cross platform applications that you can use on Mac OS X, Windows, and Linux. It uses the C++ programming language and has a nice GUI builder, so it is a popular choice for many open source-centric developers.

Getting ready

You will need the following:

- ▸ BeagleBone Black powered down.
- ▸ A 5V DC power supply. You can also use a 5V "wall wart" power adapter with a USB port on it as long as it can deliver 1A.
- ▸ A microSD card (4GB or greater).
- ▸ An SD card reader. You will insert the microSD card into the card reader and the card reader into an SD port on your desktop machine.
- ▸ A board connected to either an HDMI monitor or an LCD cape (as explained earlier in this chapter).

 If you had it connected, ensure that you remove the Ethernet cable before proceeding with this recipe as an Ethernet connection requires more current and will likely cause the software flashing to fail.

How to do it...

The following steps are used to flash the OS to your internal drive:

1. Using the `wget` command, get the software and put it on your desktop computer.

    The latest version of the shipping OS, Debian 7 (Wheezy), is available at `http://beagleboard.org/latest-images`. So, you need to get the exact URL and append it accordingly in the following command:

    ```
    $ wget https://rcn-ee.com/rootfs/bb.org/release/YEAR-MONTH-DAY/
    lxde-4gb/BBB-eMMC-flasher-debian-7.8-lxde-4gb-armhf-YEAR-MONTH-
    DAY-4gb.img.xz
    ```

    The preceding link references a Rev. C board, the currently shipping version. If you have another version of the BBB, you can find software for prior releases at `http://elinux.org/Beagleboard:BeagleBoneBlack_Debian#Debian_Build_Instructions`.

    Debian testing version

    You can also alternatively install Debian 8 (Jessie) using the same steps as the following, substituting the URL and appending the month, day, and year accordingly:

    ```
    https://rcn-ee.com/rootfs/bb.org/testing/YEAR-MONTH-
    DAY/lxqt-4gb/BBB-eMMC-flasher-debian-8.0-lxqt-4gb-
    armhf-YEAR-MONTH-DAY-4gb.img.xz
    ```

2. Next, unpack, unzip, or unarchive the downloaded file using your favorite archive tool. On my Mac, I use Unarchive since it's easy to use and flexible. After unarchiving, there will be an `.img` file available in your chosen folder.

3. Now, we will flash the `.img` file to the microSD card. The easiest method is to use a GUI-type tool such as Pi Filler (originally designed for Raspberry Pi but works equally well on the BBB) for the Mac, or Win32 Diskimager on your Windows box.

    Wait for a prompt from the imaging software before actually inserting the SD card into the desktop's slot. Depending upon the speed of your desktop box's environment, the flashing/writing process will take anywhere from 15 to 30 minutes.

4. Remove the SD card from your desktop after the flashing finishes and then remove the microSD card. Ensure that your BBB is powered down and then insert the card into the microSD slot on the BBB.

5. Press and hold the *Boot* switch, which is the small button on the BBB above the microSD card slot. Take a look at the the following image to confirm that you are pressing the *Boot* switch and not one of the other switches:

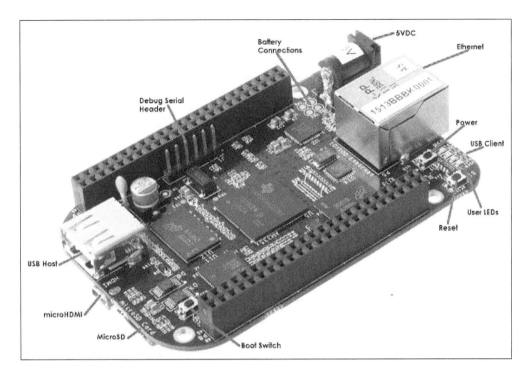

6. While holding this button down, insert the 5V supply into the power jack.

7. As the board boots up, the array of LEDs next to the Ethernet jack at the other end of the board will begin flashing in a sweeping pattern.

8. When the boot completes, all four LEDs should be lit and not blinking. Remove the power cable and then remove the microSD card from the BBB.

9. Now, plug the 5V supply back into the board again. The BBB will boot directly from the eMMC.

10. In your terminal window, we will now SSH into the board with the following command:

```
$ ssh debian@192.168.7.2
```

11. When the login prompts appear, use the following credentials:

```
username: Debian
```

```
password: temppwd
```

You should now be ready for action with the default graphical desktop showing the BeagleBone Black logo in the lower-right corner of the screen. This means that you are almost ready to go....

There's more...

Good practice to manage your system OS and files includes having enough room to add more packages, being able to clone your eMMC, and backing up your code image.

Expand your partition

Unless you use an SD card larger than 8 GB, you're likely to run out of space quickly on your card even after a modicum of packages are installed. So, save yourself a whole lot of hurt and expand your partition size....now! The following steps will be useful:

1. Change to the root user with this command:

   ```
   $ sudo -i
   ```

2. Check the disk space usage using the following command:

   ```
   root@beaglebone:~# df -h
   ```

3. Go to this directory as follows:

   ```
   # cd dir: /opt/scripts/tools
   ```

4. Check the available files using this command:

   ```
   # ls
   ```

   You will see the grow_partition.sh script. This is a bash script included in the BBB distribution that will run a routine to expand your SD card space.

   Now, run the following:

   ```
   # bash grow_partition.sh
   ```

   Alternatively, you can also run the following command:

   ```
   # sh grow_partition.sh
   ```

5. Finally, running ls again on your drive will show a higher percentage of available space:

   ```
   # ls
   ```

Backing up a code image to a file

1. Insert a microSD card into your desktop machine's card reader and confirm that it's recognized.

2. On your desktop box (Mac, in our case), open **Terminal** and type the following:

```
$ diskutil list
```

3. From the list shown, write down the ID for your SD card. In my case, it looks similar to this:

```
/dev/disk1
```

4. Now, we will run a routine that backs up the content of the card to your desktop and simultaneously archives it to save space:

```
sudo dd if=/dev/rdisk1 bs=1m | gzip -9 > ~/Desktop/backupimage.
img.gz
```

5. Input your password at the prompt. When you do so, the routine will run and may take several minutes depending on the amount of data you're backing up.

OS image flashing – the SD card boot

In this section, you will learn the recipes to load the OS and boot from a microSD card. Much of the process is similar to how we flash the eMMC internal drive; however, it is important to take note of the differences.

Getting ready

You will need the following:

▸ BeagleBone Black powered down

▸ A 5V DC power supply or a USB tethered to the BBB.

▸ A MicroSD card (4 GB or greater)

▸ An SD card reader. You will insert the microSD card into the card reader and the card reader into an SD port on your desktop machine.

▸ A board connected to either an HDMI monitor or an LCD cape (as explained earlier in this chapter).

How to do it...

Perform the following steps:

1. Using the `wget` command, get the latest software image and put it on your desktop computer.

   The latest version of the shipping OS is at `http://beagleboard.org/latest-images`. So, you will need to get the exact URL and append it accordingly in the following command. Note the URL difference from the prior recipe for flashing the internal drive:

   ```
   $ wget https://rcn-ee.com/rootfs/bb.org/release/YEAR-MONTH-DAY/
   lxde-4gb/bone-debian-7.8-lxde-4gb-armhf-YEAR-MONTH-DAY-4gb.img.xz
   ```

   The preceding link references a Rev. C board, which is the currently shipping version. If you have another version of the BBB, you can find software for prior releases at `http://elinux.org/Beagleboard:BeagleBoneBlack_Debian#Debian_Build_Instructions`.

   Debian testing version

   You can also alternatively install Debian 8 (Jessie) using the same steps by substituting the following URL and appending the month, day, and year accordingly:

   `https://rcn-ee.com/rootfs/bb.org/testing/YEAR-MONTH-DAY/lxqt-4gb/bone-debian-8.0-lxqt-4gb-armhf-2015-05-04-4gb.img.xz`

2. Next, unpack, unzip, or unarchive the downloaded file using your favorite archive tool. On my Mac, I use Unarchive as it's easy to use and flexible. After unarchiving, there will be an `.img` file available in your chosen folder.

3. Now, we will flash the `.img` file to the microSD card. The easiest method is to use a GUI-like tool such as Pi Filler for the Mac or Win32 Disk Imager on your Windows box.

   Wait for a prompt from the imaging software before actually inserting the SD card into the desktop's slot. Depending on the speed of your desktop box's environment, the flashing/writing process will take anywhere from 15 to 30 minutes.

4. Remove the SD card from your desktop after the flashing finishes and then remove the microSD card. Ensure that your BBB is powered down and then insert the card into the microSD slot on the BBB.

   Either with the USB tether or a 5V power supply, power up the BBB.

5. In your terminal window, we will now SSH into the board with this command:

   ```
   $ ssh debian@192.168.7.2
   ```

6. When the login prompts appear, use the following credentials:

   ```
   username: debian
   ```

   ```
   password: temppwd
   ```

Updating your current OS kernel

Sometimes, you want to stick with what you have already installed as it runs fine and does the job. But more often than not, you want the latest and greatest kernel, including updating to Debian 8.0, aka Debian Jessie. The following steps show you how:

1. Ensure that you are logged in as the root user with the following command:

   ```
   $ sudo -i
   root@beaglebone:~#
   ```

2. Check the version of the kernel that you have currently installed:

   ```
   # uname -r
   3.8.13-boneXX
   ```

3. Navigate to the directory with the update kernel script:

   ```
   # cd /opt/scripts/tools/
   ```

4. Run a command on the kernel you currently have installed that `pulls` down to your local drive information regarding any changes:

   ```
   # git pull
   ```

    We will explore the `git` command in a later chapter.

5. Now, we will run the script that takes advantage of the information we just pulled down and updates our OS:

   ```
   # ./update_kernel.sh
   ```

6. Time to reboot! Run the following command:

   ```
   # reboot
   ```

7. When the login prompts appear, use the following credentials:

   username: debian

   password: temppwd

8. Finally, verify that the script did what we expected through the following command:

   $ uname -r

   3.8.13-boneXX

Compare the preceding screen output with the version you wrote down in Step 2 of this recipe. You should, hopefully, see the new version kernel goodness.

See also

If you know a specific version you want, you can also update or modify your kernel with an alternative method using a series of command-line steps:

1. Log in as root as follows:

   $ sudo -i

2. Check the kernel version with this command:

   # uname -r

3. Update your repositories with this command:

   # apt-get update

4. Find available kernel versions using this:

   # apt-cache search linux-image

   The screen output will deliver a long list of kernel options. Scroll the list until you find one with the label: Linux kernel, version 3.8.13-boneXX (with the XX being a two-digit number).

5. Install the kernel you want by explicitly specifying a version number from the list in the prior step as follows:

   # apt-get install linux-image-x.x.x-xx

6. Reboot your board as follows:

   # reboot

   $ uname -r

   Your new kernel should now be installed on your board.

2
Basic Programming Recipes

As the next step in learning how to control and manipulate your BeagleBone Black, we will take a look at the following languages, tools, and simple programming recipes in this chapter:

- ▶ Introduction to BoneScript
- ▶ Toggle LED
- ▶ Using the Cloud9 IDE
- ▶ Node.js basic recipes
- ▶ Adding a new module to Node.js
- ▶ Using Node.js with Johnny-Five
- ▶ Python basic recipes
- ▶ Adding libraries
- ▶ Running a Python script to control the LEDs

Introduction

In the first chapter, our objective was to ensure that all you new chefs were ready with sharpened knives and the right combination of seasonings, or at least equipped with a basic working environment with happy, flashing blue LEDs on your BeagleBone Black and some command-line controls.

In later chapters, you will learn how to use other physical pieces of the system, including controlling the physical pins on the board. Before we get there, however, you will need to take a quick dip into a handful of recipes using programming languages that are typical and essential for building robust, compelling projects on BeagleBone Black. So, give a big round of applause to your soon-to-be faithful friends: BoneScript, Node.js, and Python.

Introduction to BoneScript

BoneScript is BBB's handy Node.js library. What is Node.js, you ask? Also, why bother with another library? We will talk more about Node.js in the next section. However, as far as another library goes, we're bothering with it because it's designed to work seamlessly with the hardware of your board, making physical computing development under embedded Linux faster and simpler. Using Arduino-like functions, BoneScript exploits the vast developer base of JavaScript.

Typically, your intention in using Node.js and BoneScript on BBB—just as it is with Python in the next section—is to gain access to the header pins, the **General Purpose In/Out** (**GPIO**) pins. Although we will discuss more about GPIOs in a later chapter, for now our plan is to briefly explore some fundamental methods to control the hardware.

Toggle LED

In this section, let's do a quick and easy recipe with BoneScript, one that turns on and off the on board LEDs, also known as USR LEDs. We will tackle more complex recipes with BoneScript in the next chapter.

How to do it...

In order to do this, perform the following steps:

1. Remove all cables and power from your BBB.
2. Power up your board via the mini USB using your desktop USB port.
3. On the BEAGLEBONE_BLACK device that appears on your desktop, browse to and open the START.htm file (some versions of the OS may have a slightly different file name, such as BASIC_START.htm).

 Note that on Debian 8 (Jessie), your board will be labelled BEAGLEBONE on the desktop and not BEAGLEBONE_BLACK.

4. Scroll down the page to `BoneScript interactive guide`, where you'll see an embedded script that you can run to interact with BBB.

5. Click on **Run**.

6. All the LEDs should stay on for two seconds. Let them return to blinking.

7. Now change **USR0** from `b.HIGH` to `b.LOW`.

8. Change the timing from `2000` to `12000`.

9. You should now see two differences from the default script that you just ran. Firstly, the LEDs now stay on for longer (12 seconds), and the **USR0** LED—the LED closest to the **Reset** button—now remains off.

Voila! You're talking to the hardware using JavaScript and BoneScript.!

See also

If you run into any errors while running your BoneScript recipes, such as **Cannot find module 'bonescript'**, you may need to do two things:

1. Check the version of BoneScript that you are running on your board using the following code:

   ```
   $ node -pe "require('bonescript').getPlatform().bonescript"
   ```

2. Install the latest version of BoneScript; to do this, you need to be the root user first. Then, you can execute the following command:

   ```
   $ sudo -i
   # TERM=none npm install -g bonescript
   ```

Using the Cloud9 IDE

As the name implies, Cloud9 is a cloud-hosted toolkit. For BBB, it provides an integrated, open source development environment to build BoneScript-powered (JavaScript) code. Its strengths are JavaScript and Node.js (which it actually uses on the backend; we'll discuss this in the next section), though it is also very flexible with other programming languages such as PHP, Ruby, and Python.

The IDE comes preloaded and ready to use immediately on the BBB firmware with no setup necessary. With your board still connected via USB, let's do a snappy recipe.

How to do it...

1. To load the IDE, open a browser window to the following URL:
    `http://192.168.7.2:3000/ide.html`. The IDE will open to a window like this:

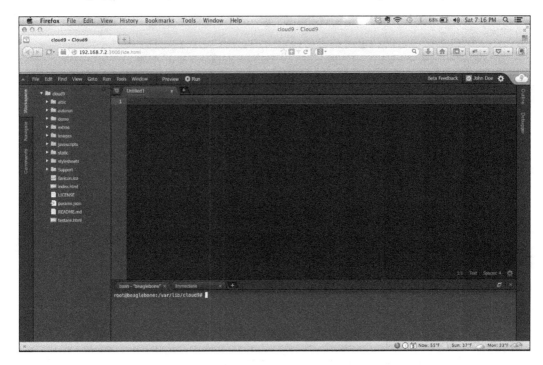

2. Next, change the color settings to improve readability in the UI. The default black
    scheme is funereal; let's change it to **Cloud9 Bright Theme** instead.

Not all UI screens change to the new color scheme; there's a temporary bug
in this beta release of Cloud9's IDE.

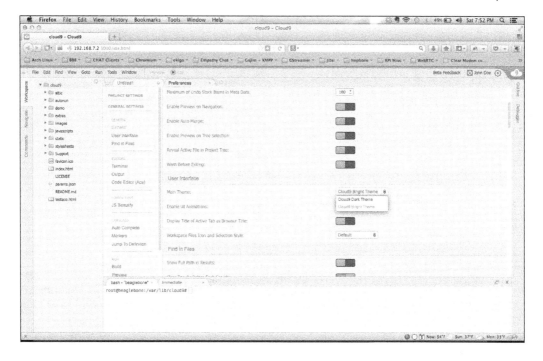

3. One handy feature in the lower portion of the screen is a command shell window. This gives the user an integrated command-line control within the IDE proper without the need to pop open another window for a shell application.

4. Unless you want to customize the UI or listen to the audio tutorials, close the **Welcome** tab.

5. Create a new file by clicking on the **+** sign.

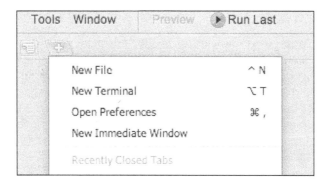

6. Copy and paste the following code in the new window:

```
var b = require('bonescript');
var ledPin = "USR0";

b.pinMode(ledPin, b.OUTPUT);

var state = b.LOW;
b.digitalWrite(ledPin, state);

setInterval(toggle, 1000);

function toggle() {
    if(state == b.LOW) state = b.HIGH;
    else state = b.LOW;
    b.digitalWrite(ledPin, state);
}
```

For you Arduino users, the code feels kind of familiar, right? For those of you who are brand new to physical computing and hardware, let's break down some of the lines before executing the script.

At the outset of the code, we needed to establish certain ground rules, namely that we will be using the functionality of BoneScript. So, we had to include the BoneScript library with all its functionalities and coding shortcuts with the following script:

```
var b = require('bonescript');
```

Next, we needed to establish which pin or pins we intended to use (USR0) and then create a variable of it so as to not have to write the pin name repeatedly throughout the script. The following code helped us do this:

```
var ledPin = "USR0";
```

Once we had an anointed pin to play with, we needed to set its mode—in other words, initialize it—so that we could interact with it and declare whether it will be an input or output pin. If we were controlling a button, the pin would need to be recognized as an input; however, in our case we had an LED, which needed to be in the output mode. Note also b., which is used in the notation. This was used to tell the code interpreter—Node.js—that the subsequent function will be found in the BoneScript library. For this, we used the following code:

```
b.pinMode(ledPin, b.OUTPUT);
```

With the pin initialized, we declared whether the pin began in a state of being on (HIGH) or off (LOW). At this point, we also needed to tell the interpreter that we would actually be writing to the pin, as opposed to collecting data from it or reading it, with the following script:

```
var state = b.LOW;
b.digitalWrite(ledPin, state);
```

Our task moved on to telling the interpreter how often we will be doing a particular thing. In our case, we toggled the light on and off in 1000-millisecond intervals by executing the following script:

```
setInterval(toggle, 1000);
```

It was great that we knew the frequency of our toggle event, but as we did not yet tell the interpreter what the `toggle` term actually does, we had to explain its meaning. We described it as a function that alternates between the states of `HIGH` and `LOW`, which was applied to the pin that we declared at the beginning of our script with the following lines of code:

```
function toggle() {
    if(state == b.LOW) state = b.HIGH;
    else state = b.LOW;
    b.digitalWrite(ledPin, state);
}
```

Okay! For the moment, that's enough of a script breakdown. If you have not already jumped ahead, let's continue with the recipe's steps and take a look at how these lines actually affect the LED.

Now, perform the following steps:

1. Create a new directory called `projects` and save the file in it, naming the file `major_tom_blinks.js`.

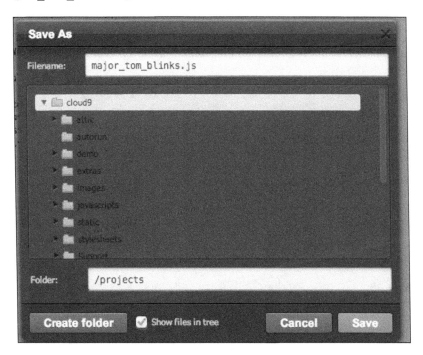

2. Now, run the file in the terminal window at the bottom of the IDE. First, ensure that you navigate to the proper directory using the following lines of code:

```
$ cd projects
$ node major_tom_blinks.js
```

3. The USRO LED (which is the on board LED closest to the reset button) should now have changed its constant "heartbeat"-patterned blink to slower, steadier 1-second blink intervals.

4. Now, press *Ctrl + z* or click on the **Stop** button in the terminal pane window at the bottom of the IDE. Don't forget to do this; otherwise, you're likely to run into some errors or confusion in the upcoming recipes.

5. Finally, it's a good idea to reset the LEDs so that you end up where you started. For now, the easiest way to do this is by running the restore script at `http://beagleboard.org/Support/BoneScript/demo_blinkled/`.

See also

You can find more information at `http://beagleboard.org/Support/BoneScript`.

Node.js basic recipes

JavaScript on the server; let that sink in for a moment....

What is Node.js? The quick and dirty answer is that it's a unique and very fast server environment to handle requests from client applications and apps that are authored in Javascript. It's Javascript on the server. More specifically, it's an I/O framework that:

- Is event-driven
- Is nonblocking
- Runs on the V8 JavaScript engine
- Executes JavaScript code on the server side
- Is rich in robust developer libraries and modules

Node's speed makes it particularly useful in physical computing scenarios as it can handle requests in real time. After all, when a gust of sudden wind blows and your BBB-powered drone starts teetering midair, you don't want to rely on a poky LAMP stack and keep those gyros compensating.

The good news about Node.js—and we'll often just call it node—is that you don't have to install it because it comes preloaded on the BBB firmware. The bad news about Node.js is that it can be a bit confusing to understand for beginners; its sheer simplicity is daunting! However, once you review some recipes, you'll likely find yourself a new fangirl/fanboy of node.

Adding a new module to Node.js

Here is a recipe to add a new module into Node.js. In this case, we'll use Nodemailer, a powerful and highly customizable API e-mail engine. We chose this module because we wanted to actually have the script do something interesting and not just spit out another onscreen print command. At the end of this recipe, you will be able to run a script that sends an e-mail to your inbox.

Getting ready

Open up **LXTerminal**. Alternatively, open up the Cloud9 IDE in the manner described in the previous section.

How to do it...

Create a directory for your projects using the following command:

```
$ mkdir projects
```

Perform the following steps after creating a directory for your project:

1. Browse to this new directory and make another `emailer` directory using the following command:

    ```
    $ cd projects
    $ mkdir emailer
    ```

2. Now, go to the new directory with the following command:

    ```
    $ cd emailer
    ```

3. Although it's not mandatory, the following command is the proper first step to setting up your node environment:

    ```
    $ npm init
    ```

    You will see a series of prompts that you can fill out; you can skip them by hitting the return (*Enter*) key on your keyboard.

    What you will do with these prompts and inputs is create the metadata to populate a file called `package.json`. This file's purpose is to give information to `npm`, which allows it to identify the project as well as handle the project's dependencies.

4. Next, we will use the following command to install the star of the current show: a node package called `nodemailer`:

    ```
    $ sudo npm install nodemailer --save
    ```

5. Navigate to the new directory created by the installation and open up a `nano` window with a new filename, as described here:

```
$ cd node_modules/nodemailer
$ sudo nano nodemailer-test.js
```

6. Copy and paste this code in the nano window:

```
//This code has been modified from the nodemailer github example.

var nodemailer = require('nodemailer');

var transporter = nodemailer.createTransport({
    service: 'Gmail',
    auth: {
        user: 'gmail.user@gmail.com',
        pass: 'user_password'
    }
});

// setup e-mail data with unicode symbols
var mailOptions = {
    // sender address
    from: 'Ground Control <your_name@gmail.com>',
    // list of receivers
    to: 'sender_name1@some_domain.com, another_address@
anotherdomain.com',
    // Subject line
    subject: 'This is Ground Control to Major Tom',
    // plaintext body
    text: 'Can you hear me, Major Tom?',
     // html body
    html: '<b>Can you hear me Major Tom?</b>'
};

// send mail with defined transport object
transporter.sendMail(mailOptions, function(error, info){
    if(error){
        return console.log(error);
    }
    console.log('Message sent: ' + info.response);

});
```

The preceding code is a modification of nodemailer's GitHub example. Also note: if you run into problems copying and pasting the code, you can download the code from `https://github.com/HudsonWerks/Nodemailer/blob/master/examples/nodemailer-test.js`.

Finally, if you use Gmail for your account in this example and run into login errors, there are numerous troublehooting tips here: `https://github.com/andris9/nodemailer-wellknown/issues/3`.

7. Save the new file using the keyboard command, *Ctrl + x* with `nano`, and then type `Y` for "yes".

   Then, press the return (*Enter*) key.

8. Now, run the following command:

   ```
   $ node nodemailer-test.js
   ```

9. Ta-da! If all went well, you should receive an e-mail from Ground Control in your inbox.

There's more...

▶ *6 things you should know about Node.js*: This is perhaps the best (and most succinct) article on why Node.js has become a freight train for rapid, robust development, and can be found at `http://www.javaworld.com/article/2079190/scripting-jvm-languages/6-things-you-should-know-about-node-js.html`.

▶ *The Node Beginner Book*: The author of this book provides the first 21 pages for free and charges for the rest of the book, which is definitely worth the $20.00. You can find it at `http://www.nodebeginner.org/`.

▶ *Mixu's Node book*: Although it was originally written several years ago, it remains an excellent in-depth introduction to Node.js. This can be easily found at `http://book.mixu.net/node/`.

▶ *From Java to Node.js*: You can find this at `https://n0tw0rthy.wordpress.com/2013/01/08/from-java-to-node-js/`.

▶ For further ideas on which modules are out there, explore the extensive list of node modules found at `https://github.com/nodejs/node/wiki`.

See also

To explore this particular module, including nodemailer's wide variety of features and customization options, check out `https://github.com/andris9/Nodemailer`.

Using Node.js with Johnny-Five

In this section, we will cover a recipe for Johnny-Five, a unique library built in JavaScript/ Node.js that is increasingly getting the attention of the open source software world. Although positioned as a robotics library, Johnny-Five is a great tool set to scratch the itch that many JS developers have for hardware now.

One of its principal advantages is that it greatly simplifies the process of managing pins and allows a programmer to use more obvious naming conventions in their code, such as *LEDs*, *buttons*, sensors, and servos, rather than *high pins*, *low pins*, and so on. Although it does not yet have out-of-the-box ease that BoneScript has for BBB, you should consider it a viable and, in some ways, more robust alternative. It is also a more modular library than BoneScript as the code can be easily ported to a variety of platforms. Finally, if you are an Arduino aficionado, you will appreciate its familiarity as it is based on the Arduino Firmata protocol.

How to do it...

Perform the following steps to use Node.js with Johnny-Five:

1. As usual, good practice before installing a new package is to update your repositories. You can use the following command line for this:

    ```
    $ sudo apt-get update
    ```

2. Next, we will install Johnny-Five as root user using npm (node package manager) and not apt-get, as follows:

    ```
    $ sudo -i
    # npm install johnny-five
    ```

3. Then, we will add a BeagleBone-specific plugin with the following command. This will make our board's I/O pins easily accessible:

    ```
    $ npm install beaglebone-io
    ```

4. In a terminal window, open up the nano editor with a new filename using this command:

    ```
    $ sudo nano johnny5_led1.js
    ```

5. Copy and paste this code in the nano window:

    ```
    var five = require('johnny-five');
    var BeagleBone = require('beaglebone-io');
    var board = new five.Board({
      io: new BeagleBone()
    });
    ```

```
board.on('ready', function() {
  var led = new five.Led();


// turn the LED off and on in 1000ms increments
  led.blink(1000);


  this.repl.inject({ led: led });
});
```

 If you run into problems copying and pasting the code, you can download the code from `https://github.com/HudsonWerks/Johnny-Five/blob/master/johnny5_led1.js`

6. Save the new file using the following keyboard command with `nano`, *Ctrl* + *x*; when prompted type `y` for yes and then press return (*Enter*) key:

7. Now, run the following script:

   `$ sudo node johnny5_led1.js`

   The onboard LED (USR3) should begin blinking at 1-second (1000ms) intervals.

We will not break down every part of the script here; you can further investigate Johnny-Five in the *There's More...* section. However, one thing we will point out is a feature of the code that expresses Johnny-Five's modularity over BoneScript, specifically the following line:

```
var board = new five.Board({
  io: new BeagleBone()
```

With Johnny-Five, this code snippet is all you need to change if you want to run the same script on the Raspberry Pi, Arduino, or UDOO board or a huge range of other SOCs. "Write once, run anywhere" is getting closer....

There's more...

For more insight into Johnny-Five, it's best to start by exploring their wiki, which is full of examples and documentation, at `http://johnny-five.io/`. In addition to the BeagleBone Black, you will notice that the library supports a host of SOCs and microcontrollers.

Learn more about the Johnny-Five `beaglebone-io` plugin and the specific pin mapping for the board at `https://github.com/julianduque/beaglebone-io#beaglebone-io`.

Python basic recipes

In addition to your JavaScript chops, some of you reading this most likely have some Python skills. We'll take a look at a similar recipe to activate the onboard LEDs; this time, however, we will do this from a Python perspective.

Getting ready

Let's confirm that you have Python installed and working properly along with its IDE. After this, perform the following steps:

1. Open a terminal window and type the following:

    ```
    $ python
    ```

2. At the >>> prompt, type:

    ```
    >>> print "This is Ground Control"
    ```

3. Now, you should see this:

    ```
    This is Ground Control
    ```

4. To quit, press *Ctrl + z*.

Adding libraries

The current Debian distribution includes the Adafruit_BBIO and PyBBIO libraries, both of which are extremely useful and commonly used on BBB to control the pins of your board with Python. We will work with these libraries in the next section.

If you're using the current Debian 7 Wheezy distribution or Debian 8 Jessie, you can skip to the next section. However, if you have some other version of an OS, here are the steps to install the two libraries.

How to do it...

Part One: Installing Adafruit _BBIO library. Perform the following steps:

1. Log in as the root user with this command:

    ```
    $ sudo -i
    ```

2. Using the following command, ensure that you update your package list:

    ```
    # apt-get update
    ```

3. Now, install the library's dependencies through the following command:

```
# apt-get install build-essential python-dev python-setuptools
python-pip python-smbus -y
```

 For instructions on installing a software patch to make extra pins accessible with the library (the SPI and UART pins, in particular), refer to the further chapters.

4. Now, we can install the library itself with the following command:

```
# pip install Adafruit_BBIO
```

5. Test your package installation by typing out this command:

```
# python -c "import Adafruit_BBIO.GPIO as GPIO; print GPIO"
```

Your output should look similar to this:

```
<module 'Adafruit_BBIO.GPIO' from '/usr/local/lib/python2.7/dist-
packages/Adafruit_BBIO/GPIO.so'>
```

Part Two: Installing PyBBIO library. Perform the following steps:

1. Log in as the root user with the following command line:

```
$ sudo -i
```

2. Ensure that you've updated your package list using the following command:

```
# apt-get update
```

3. Now, install the library's dependencies with this command:

```
# apt-get install python-serial python-setuptools python-dev
python-smbus python-pip
```

4. Now, we can install the library itself. Use the following command for this:

```
# pip install --upgrade PyBBIO
```

5. Test your package installation via the following command line:

```
# python -c "import bbio as GPIO; print GPIO"
```

If all went as hoped with the installation, your output should look similar to this:

```
PyBBIO initialized
<module 'bbio' from '/usr/local/lib/python2.7/dist-packages/
PyBBIO-0.9.4-py2.7-linux-armv71.egg/bbio/__init__.pyc'>Finished
PyBBIO cleanup
```

Running a Python script to control the LEDs

In the next chapter, we'll look at more robust ways to begin using the GPIO pin library. In the meantime, let's wrap up by doing an on board LED blink similar to the recipe we did earlier in the chapter.

However, instead of BoneScript, we'll do a variation of the recipe in Python and specifically pull on the PyBBIO library's functionality. This recipe will work on both Debian Wheezy and Jessie.

How to do it...

Perform the following steps to run Python scripts to control LEDs:

1. Open up **LXTerminal**.

2. Create a python project directory within the `bbb_recipe_book` directory and navigate to it as follows:

   ```
   mkdir python

   cd bbb_recipe_book/projects/python
   ```

3. Create a new Python file using the following code (note the `.py` file format):

   ```
   sudo nano major_tom_blinks.py
   ```

4. Copy and paste the following code into the window:

   ```python
   #!/usr/bin/python


   # Blinks one of the Beaglebone Black's on-board LEDs until CTRL-C
   is pressed. These LEDs include USR0, USR1, USR2, USR3


   # Import PyBBIO library
   from bbio import *
   #import the time module which allows us to set the timing for a
   loop event
   import time


   #Create variable called ledPin which refers to one of the
   designated onboard USR LEDs. You can change the number to any of
   the USR LEDs listed above.
   ```

```
ledPin = "USR3"


# Create a setup function
def setup():
    # Set one of the USR LEDs as output
    pinMode(ledPin, OUTPUT)


# Set up a loop and the blink timing to two second intervals
while True:
    # Start the pin state at LOW = off
    digitalWrite(ledPin, LOW)
    # Hold this state for 2 seconds
    time.sleep(2)
    # Change the pin state to HIGH = on
    digitalWrite(ledPin, HIGH)
    time.sleep(2)
```

 If you run into problems copying and pasting the code, you can download the code from `https://github.com/HudsonWerks/Python-examples/blob/master/major_tom_blinks.py`

5. Run this script:

   ```
   $ sudo python major_tom_blinks.py
   ```

6. The on board USR3 LED should now be blinking at regular 2-second intervals.

7. To quit the script, press *Ctrl + z* on your keyboard.

There's more...

Python is a big subject, and the web is jammed with great resources to learn it more deeply. Here is a small, select sample of starting points to teach yourself Python:

▸ MIT's online course is on demand, free, and taught by one of their computer science department's favorite teachers, Prof. John Guttag. You can find it at `https://www.edx.org/course/introduction-computer-science-mitx-6-00-1x-5`.

- ▸ Coursera has several strong online courses. Most of their courses are not available on demand but for specific schedules throughout the year. Here are two excellent Python courses offered:

  - ❑ University of MICHIGAN offers Python in their *Programming for Everybody* series. You can find it at `https://www.coursera.org/specializations/python`.

  - ❑ Rice Unversity's 8-week course is another excellent introductory dive to be found at `https://class.coursera.org/interactivepython1-003`.

- ▸ Python.org is an excellent place to get started with its tons of links on the beginners' page at the link, `https://wiki.python.org/moin/BeginnersGuide/Programmers`.

3
Physical Computing Recipes Using JavaScript, the BoneScript Library, and Python

Now that you're armed to the...er, fingertips with your Linux commands and can happily control your BeagleBone Black remotely like a pro, it's time to get physical with the board. So, to begin with our exercises in physical computing, we're whipping up some essential recipes on the following topics:

- ▸ Controlling external LEDs
- ▸ Using buttons – button press function
- ▸ Using analog sensors
- ▸ Variable resistance sensor – photocell
- ▸ Using motors

Our programming language of choice will principally be JavaScript in tandem with BoneScript, which is a Node.js and browser-side library. We will also include or reference a few Python script analogues to broaden our skills with the hardware.

Introduction

The basics of physical computing typically require understanding and shaping input and output on your hardware. We will begin with taking a look at the old chestnut, manipulating LEDs, an experience you're likely to have some familiarity with if you have read the last chapter, or if you're an Arduino or Raspberry Pi user. Next, we'll play a bit with buttons because who doesn't like to push a button? Then, it gets more interesting as we add sensors to the mix. After this, we'll give you some basic recipes for locomotion that use some motors. Finally, we'll wind it up with the ingredients and steps for setting up a connection between your BBB and an Arduino board.

We'll march across the BBB, draft the large army of pins that the board has at our disposal, the GPIOs, ADCs, PWMs, and UARTs, a phalanx that makes the Raspberry Pi look feeble. All of these acronyms may seem impenetrable; however, throughout the course of this book we will steadily learn something about all of them.

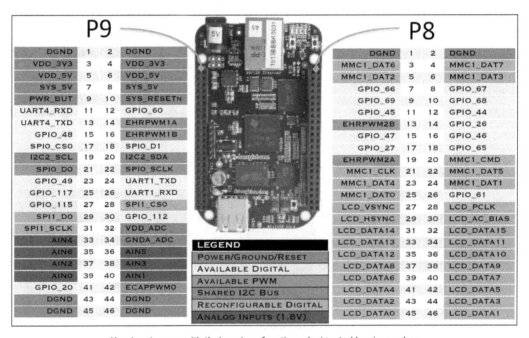

P9

DGND	1	2	DGND
VDD_3V3	3	4	VDD_3V3
VDD_5V	5	6	VDD_5V
SYS_5V	7	8	SYS_5V
PWR_BUT	9	10	SYS_RESETN
UART4_RXD	11	12	GPIO_60
UART4_TXD	13	14	EHRPWM1A
GPIO_48	15	16	EHRPWM1B
SPI0_CS0	17	18	SPI0_D1
I2C2_SCL	19	20	I2C2_SDA
SPI0_DO	21	22	SPI0_SCLK
GPIO_49	23	24	UART1_TXD
GPIO_117	25	26	UART1_RXD
GPIO_115	27	28	SPI1_CS0
SPI1_DO	29	30	GPIO_112
SPI1_SCLK	31	32	VDD_ADC
AIN4	33	34	GNDA_ADC
AIN6	35	36	AIN5
AIN2	37	38	AIN3
AIN0	39	40	AIN1
GPIO_20	41	42	ECAPPWM0
DGND	43	44	DGND
DGND	45	46	DGND

P8

DGND	1	2	DGND
MMC1_DAT6	3	4	MMC1_DAT7
MMC1_DAT2	5	6	MMC1_DAT3
GPIO_66	7	8	GPIO_67
GPIO_69	9	10	GPIO_68
GPIO_45	11	12	GPIO_44
EHRPWM2B	13	14	GPIO_26
GPIO_47	15	16	GPIO_46
GPIO_27	17	18	GPIO_65
EHRPWM2A	19	20	MMC1_CMD
MMC1_CLK	21	22	MMC1_DAT5
MMC1_DAT4	23	24	MMC1_DAT1
MMC1_DAT0	25	26	GPIO_61
LCD_VSYNC	27	28	LCD_PCLK
LCD_HSYNC	29	30	LCD_AC_BIAS
LCD_DATA14	31	32	LCD_DATA15
LCD_DATA13	33	34	LCD_DATA11
LCD_DATA12	35	36	LCD_DATA10
LCD_DATA8	37	38	LCD_DATA9
LCD_DATA6	39	40	LCD_DATA7
LCD_DATA4	41	42	LCD_DATA5
LCD_DATA2	43	44	LCD_DATA3
LCD_DATA0	45	46	LCD_DATA1

LEGEND

POWER/GROUND/RESET
AVAILABLE DIGITAL
AVAILABLE PWM
SHARED I2C BUS
RECONFIGURABLE DIGITAL
ANALOG INPUTS (1.8V)

Header pin array with their various functions designated by pin number

Although we will have a dash of Python code here and there, the recipes in this chapter will primarily consist of BoneScript/JavaScript ingredients and its powerful potions for physical computing. For an extensive documentation of the BoneScript Library and its up-to-date reference, refer to `http://beagleboard.org/Support/BoneScript`.

Before we head off to the recipe land (and since this chapter is actually about how to make some basic electrical circuits), we need to take a quick look at some of the foundational principles of electricity and current. Knowing a few things about them will prevent you from accidentally frying your board.

The essentials of electronics

How much power does an LED need? What would happen if I ran a 5V circuit with a 3V power supply? Will my 12V battery pack keep the robot going long enough to get the data I need? Also, most importantly, can I attach the Spottiswoode Great Induction Coil Cape to pins *9_11* and **37** on the BeagleBone Black?

 The earlier versions of BeagleBones were larger than the Black version. However, you should never connect an old or new BeagleBone Black to a Spottiswoode Great Induction Coil.

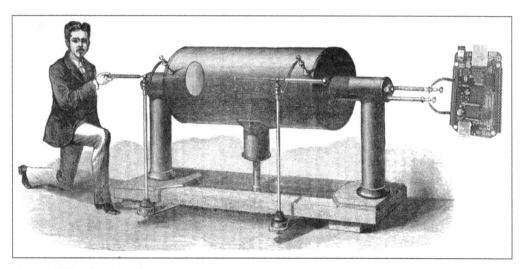

Source: William Spottiswoode and induction coil from Wikimedia Commons / The London, Edinburgh, and Dublin Philosophical Magazine, 1877. Image composite by Charles Hamilton.

To discover the answer to these and other (potentially) board burning questions, you need to know a bit about the three pillars of electronics wisdom and wiring: current, voltage, and resistance:

- **Current**: The continuous flow of electrons, or the rate of "charge" through a given point in a circuit.

- **Voltage (potential difference)**: This indicates the size of the electrical potential in your circuit that allows electrons to flow. Specifically, voltage is the difference in the electrical potential between two given points that allows electrons to move. This is why it is known as the potential difference.

- **Resistance**: This denotes that electrons get hung up from Point-A to Point-B, that is, there is friction that can impede their free flow of current, which we call resistance.

How do all these things relate to one another when it comes to circuitry?

The easy answer is Ohm's law. Much ink has been spilled in explaining this foundational principle of electricity; we will only say a few words and quickly throw a formula at you, the only one you will see in this book: $V = I \times R$.

Knowing how to use this basic formula will help you determine the right combination of current and resistance to apply when you wire up your BBB circuits. Here is the breakdown of the formula:

- **V**: This specifies voltage (expressed in volts)

- **I**: This indicates current (expressed in amps)

- **R**: This denotes resistance (expressed in ohms and commonly seen as Ω)

As long as we know any two of the three variables, we will use Ohm's law to calculate the third and remaining number. Typically, you will need to use Ohm's law to determine the right resistor to use when you wire up a circuit.

There are numerous and exhaustive free examples available online that show you how to use Ohm's law for your projects. Here are a few excellent ones:

- Sparkfun's tutorial on *Voltage, Current, Resistance, and Ohm's Law* is one of the best for beginners and is available at `https://learn.sparkfun.com/tutorials/voltage-current-resistance-and-ohms-law`

- Collin Cunningham, formerly of *Make magazine* and now an Adafruiter, gives us the video version skinny at `https://www.youtube.com/watch?v=-mHLvtGjum4`

- A very handy online Ohm's law calculator tool is available at `http://www.onlineconversion.com/ohms_law.htm`

If you take nothing else from this section, at least heed this one warning: be very careful how you power your BeagleBone Black; otherwise, you may damage it.

Header pins and pinmuxing

The magical thing about microcomputers is that they give you the ability to interact with the physical world. This interaction is essentially possible via the GPIOs and other pins. These pins are intended to generate different voltage levels and pulses. This is the essential purpose of programming a GPIO: you will tell the board to generate a specific level of voltage or pulse on a specific pin.

Perusing our complement of I/O pins, we can count two rows of 46 pin slots on the two expansion headers. If you look closely, you will see that one block is labeled **P8** and the other one **P9**. All the references to a specific pin begin with this block number first, followed by a number between *1* and *46*. Therefore, the example pins look similar to *P8_2*, *P8_15*, *P8_24*, *P9_2*, *P9_15*, and so on.

But what do you do with all these pins? Not all of them are actually available. Some have been drafted for other purposes. According to the BBB reference manual, the board has the following breakdown for pin purposes and availability:

# of Pins	Purpose of pins
65	General purpose and digital IO pins
8	PWMs
4	Timers
7	1.8V analog inputs
4.5	UARTs
2	I2C
?	SPI
2	5V
2	3.3V

 The BBB also includes another six male pins to accommodate a serial debug cable on the main board (not the headers).

To understand the nitty-gritty of the pins that may be available, you can refer to the *BeagleBone Black System Reference Manual* at `http://elinux.org/Beagleboard:BeagleBoneBlack`. *Page 84* describes the pins on the **P8** header, and *page 86* describes the pins on the **P9** header. There are also numerous reference guides online that help you understand the BBB's pin layouts. Skip to the *There's more...* section for additional sources. In the meantime, the following image a snapshot view of the board's entire *pinmux*. You can also refer back to the pin mapping diagram at the beginning of this chapter.

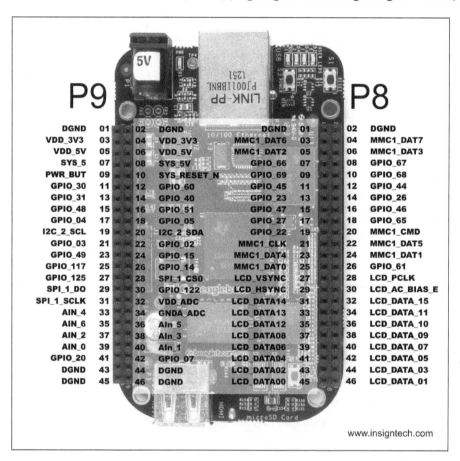

The process of pinmuxing

A common frustration among new BBB users is that the pins do not always respond as expected. This is because, by default, some header pins are assigned to specific tasks, such as the HDMI output, some are used for multiple purposes, and many of its functions are only available after some tweaking. For example, pin *21* on the *P9* header wants to be a GPIO at some time, whereas at other times, it wants to be a PWM, a UART, an I2C, or a SPI pin.

So, how do you get around this pin schizophrenia? Well, you have to reconfigure it for this purpose, a process known as pin multiplexing or **pinmux**. Pinmuxing is fairly straightforward and can be easily handled from the command line. We will encounter this technique later in this and subsequent chapters.

Although the BBB's sophisticated pin design can accept different types of signals, in this chapter, we will mainly take a look at the two types that are commonly used in physical computing:

- **Pulse width modulation** (**PWM**)
- **Analog to digital converter** (**ADC**)

Within our toolset is another software application that electronics and hardware makers rely heavily on: Fritzing. You may already be familiar with it, but if not, Fritzing is an extremely handy open source graphical tool for creating diagrams of breadboards, schematics, and PCB layouts without the need for traditional engineering schematics.

 Before wiring up your breadboard, it's a good idea to reset the BBB each time you perform a new recipe by powering it down. This ensures that the pins are reset to their input state. Otherwise, if the pin is being used as an input in a new recipe that was previously used as an output, you may damage your BBB.

There's more...

Here are some of the sources and links to the BeagleBone Black's pin layouts:

- One of the best pin-mapping guides is Eskimon's interactive overlay at `http://eskimon.fr/beaglebone-black-gpio-interactive-map`.
- The full expansion header layout is at `http://elinux.org/Beagleboard:Cape_Expansion_Headers`
- A more succinct diagram of GPIOs is available at `http://stuffwemade.net/post/beaglebone-pinout-new`.
- Collars that you can attach to the BBB that provide easy call outs for the GPIO pins is available at `http://www.doctormonk.com/2014/01/beaglebone-black-collars.html`.
- Take a look at how to use BeagleBone Black GPIOs at `http://www.armhf.com/using-beaglebone-black-gpios/`.
- A quick guide on how to pinmux is available at `http://beaglebone.cameon.net/home/pin-muxing`.

▶ Derek Molloy's *Beaglebone: GPIO Programming on ARM Embedded Linux* tutorial and video is another comprehensive and thoughtful introduction available at `http://derekmolloy.ie/beaglebone/beaglebone-gpio-programming-on-arm-embedded-linux/`.

Controlling external LEDs

In the last chapter, we looked at a quick blink recipe on how to control our on board LEDs. Now, the objective is to have an external LED on a breadboard blink. First, we will take a look at the circuit symbol of a basic LED so that we can recognize its proper usage, as shown in the following diagram:

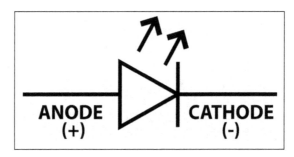

The typical symbol for a light-emitting diode (LED)

In the following image, you will see what a real-life LED actually looks like. Not so straightforward as looking at the symbol, right?

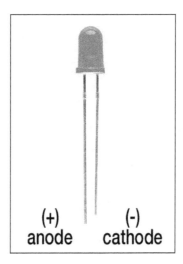

With LEDs, polarity matters to have a working circuit. Pay attention to the fact that the anode is the longer end, whereas the cathode is the shorter end. Although mixing them up will not cause any damage, the circuit will not work.

Getting ready

You'll need the following items to supplement your now happily perking BBB:

- **LED**: Just a plain vanilla, inexpensive LED is fine; this is the type you'll find for pennies at your local hobby store or online. You may already have a bunch in your kit.
- **Resistor**: Anything from 700 (700Ω) to 1k is fine. We will use a 700Ω version here (violet/black/brown/gold bands).
- **2x jumper wires**: These are easy to connect to the breadboard.
- **Breadboard**.

How to do it...

Now, let's begin with the following steps:

1. From our fritzing tool, here's the diagram we made for our wiring:

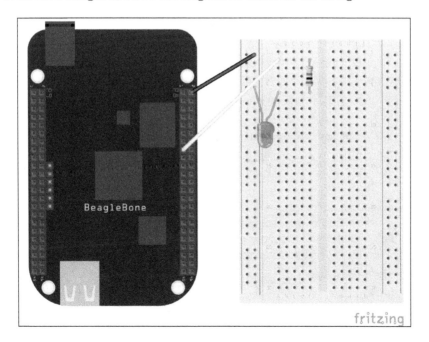

2. Now, wire up your breadboard using the following steps:

    1. First, put the Ground wire into GND (*P8_2*) on the BBB.

    2. Then, insert the other wire to the *P8_15* pin on the BBB.

    3. On the breadboard, put the LED's shorter end—the cathode (-) pin—into the GND rail and the longer end—the anode (+) pin—into the sixth slot of the breadboard.

    4. Now, insert your resistor and make sure that the top end is aligned in the slot with the GPIO wire and the bottom end is aligned with the LED's anode.

3. Open up Cloud9 IDE at `http://192.168.7.2:3000` and create a new file called `blink_LED.js`.

4. Then, copy and paste the following code into the open IDE window:

```
// Setup
var b = require('bonescript'); // Call library
var LED = "P8_15"; // Pin choice
var state = 0; // LED state
b.pinMode(LED, 'out'); // Pin function

setInterval(blink, 500);
function blink() {
   state = !state;
   b.digitalWrite(LED, state);
```

5. Before running the code, let's take a closer look at the parts. First, as noted in the prior chapter, you need to invoke the BoneScript library so you have access to all its functions:

```
// Setup
var b = require('bonescript');
```

Please keep in mind that anything after the `//` are comments, and isn't functional code.

6. Now, select the pin number where your LED is wired. You can change this option easily; just be sure to choose from an available pin. Then, make the change on your board as well. Refer to the pin layout reference diagram at the beginning of this section for more background on the pin outs, as shown in the following code:

```
var LED = "P8_15";
```

7. This line defines the variable state of our pin, which in this case has a LED connected to it. Naturally, the state will vary as either on or off, where 0 is equal to off and 1 is equal to on:

    ```
    var state = 0;
    ```

8. Following this, as the pin has no preassigned value, here, we have to use `pinMode` to tell the pin (P8_15) what type of pin it's supposed to be, either an `INPUT` (this would be used with a button) or an `OUTPUT`. In this case, as we will control a LED, our GPIO will be an output, as follows:

    ```
    b.pinMode(LED, b.OUTPUT);
    ```

    You can also write it this way:

    ```
    b.pinMode(LED, 'out');
    ```

9. From the setup code, we then shift to instructing the LED to evoke the blink function (which we'll define in the next section of code). Then, flash on/off according to whatever interval we specify (in this case, every 500 milliseconds). This line is analogous to the commonly seen `loop` function in Arduino scripts. However, JavaScript and the event-driven Node.js environment greatly simplifies the code, as follows:

    ```
    setInterval(blink, 500);
    ```

10. Finally, we will define the `blink` function. The `!` before the `state` value inverts the value, and as the LED begins with a 0 (off) state (this isn't the same as 0 changing to 1 (on)). The last line (`b.digitalWrite`)—which happens to be Arduino-friendly syntax—establishes an output statement for the LED and its on/off state, as shown in the following code:

    ```
    function blink() {
        state = !state;
        b.digitalWrite(LED, state);
    }
    ```

11. Finally, let's see what the script does. Click **Run** in the Cloud9 IDE. Your LED should now be blinking merrily at 500 millisecond increments.

 You can find more documentation on the BoneScript library functions at `http://beagleboard.org/support/bonescript`.

Writing an alternative script with Python

Starting from *step 3*, here's the Python version of the recipe that uses the Adafruit library:

1. In the Cloud9 IDE terminal window, open a new file window in the editor and name it `blink_LED.py`.

2. Copy and paste the following code to the window:

```
import Adafruit_BBIO.GPIO as GPIO
import time

GPIO.setup ("P8_15", GPIO.OUT)

while True:
        GPIO.output("P8_15", GPIO.HIGH)
        time.sleep(1.0)
        GPIO.output("P8_15", GPIO.LOW)
        time.sleep(1.0)
```

3. Now, save the script.

4. Click Run in the Cloud9 IDE. Your LED should begin blinking.

There's more...

You can find more support in these tutorials:

▶ Sparkfun's multipage tutorial on LEDs provides a top-notch further study at `https://learn.sparkfun.com/tutorials/light-emitting-diodes-leds`

▶ For a beginner, instructables delivers excellent and additional background on LEDs at `http://www.instructables.com/id/LEDs-for-Beginners/`

Using buttons – button press function

Buttons come in all shapes and sizes. Some are quiet. Some are noisy. Some are expensive. Some cost pennies. We'll not only use the cheap and peppy, penny variety, but also show an example with a more interesting, whizzy personality and make it do something more than just turn the switch on and off.

Pull-up, pull-down, and floating

Frequently when wiring up circuits, you will hear references to pull-up, pull-down, and floating configurations. When your design is a pull-up circuit, this means that the resistor holds the positive or supply voltage (VCC) until you push the button pulling it up to ground. This is the most common scenario, and one you encounter when you design a circuit with a button press to activate something.

In the pull-down version of a circuit, the resistor in the circuit remains at ground unless you push (or pull down) the button, causing the circuit to switch from ground to positive or supply voltage (VCC).

Floating means the circuit is neither tied to ground or a particular voltage. This can create a situation where a pin may accumulate some kind of charge on it, thus throwing off incorrect values. You can create a more reliable circuit by writing code to correct for these potential false readings.

The purpose of this recipe is to read the state of a button press and have it turn an LED on and off. When the button is not pressed, the state of the input pin will be a 1 or high due to the resistor pulling the pin up. When the button is pressed, the input pin will be grounded low and have the value as 0.

Getting ready

You'll need the following items for this recipe:

- **1 x LED**: This is the same one you used in the previous section.
- **1 x pushbutton**: This is a simple, one button, four-pronged tactile switch. By default, the button pins are open (disconnected) and momentarily closed (connected) when the button is pressed.
- **Resistors**: 2x 700 (700Ω) to 1k will be fine. We will use the 700Ω here (violet/black/brown/gold bands).
- **5 x jumper wires**: This is easy to connect to the breadboard.
- **Breadboard**.

How to do it...

1. Wire your board and breadboard in the following manner:

    1. Connect the GND wire to GND at *P9_2* on the BBB and the other end to GND in the first slot at the top of the second row on the breadboard.

    2. Insert a red wire into the 3V slot at *P9_3* and the other end into the power rail on the breadboard.

    3. The button will use the next wire. Connect a wire to the pin on the *P9_15* BBB and to the first slot in the same row in the upper-left corner of the button on the breadboard.

    4. Take another wire and connect one end to *P8_11* on BBB and the other end to row 2 and column 1 on the breadboard.

    5. The last wire serves as Ground for the button. Connect one end of this wire to the GND rail and the other end next to the button's GND leg.

    6. On the breadboard, connect the LED's cathode pin (the shorter end) to the GND rail and the anode or the positive lead (the longer end) into the sixth row of the breadboard

    7. Insert one resistor to regulate the current to the LED and the other to regulate the flow through the button, as shown in the following image:

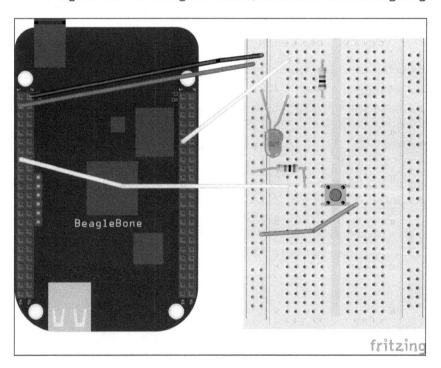

2. Now, open your Cloud9 IDE at `http://192.168.7.2:3000` and create a new file called `button-led.js`.

3. Then, use the following code to turn the LED on and off with a push button. Copy and paste it into the open IDE window:

```
// Setup
var b = require('bonescript'); //Read library
var LED = "P8_11"; //Pin where LED is connected
var BUTTON = "P9_15";

b.pinMode(LED, b.OUTPUT);
b.pinMode(BUTTON, b.INPUT);

setInterval(readBUTTON, 10);

function readBUTTON() {
    b.digitalRead(BUTTON, writeLED);
}

function writeLED(x) {
    b.digitalWrite(LED, !x.value);
}
```

- Before running the code, let's look at how the script breaks down. First, as always, evoke the BoneScript library with the following code:

```
// Setup
var b = require('bonescript'); //Read library
```

- Now, choose the pin number where your LED is wired. You can change this option easily; just be sure to choose from an available pin (see the pin layout reference diagram at the end of this section for more background on the GPIOs):

```
var LED = "P8_11"; //Pin where LED is connected
```

- Then, we will set the pin number for the button, as follows:

```
var BUTTON = "P9_15";
```

❑ Now, we will tell the previously specified pins to function in an OUTPUT mode for the LED and in an INPUT mode for the button, as shown in the following code:

```
b.pinMode(LED, b.OUTPUT);
b.pinMode(BUTTON, b.INPUT);
```

You can also write it this way:

```
b.pinMode(LED, "out");
b.pinMode(BUTTON, "in");
```

❑ Now, we need to check the status of the button at specific intervals, in this case, every 10 minutes, as shown in the following code:

```
setInterval(readBUTTON, 10);
```

❑ Then, we need to define another function, as shown in the following code, this time one that triggers an event based on when the button is pressed:

```
function readBUTTON() {
b.digitalRead(BUTTON, writeLED);
}
```

❑ Finally, we will define a function for the LED when the button is pressed with the following code:

```
function writeLED(x) {
   b.digitalWrite(LED, !x.value);
}
```

4. Finally, we run the script by clicking the **Run** button. Your LED should now be blinking. Change the interval value to speed it up or slow it down.

 If you get an error in the IDE's console window, sometimes the fix is as simple as clicking on the **Resume** button in the upper-right corner panel or just restarting the script. You can also turn off the debugger to keep the script running.

There's more...

The ultimate circuit/resistor/capacitor cheat sheet—we recommend a couple of very useful smartphone apps that serve as exceptionally handy reference tools for resistor and capacitor codes, circuit calculators, and other useful component values. First, is AdaFruit's **Circuit Playground** app for iPhone and Android. Although not free (but available for just a few dollars), it sure beats getting it wrong on those resistor color value bands. Second, for the Android platform only is Electrodroid, which has free and pro (USD $2.99) versions available in the Google Play store.

Using analog sensors

Now it's time to grab some analog data. Wait a second? Analog? Isn't the world we live in—including the BBB's—all digital? Mostly, yes. But the world of sensors is vast, and many of the most ubiquitous, most useful, and least costly sensors are analog devices. A great deal of the embedded sensing world—motion, temperature, humidity, light intensity, pressure, and accelerometers—consists of analog animals. So, how do we capture all that analog data goodness?

With ADC (analog to digital converter) pins, of course. And the BBB comes with seven pre-assigned analog inputs on our board, so it's nearly plug and play! Well, not quite. But at least we don't have to fuss with pin muxing right away.

Temperature sensors

For this recipe, we're using the TMP36, a very low cost (USD $1.50) analog temperature sensor that you can find at many different electronics stores or suppliers. It outputs an analog voltage that is proportional to the ambient temperature. We will write a script that takes that proportional value and reads back the temperature into the Cloud9 console.

Getting ready

- **Temperature sensor**: Available at SparkFun (`http://bit.ly/OCGFDj`)
- **3x jumper wires**: Easy to connect to the breadboard
- **Breadboard**

How to do it...

1. Make sure your BBB is powered down first, then wire up your breadboard. Here's what your wiring should look like:

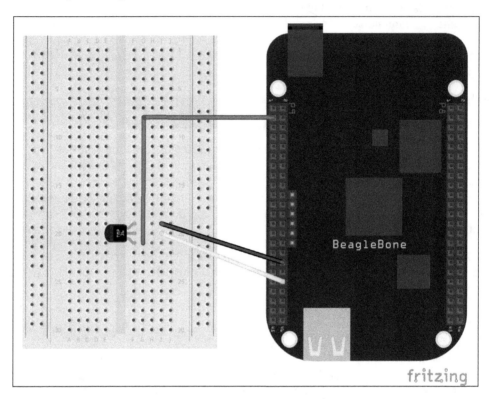

Be sure that you...

> Put the GND into the special analog ground GNDA_ADC on the BBB. In our diagram, that's the black wire into pin *P9_34*.
>
> Put the 3V into the 3V on the BBB. In our case, that's the red wire into pin *P9_3*.

Very Important!

The analog inputs on the BeagleBone Black accept a maximum of 1.8V. Never apply more voltage than 1.8V to the analog pins or you will damage your board.

For the sensor (markings facing you), match up the pins as follows:

> Pin 1 (left pin): Power/3.3V
>
> Pin 2 (middle pin): Analog pin on the BBB which in our recipe is pin *P9_38*, or *AIN3*
>
> Pin 3 (right pin): Ground pin on the BBB

2. Open up Cloud9 IDE at `http://192.168.7.2:3000` and use the following code to begin capturing temperature readings:

```
//Setup
var b = require('bonescript'); // Read library
var TMP36 = "P9_38"; // Pin location for sensor

//Check the temperature every 4 seconds
setInterval(readTMP, 4000);

//Define the 'readTMP' function
function readTMP() {
  b.analogRead(TMP36, writeTMP);
}

//Define the 'writeTMP' function
function writeTMP(x) {
  var millivolts = x.value * 1800; // 1.8V
  var temp_c = (millivolts - 500) / 10;
  var temp_f = (temp_c * 9/5) + 32;
  console.log("Current temperature is " + temp_c + " C and
  " + temp_f + " F");
}
```

3. The code is broken down as follows:

   ❑ Evoke the BoneScript library:

   ```
   // Setup
   var b = require('bonescript');
   ```

   ❑ Now, choose the pin number where your sensor is wired. See the pin layout reference diagram at the end of this section for more background on the ADC input options:

   ```
   var TMP36 = "P9_38"; // Pin location for sensor
   ```

❑ Then, we'll check the temperature at specific intervals, in this case, every four seconds:

```
setInterval(readTMP, 4000);
```

❑ Now, we define the readTMP function:

```
function readTMP() {
    b.analogRead(TMP36, writeTMP);
}
```

❑ Finally, we define the writeTMP function, which is where the voltage data captured is turned into temperature readings. We calculate the temperature from the voltage in millivolts with a simple formula, *Temp C = 100 x (reading in V) - 50*:

```
function writeTMP(x) {
    var millivolts = x.value * 1800; // 1.8V
    var temp_c = (millivolts - 500) / 10;
    var temp_f = (temp_c * 9/5) + 32;
    console.log("Current temperature is " + temp_c + " C and
    " + temp_f + " F");
}
```

4. When you are ready to run the code, just click the **Run** button in the IDE. Your output should look like the following (with your local temperature, of course):

```
Current temperature is 20 C and 68 F
Current temperature is 22.4 C and 72.32 F
```

 If you get some funky temperature readings, reboot your board and rerun the script.

There's more...

You can try exactly the same exercise, this time with Python—https://learn.adafruit.com/setting-up-io-python-library-on-beaglebone-black/adc.

See also

> ▸ More support for analog inputs can be found at *Reading the analog inputs*—`http://beaglebone.cameon.net/home/reading-the-analog-inputs-adc`

Variable resistance sensor – photocell

Capturing the data generated from light sensors is one of those satisfying and highly useful examples of physical computing. Some of you may have used light sensors—also known as CdS cells, photoresistors, and photocells—in your Arduino or Raspberry Pi projects. If so, this recipe will be a snap for you.

A photocell is a variable resistor, which in this case means that it varies its resistance according to the intensity of light exposed to it. The value of that variable resistance is turned into data, which in turn means the sensor functions as an effective measurement tool for ambient light. In this recipe, we show you how to read analog values captured from a light sensor using BoneScript along with an alternative Python script.

 CdS stands for Cadmium Sulfide, a compound that is non-ROHs compliant due to the cadmium, a chemical severely restricted in Europe as hazardous waste.

Getting ready

Rustle up the items in the list below for this recipe:

▸ **Photoresistor (photocell)**: Nothing fancy for our purposes here. We're using one that costs less than USD $1.50 in many electronics stores such as SparkFun (`http://bit.ly/1kwejIt`).

▸ **Resistor**: 10,000 (10kΩ); brown/black/orange/gold bands

▸ **3x jumper wires**: Easy to connect to breadboard.

▸ **Breadboard**.

How to do it...

1. First, make sure your BBB is powered down, then wire up your breadboard. Here's what your wiring should look like:

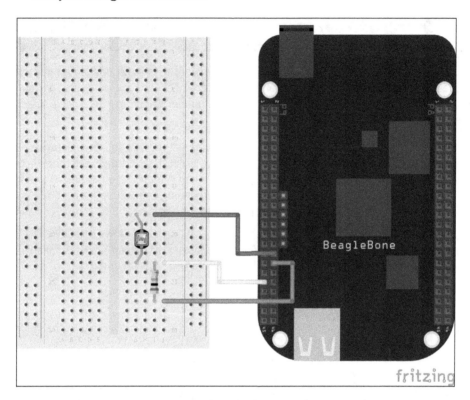

We wire this sensor up differently from the temperature sensor, so take care with the diagram. If you are reading this recipe and want to see color versions of the fritzing diagrams for better clarity on the wiring, you can find them online at `http://bit.ly/1MP2UNo`:

> **Light sensor**: Plug the light sensor's wires into the breadboard, positioning the wires four or five slots apart from one another for easier wiring management.
>
> **Resistor**: Plug the 10k resistor into the breadboard a couple of columns in front of the photocell with one end of the resistor aligned with the bottom wire of the sensor.
>
> **Voltage wire**: Plug the red wire into the *P9_32* slot on the BBB. This is one of the board's specially designated pins (labeled VDD_ADC) for 1.8V reference voltage, a low power source for analog sensors like this. The other end of the wire should be inserted into the breadboard aligning with the phototcell's top wire.

Ground wire: The blue wire is for ground (GND), and for this we will also use a special ground pin at *P9_34* for 1.8V (GNDA_ADC).

VERY IMPORTANT!

The analog inputs on the BeagleBone Black accept a maximum 1.8V. Never apply more voltage than 1.8V to the analog pins or you will damage your board.

Sensor pin: Plug one end of the yellow wire into *P9_37* on the BBB, and the other end into a breadboard slot in front of the resistor. It should align with the bottom wire of the light sensor.

2. Open up Cloud9 IDE at `http://192.168.7.2:3000`.

3. Create a new file called `light_sensor.js`, and paste the following BoneScript code into the window:

```
var b = require('bonescript');
function lightSensor() {
  b.analogRead('P9_37', lightValue);
}

function lightValue(reading) {
    var millivolts = reading.value * 1800;
    console.log("Light output in millivolts: " + millivolts +
    "\n");

}

setInterval(lightSensor, 1000);
```

4. Press the **Run** button to begin capturing light intensity readings. Your console output should look something like this. Your readings, of course, will vary according to the strength of your light source:

```
Light output in millivolts: 1387

Light output in millivolts: 1386

Light output in millivolts: 1159

Light output in millivolts: 608
```

Moving your hand over or close to the sensor should make the output numbers rise and fall based on how the light source hits the sensor. Notice that doing all this requires very few lines of code. So, let's take a quick look at what some of the parts of the script are doing

5. Besides evoking the BoneScript library, the first section defines a `read` function on a specific analog pin that we will reference on the BBB:

```
var b = require('bonescript');
function lightSensor() {
   b.analogRead('P9_37', lightValue);
}
```

6. In the next section, we define a function that determines how the sensor data being captured will be crunched. That data is expressed in millivolts and varies at a constant rate:

```
function lightValue(reading) {
   var millivolts = reading.value * 1800;
   console.log("Light output in millivolts: " + millivolts +
   "\n");
}
```

The \n in the code simply creates a space between each output for better legibility.

Optional Python code

Besides the code above, you can also test your light sensor with a Python script available on our Github repository. There is a `ReadMe` file on the repo, but here are the basic steps:

1. Download the Python code with the following command:

```
$ git clone https://github.com/HudsonWerks/light-sensor.git
```

2. Browse to the directory with the Python script and run it:

```
$ cd light_sensor
$ sudo python light_sensor.py
```

Your output should be very similar to what you saw in the BoneScript example.

Using motors

Whether it's a robot, an RC toy, a CNC, a 3D printer, or a high-end industrial machine, motion control is one of the most popular subjects in physical computing.

In our examples, we'll be using BoneScript to run our devices, beginning with a DC motor and then following with a servomotor.

However, first you should learn a little about the type of pins that we will use in the following recipes.

DC motors

They're fun. They're cheap. They're everywhere. The little motors that have been driving toys for decades still remain a mainstay for projects where locomotion is part of the picture. Understanding how to drive a DC motor requires more complex and powerful mechanisms, such as robotics.

Getting ready

You will need several items for this recipe:

- **DC motor**: This is a standard issue 2-lead motor prevalent in toys and cheaper RC devices.
- **H-Bridge IC motor driver**: This Texas instrument component *SN754410* is available at Sparkfun (`https://www.sparkfun.com/products/315`) and other similar sources for approximately 2.50 USD. It is also commonly used in the L293D version. This little circuit is an important piece of the puzzle because it is the mechanism used to send the voltage that drives the motor's direction and regulates its speed. More details about this IC are described later in this recipe.

  - **13x jumper wires**
  - **1x pushbutton/switch**
  - **1x 1k resistor**
  - **9V battery and holder**
  - **Breadboard**

How to do it...

Perform the following steps to test the DC motors:

1. Make sure that your BBB is powered down first and then wire your breadboard as follows. Clearly, this is a thicket of wires, so be methodical as you follow the diagram:

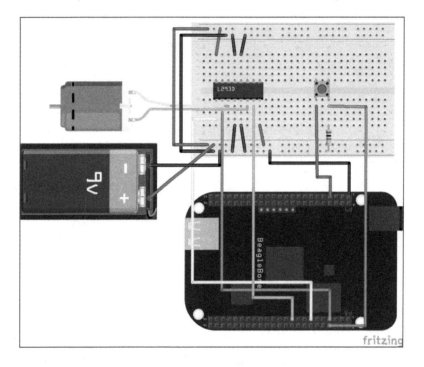

To help with the diagram above, here are some further details for the wiring setup:

Hardware	Pin#	Color	Location/purpose
BBB	P8_7	Blue	Pin 2 (1A, motor logic 1) on H-bridge
BBB	P8_13	Yellow	Pin 1 (1,2EN/PWM) on H-bridge
BBB	P8_19	Green	Pin 7 (2A, motor logic 1) on H-bridge
BBB	P8_8	Blue	GND on breadboard button—aligned with 1k resistor
BBB	P9_1	Black	GND on breadboard rail
BBB	P9_7	Red	5V power to button
Motor Wire 1			Attached at pin 3 (1Y) on H-bridge
Motor Wire 2			Attached at pin 6 (2Y) on H-bridge
Battery wire 1		Black	GND rail on breadboard
Battery wire 2			RED to PWR rail on breadboard

Hardware	Pin#	Color	Location/purpose
Bus wire 1	Black		GND
Bus wire 2	Red		VCC

2. Open the Cloud9 IDE at `http://192.168.7.2:3000` and navigate to **File | New From Template | Javascript**.

3. Save the new file as `DC_motor1.js`.

4. Paste the new document to the following BoneScript code:

```javascript
var b = require('bonescript');

var enablePin = "P8_13"; //pin 1 (1,2EN/PWM) on H-Bridge
var motorPin1 = "P8_7"; //pin 2 (1A, motor logic 1) on H-Bridge
var motorPin2 = "P8_19"; //pin 7 (2A, motor logic 1) on H-Bridge
var buttonPin = "P8_8"; //pin for button

b.pinMode(enablePin, b.OUTPUT);
b.pinMode(motorPin1, b.OUTPUT);
b.pinMode(motorPin2, b.OUTPUT);

b.pinMode(buttonPin, b.INPUT);


function loop() {
    // if the button is high, motor will turn off
    if (b.digitalRead(buttonPin) == b.HIGH) {
        b.digitalWrite(enablePin, b.HIGH);
        b.digitalWrite(motorPin1, b.LOW); // set pin 2 on
        H-Bridge low
        b.digitalWrite(motorPin2, b.HIGH); // set pin 7 on
        H-Bridge high
    }
    // if the button is low, motor will turn on
    else {
        b.digitalWrite(enablePin, b.LOW);
        b.digitalWrite(motorPin1, b.LOW);
        b.digitalWrite(motorPin2, b.HIGH);
    }
}

setInterval(loop, 50);
```

5. To start your engines, click on the **Run** button in the IDE. The motor should rotate when you press the button and stop when you release it.

How it works...

Here is some context for what's happening with the wiring:

1. **H-Bridge motor driver**: Although our component can drive two motors (one on each side of the chip), in our example, we will only run one. Besides controlling the direction and speed, the motor driver also protects the BBB from the higher output needed to drive the motor. The name *H-Bridge* is derived from the way the circuit is typically drawn with four switches. When switch 1 (s1) and switch 4 (s4) are closed and switch 2 (s2) and switch 3 (s3) are open, then a positive voltage flows across the motor. To reverse the direction of the motor, the switches are then reversed from their open or closed state.

   In the following illustration, the image on the left-hand side shows the voltage flowing across s1 and s4 for one motor direction and on the right-hand side across s2 and s3 for the reverse direction. In our recipe's code, we will only turn the motor in one direction, so the voltage will only flow across one bridge circuit, as shown in the following image:

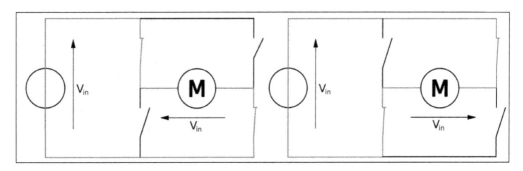

 The preceding image has been taken from Wikipedia.

The H-bridge controller has 16 pins for interfacing, although only a few of them are used in our recipe:

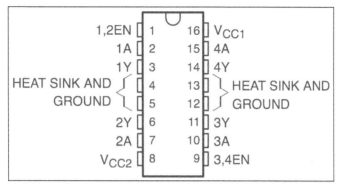

Pin outs on H-bridge

2. **DC power**: Instead of powering from the BBB directly, we offload the power for the motor to a separate 9V battery source. This both ensures a reliable and consistent voltage to the motor and removes any possibility of damaging the board.

Servo motors

For those new to servomechanisms, commonly referred to as servos, it may be useful to understand the basics of the device because the ingredients in the recipe reveal the unique nature of this type of motor.

Servos are typically used as actuators in embedded electronics scenarios, such as CNC machinery, robotics, and automated manufacturing, and even for radio-controlled toys. For their size, these motors are incredibly powerful, deliver a considerable torque, and consume a small amount of power.

A servo is really just a motor with an output shaft connected to a sensor. The sensor provides feedback of a position to control the motor's motion and final position. The shaft is able to turn around 180 degrees.

In order to run properly, the servo requires a fairly robust controller. Communication between the servo and the controller can be either digital or analogue. On the BBB front, the servo requires PWM to send pulsed signals, which we discuss later in this section. The length of the pulse drives the position of the motor.

Regardless of the signal type, the input signal's purpose is to send data that determines the motor output shaft's position. In more sophisticated servos, the signal also includes data on the speed. However, in our recipe, we will use a low cost servo that is typically used in RC toys. These kinds of devices handle only shaft position.

Servos are also distinctive for their three wires:

- ▶ **Power (+5 volts)**: This is often red
- ▶ **Ground**: This is sometimes black, but more often, this is brown in cheaper servos
- ▶ **Control**: This is commonly yellow or white

A crash course in pulse width modulation

Pulse width modulation (PWM) is a way to send very fast on/off digital signal pulses to a pin. These pulses can be modulated in order to smoothly control certain kinds of device like. LEDs, audio components, and motors.

When coding a PWM-driven device or component, you are basically setting a pin HIGH or LOW in rapid succession. Often, you will find that three control parameters can be set:

- ▶ **Duty cycle**: This is the percentage of time when the pin is HIGH or on over a specific span of time. In your code, you express duty cycle as a percentage. For example, 100 percent would be high power being applied and would be fully on. Whereas, a low duty cycle of 1 percent would result in low power since power is off for most of the cycle.
- ▶ **Period**: This is the combined time it takes to complete an on/off cycle.
- ▶ **Frequency**: In our case, frequency is how many times per second the pulse signal went ON (HIGH) and OFF (LOW). Taking the inverse of the *period* gives us the frequency. Getting the frequency setting right is crucial since some devices may not work properly if your setting is too high or too low.

Working with servos comes with taking care with the power input into your board. Under no circumstance do a 5V draw to run the motor or you will likely meet Merlin's magic smoke. And nothing cuts BBB recipes down to size like magic smoke.

 Inside every servo, there is a potentiometer that provides feedback to the motor about its position on its 180-degree sweep.

Getting ready

You'll need a few things for this recipe:

- **Servo**: These small but mighty motors come in many varieties and price ranges. If you already have fancy ones in your kit, congratulations! If not, purchase either a standard or mini size because our recipe will work with both these sizes. AdaFruit and Sparkfun have vetted collections, although you can certainly get them cheaper on Amazon.
- **Resistor**: 10,000 (10kΩ) version with brown/black/orange/gold bands
- **6x jumper wires**
- **Breadboard**

How to do it...

1. Make sure your BBB is powered down first, then wire up your breadboard according to the following fritzing diagram:

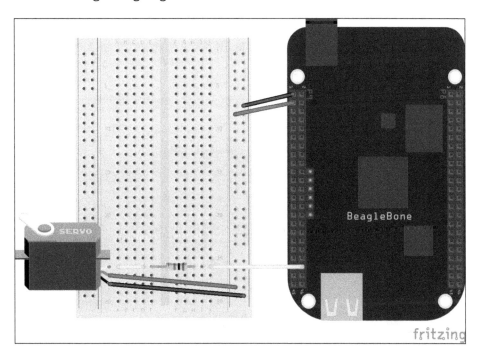

2. Here are the details for the wiring if the diagram isn't clear:

    ❑   Connect your 10k resistor to row 5 of your breadboard with the ends
        spanning the bridge. In this recipe, the resistor is not vital, but it is good
        practice to keep the voltage under control and protect the board if the servo
        is malfunctioning.

    ❑   For the servo cable, attach three jumper wires and match them as follows:

        The brown servo lead (GND): This is the black jumper wire

        The red servo lead (PWR): This indicates the red jumper wire

        The orange (looks almost yellow) servo lead: This denotes the yellow
        jumper wire

    ❑   Now, attach the second set of jumper wires to the BBB as follows:

        Connect one end of the GND (black wire) to the *P9_1* pin on the BBB and the
        other end to the breadboard, following the diagram's position

        Connect one end of the 3V red wire to the *P9_3* pin on the BBB and the
        other end to the breadboard, following the diagram's position

    ❑   Now we'll hook up the yellow jumper wire, which we'll connect to our PWM
        output on the BBB. Connect one end to the *9_42* pin on the BBB and the
        other end to the breadboard in the same row and on the left-hand side of the
        resistor, following the diagram's position. We could also have used *P9_14*,
        P9_16, *P8_13* or *P8_19*.

    ❑   Finally, attach the servo + jumper wires to the breadboard as follows:

        GND black wire into the GND rail coming from the BBB

        3V red wire into the 3V power rail coming from the BBB

        PWM yellow wire into breadboard on the other side of the resistor

3. Open the Cloud9 IDE at `http://192.168.7.2:3000`:

    Use the following code to begin firing up the servo. In order to control the
    PWM signal, we need to specify the period, run, and duty cycle. Here's the
    script to run the servo:

    ```
    #!/usr/bin/env node

    // Include the bonescript library
    var b = require('bonescript');

    // Servo motor's PWM pin
    var servo = 'P9_42';
    ```

```
var duty_min = 0.03;
var duty_max = 2.5;
var position = 0;
var increment = 0.1;

// Set up the mode for the servo pin
b.pinMode(servo, b.ANALOG_OUTPUT);
updateDuty();

console.log('Use keyboard Control-C to stop');

function updateDuty() {
    // This function calculates and adjusts the duty cycle
    based on a desired position in range 0..1
    var duty_cycle = (position*0.115) + duty_min;
    b.analogWrite(servo, duty_cycle, 60,
    scheduleNextUpdate);

    console.log('Duty Cycle: ' +
        parseFloat(duty_cycle*100).toFixed(1) + '%' + '
        Position: ' + position);

}

function scheduleNextUpdate() {
    // adjust position by increment and
    // reverse if it exceeds range of 0..1
    position = position + increment;
    if(position < 0) {
        position = 0;
        increment = -increment;
    } else if(position > 1) {
        position = 1;
        increment = -increment;
    }

    // call updateDuty after 500ms
    setTimeout(updateDuty, 500);

}
```

4. The motor will begin by first moving to a starting position, then move forward in small increments. Then, it will reset its starting point and begin moving backward in small increments. In the IDE terminal window, press *Ctrl + C* on your keyboard to stop the script.

There's more...

To check your PWM pinmux, run the following commands:

```
$ sudo -i
# cat < /sys/kernel/debug/pwm
```

Your output should look something like this:

```
platform/48304100.ecap, 1 PWM device
 pwm-0   ((null)                ):

platform/48304200.ehrpwm, 2 PWM devices
 pwm-0   ((null)                ):
 pwm-1   ((null)                ):

platform/48302200.ehrpwm, 2 PWM devices
 pwm-0   ((null)                ):
 pwm-1   ((null)                ):

platform/48300100.ecap, 1 PWM device
 pwm-0   (PWM_P9_42             ): requested enabled

platform/48300200.ehrpwm, 2 PWM devices
 pwm-0   ((null)                ):
 pwm-1   ((null)                ):
```

Note that our referenced pin in our code that we just ran, *P9_42*, is marked as requested enabled.

For an alternative method of driving the servo using Python, check out Adafruit's tutorial at https://learn.adafruit.com/controlling-a-servo-with-a-beaglebone-black.

4

Exploring GNU/Linux Recipes Using Bash, Autotools, Debugger, and systemd

Here is what we've got in store as recipes in this chapter:

- ▸ The basic shell script
- ▸ Epoch Time shell script
- ▸ Compile and install
- ▸ Compile and install Git from source
- ▸ Debugging
- ▸ Debug a simple C-code application from the command line using GDB
- ▸ Debug an application remotely from Eclipse and GDB server
- ▸ systemd services
- ▸ Basic commands for systemd services
- ▸ Optimize boot time
- ▸ Create a systemd service to run at boot time

Introduction

In our last chapter, we jumped right into how to make our hardware dance or at least blink for us. This time, you will learn more about how to bend the software to your will.

We'll build on some foundational principles first and then head towards greater complexity of scripts, including how to compile an open source software package, install it on your system, and troubleshoot it when things go out of whack. Lastly, we'll examine some core, system-level software called `systemd`, a framework that has become an essential ingredient in modern Linux distributions.

The basic shell script

Shell scripts

A shell script has a myriad of purposes on a Linux box. You can have them run at bootup so that they initiate commands or processes without you having to manually start them. They can be used to run a sequence of events. They can manipulate files, execute a program, print text, and walk your dog. Well, the last part is true if your dog is a robot. However, we're getting ahead of ourselves.

It's time for our friend Major Tom. We've missed him, but let's bring him back to earth for a moment with a very simple shell script.

How to do it...

Perform the following steps:

1. Create a new directory as follows:

   ```
   $ mkdir bin
   ```

2. Then, let's move to the new directory using the `cd` command:

   ```
   $ cd bin
   ```

3. Now, create a new file that will become our shell script, as shown in the following code:

   ```
   ~/bin$ sudo nano major_tom_bash_script
   ```

4. At the beginning of the file, it's a requirement to tell the shell the kind of script that we'll run so that it can interpret the code accordingly. It could have been another recipe using Python, but in this case, we've got a bash script:

```
#!/bin/bash
```

5. Next, it's a good practice to add a comment as follows:

```
# Major Tom bash script
```

6. On the next line of the file, enter the `echo` string command, which outputs whatever you input to the screen:

```
echo "Commencing countdown, engines on."
```

This is how the code looks:

```
#!/bin/bash
# Major Tom bash script
echo "Commencing countdown, engines on."
```

7. Now, save and close the file.

8. Then, from the terminal, you want to run a command that will give the shell the ability and permission to actually execute the script, as shown in the following code:

```
~/bin$ sudo chmod 755 major_tom_bash_script
```

Adding the `755` option instructs the script to allow read and execute access to everyone and write access to the file owner (you) as well. Refer to *Chapter 1, Setting Up for the First Time*, for our review of the `chmod` command.

9. Finally, it's time for the magic (`.`). This tells bash to run the script, and (`/`) tells bash where the file is located, as shown in the following code:

```
~bin$ ./major_tom_bash_script
```

10. This is how your output should look:

```
debian@beaglebone:~bin$ ./major_tom_bash_script
Commencing countdown, engines on.
```

This is a very small blast off, but still a beginning.

Epoch Time shell script

Shell scripts

A shell script has a myriad of purposes on a Linux box. You can have them run at bootup so that they initiate commands or processes without you having to manually start them. They can be used to run a sequence of events. They can manipulate files, execute a program, print text, and walk your dog. Well, the last part is true if your dog is a robot. However, we're getting ahead of ourselves.

Epoch time, more commonly known as UNIX time (also POSIX time), is widely used in Linux (UNIX) systems as a way to describe instants in time. Specifically, it measures the number of seconds that have elapsed since January 1, 1970, and is used as a timestamp reference point.

With this shell script, we can quickly compare the Epoch time on our machine with the UTC that we are more accustomed to using.

How to do it...

Perform the following steps:

Unix time can be checked on most Unix systems by typing `date +%s` on the command line. Perform the following steps:

1. First, create the following script in `nano`:

    $ sudo nano epoch-time.sh

2. Then, paste the following code in the new window:

    ```
    # Epoch time in milliseconds
    # CTRL-C TO STOP
    # WRITTEN BY CHARLES HAMILTON
    # Simple script for showing the epoch time at 10-second intervals
    on a BeagleBone Black running Debian

    #!/bin/bash

    # Resets the RTC from  the system clock
    sudo hwclock --systohc
    sudo hwclock --show
    ```

```
# Runs command for determining epoch time
for (( ; ; ))
do
        echo -n "Since Epoch [in milliseconds]: "
# OPTION 1 command. Comment out if running OPTION 2.
        echo $(($(date +%s%N)/1000000))

## OPTION 2 command. Uncomment to run this version and comment out
OPTION 1.
#        cat /sys/class/rtc/rtc0/since_epoch | sed 's/...$//'
        sleep 10
done
```

 If you run into problems while copying and pasting the code, download the script available at `https://github.com/HudsonWerks/bash-script-samples/blob/master/epoch-time.sh`.

3. Now, run the following script:

    `$ sudo bash epoch.sh`

4. Your screen output should look similar to this:

    Tue Oct 27 14:13:53 2015 -0.062322 seconds

    Since Epoch [in milliseconds]: 1445969632617

    Since Epoch [in milliseconds]: 1445969642630

    The script determines the Epoch time in milliseconds relative to the UTC time.

5. Stop the script by pressing Ctrl + C.

There's more...

For some, all you can eat is buffets with shell scripts on the menu:

▶ `http://linuxcommand.org/writing_shell_scripts.php`

▶ `http://www.tldp.org/LDP/abs/html/why-shell.html`

Compile and install

In *Chapter 1, Setting Up for the First Time*, you learned the magical `apt-get install` routine to get a package that you want on your BeagleBone Black. However, you've already encountered situations where you wanted a package (typically abbreviated as pkg) and the repository came up with nada: `E: Unable to locate package xyz`. This often implies that there is no precompiled binary for you to install, which means that we now have to put on our big girl and big boy boots and compile from source files.

Building software from original source files is one of the prerequisites when you work with SOCs, such as BeagleBone Black. This is true in part because the BBB is a Linux environment. Many software applications have to be compiled in order to use them. However, it's also a fact that you will often want a version of a tool that doesn't come with a packaged binary to suit your use case or the prototype that you'll build. Native packages (in our case, the `armh` packages) are almost always a better fit than prebuilt binaries if you have the time and fortitude to build them.

Therefore, mastering, creating, and building from source files gives you tremendous power over how you customize and optimize the software that you use on the board.

Autotools, aka the GNU build system, is a toolset to build native packages. The tool chain is familiar to Unix users for its holy triad of commands: `configure`, `make`, and `install`.

Like almost anything related to Linux, there is a universe of information about autotools and the build and compile process for the source code. As this book is a mere dust mote in that universe, we can only cover the basics here.

 Most of the software you'll want is only released in the tarball (source code) form. These are just compressed archives with extensions, such as `.tar.gz`, `.tar.xz`, or `.tar.bz2`.

Documentation standards

In the open source world, developers generally ship their source code with the README files intended to provide guidance on the compile process for their tarball. The README file can serve as a starting point to build the package from scratch. Unfortunately, these README files can often be cryptic or poorly written. Although frustrating, it is inevitable that you will frequently find yourself Googling for more information about how to install a package.

Compiling on BeagleBone Black

Although the board's 1.7 GHz ARM chip is pretty snappy for most embedded applications, compiling and installing software directly on the BBB can be pretty poky and even painful. Ideally, building a large package with multiple dependencies will be far speedier on a dedicated desktop with bushels of RAM. However, for the purposes of simplicity, we'll forge ahead with how to compile on our board.

Autotools contains several utility programs:

  ▸ **Autoconf**: This creates a configure shell script for the source code that runs tests to determine the build environment.

  ▸ **Automake**: This generates files called `Makefiles` that track the dependencies for the code that you run with a `make` utility.

  ▸ **Libtool**: This is a script that provides a frontend to the often complex assortment of shared objects, such as compilers, linkers, and libraries that an application requires. In the Windows world, developers more commonly know this animal as dynamic link libraries or DLLs.

For most occasions when you compile and install a source file package, you will rely on three common commands, which must be run in the directory where they reside:

  1. `./configure`: This runs a script that configures the `make` file. It serves to customize the package to the system where it will be running. The `./` tells the Linux shell that the script is in the current directory.

  2. `make`: This is the command that executes the make files in your source code. The make files contain the shell commands that compile the necessary files for assembling the software package.

  3. `make install`: This is simply the `make` command, but with an additional option called target. It takes the compiled files from *Step 2* and installs them.

The `make` and `make install` commands almost always require super user privileges to execute, so `sudo make` and `sudo make install` is your frequent companion.

When you run `make`, you can further refine what the script does with other targets. Here are other commonly used options:

  ▸ `make all`: This is somewhat redundant to just using `make`, but you may occasionally find a `README` file recommending it. Target compiles the entire program, including its libraries and documentation.

- ▶ `make install-strip`: This is the same as `make install`, strips out debugging symbols, and is not typically recommended unless you're certain that the program has no bugs.

- ▶ `make uninstall`: This is the opposite of `make install` because it deletes all the installed files.

- ▶ `make clean`: This cleans and erases what has been built (the opposite of `make all`).

- ▶ `make distclean`: This erases anything that the `./configure` command created.

- ▶ `make check`: This runs a test suite if one exists for the source.

- ▶ `make installcheck`: This performs installation checks on the installed program (if needed).

- ▶ `make dist`: This creates a distribution tarball for the program and outputs `PACKAGE-VERSION.tar.gz`.

See also

- ▶ For a more detailed usage of the autotools toolset and further explanation on how to change the default behaviors and the options to build customized packages in order to suit your specific purpose, refer to `https://autotools.io/index.html`

- ▶ Refer to `https://www.gnu.org/software/libtool/` for more details on Libtool

- ▶ You can deep dive into autotools arcana with a bazillion examples at `https://www.lrde.epita.fr/~adl/autotools.html`

Now, onward and upward with the recipes.

Compile and install Git from source

Our first recipe is a basic scenario of building from a source file and then installing it on your BBB. In this case, we will work with Git, the illustrious software version control system.

We could have cheated and just stuck with the version of Git that is already handily installed on the current Debian distro for the BBB. Let's check it:

```
$ git --version
git version 2.0.2
```

This tells us that the current prebuilt Git binary offered for armh on the Debian repository is version 2.0.2. Yet, if we go to the Git website (`http://git-scm.com/`), you will learn that there is a newer version. So, let's install the latest and greatest from the source.

How to do it...

Perform the following steps:

1. To get the dependencies or associated libraries, we'll need to start by grabbing the libraries that Git requires: `curl`, `zlib`, `openssl`, `expat`, and `libiconv` with the following command:

   ```
   $ sudo apt-get install libcurl4-gnutls-dev libexpat1-dev gettext
   libz-dev libssl-dev
   ```

2. As we are about to download the package source files and the compiled code, we should set up a directory where we can consistently manage everything, as shown in the following command:

   ```
   $ mkdir /home/debian/packages/
   ```

3. With the libraries installed, it's tarball time, so get Git using the following command:

   ```
   $ wget -P /home/debian/packages https://www.kernel.org/pub/
   software/scm/git/git-2.6.2.tar.xz
   ```

   The `-P` option points `wget` to the specified directory.

    The preceding tarball version will likely be superseded by the more current code. Check for the latest Git tarball at `http://git-scm.com/`. This link will likely refer you to a code repository. There, you'll look for a file with the `git-0.0.0.tar.xz` naming convention, along with another possible digit depending on the version.

4. Navigate to the directory and `untar` it as follows:

   ```
   $ cd packages
   $ tar -xf git-2.6.2.tar.xz
   ```

5. Then, go to the new directory created with the following code:

   ```
   ~/packages$ cd git-2.6.2
   ```

    In the untarred folder, search for the `INSTALL` file. This file provides guidance on alternative directories for installation purposes than the one we will perform here.

6. Now, we are ready to install git. For each stage of this process, wait for the terminal window to default back to your working prompt before proceeding. We will begin with `./configure`:

```
$ ./configure
```

7. Next, the `make` file needs our attention with the command:

```
$ sudo make
```

In this case, and if you're building the package directly on your BBB, the compilation may take more than 20 minutes; other packages can take considerably longer. So, be patient and wait for the default prompt.

8. Once all the files have been crunched and compiled, we need to install the package, a step that can often finish quickly, as shown in the following code:

```
$ sudo make install
```

9. Finally, let's see how we performed compared to our prior 2.0.2 version with the following command:

```
$ git --version
git version 2.X.x
```

Voila! The freshest baked version of Git is now at your board's disposal.

Debugging

Reality check: stuff breaks, especially with software. And when your software is broken, it makes it really hard to get things done with your hardware. So, the truth of the matter is (you already know this if you're an experienced programmer) that most of your time when you create some shiny new software thing, a considerable amount of time is spent on fixing and debugging your code.

In Linux Land, GDB (GNU project debugger) rules the roost as the standard debug tool. It is the go to app that provides a window to what is happening in the guts of another program and allows you to saunter through the source code line by line when the program runs. Conveniently, it comes preloaded on the Debian distribution for your BBB.

GDB provides four key things needed for fast and efficient debugging:

1. Starts your program and illuminates anything that may affect the program's behavior
2. Stops your program on the specified conditions
3. Investigates an error or anomaly and tells you what was happening at the time a program crashed
4. Tweaks code in your program, allowing you to quickly stomp one bug and go on to get another

See also

Check these links for more guidance on debugging:

- http://www.dirac.org/linux/gdb/01-Introduction.php
- http://www.unknownroad.com/rtfm/gdbtut/gdbtoc.html
- http://elinux.org/EBC_Exercise_28_Remote_gdb_and_more
- http://elinux.org/EBC_Exercise_14_gdb_Debugging

Debug a simple C-code application from the command line using GDB

GDB is frequently used to dig into problems you may have with a C or C++ program that you may have written. Alternatively, you can run GDB to debug an executable or binary. In this section, we will perform the former.

One of the most typical entry points to understand how to debug using GDB is by running simple examples of executables written in C or C++. Many of the software resources available for developing on hardware platforms such as BeagleBone Black, commonly rely on C or C++. These are the core, low-level (and mid-level) languages needed for deep manipulation of the machinery. Indeed, most of the binaries that you will often load to your BBB are written in one or both of these two languages. They also serve as a vital bridge between high-level and low-level programming, which we will see in later chapters.

If you are already an Arduino user or even a Raspberry Pi developer, this is old news because you already know that the Arduino processing language is largely a simplified version of C/C++. If you are a newcomer, don't worry because the examples we use are very basic and will not require advanced knowledge of C or C++. Also, any kind of in-depth analysis at either of these two programming languages is beyond the scope of this book.

We will begin by serving up a small piece of C code on the BBB so that you can see what the debugger output can show us. Then, based on GDB's forensics, we will fix the code.

How to do it...

Perform the following steps to debug a C-code application from the command line using GBD:

1. Log in as a root user with the following command:

   ```
   $ sudo su -i
   ```

2. Now, navigate to our `projects` directory as follows:

   ```
   # cd bbb_recipe_book/projects
   ```

3. Then, create a new subdirectory called `debug` and navigate to it with the following code:

```
# mkdir debug
```

```
# cd debug
```

Now, open the `nano` text editor, create the C file, and call it `major_tom_gdb.c` , as shown in the following code:

```
# nano majortom_gdb.c
```

Copy and paste the following code to the `nano` editor window as follows:

```c
//majortom_gdb.c
#include <stdio.h>
#include <stdlib.h>
#include <string.h>

size_t majortom_len (const char *s)
{
  return strlen (s);
}

int main (int argc, char *argv[])
{
  const char *a = NULL;

  printf ("The number of characters in Major Tom string a =
  %d\n", majortom_len (a));

  exit (0);
}
```

 If you run into problems copying and pasting the code, you can download the code from `https://github.com/HudsonWerks/debug-samples/blob/master/majortom_gdb.c`

4. Save and close the file and press *Ctrl + x*; when prompted type `y` for yes and then press return (*Enter*)key.

5. Now, we will compile the file using a C-compiler command with options:

```
# gcc majortom_gdb.c -g -o majortom_gdb
```

Here is a breakdown of the options in the command:

- ❑ gcc: This is the basic compile command for a C program
- ❑ -g: This generates the symbolic debugging information or symbols that GDB can understand within a compiled program
- ❑ -o: This specifies the name of the compiled file

The compiler will output a file called majortom_gdb (no file type).

 The current Debian distribution comes preloaded with the C/C++ compiler. If for some reason, you get errors that indicate that the compile will not run or is not present, install the compiler with $ sudo apt-get install g++.

Run the compiled file in gdb using the following code:

```
# gdb ./majortom_gdb
```

This is how the output should look:

```
GNU gdb (GDB) 7.4.1-debian
Copyright (C) 2012 Free Software Foundation, Inc.
License GPLv3+: GNU GPL version 3 or later <http://gnu.org/
licenses/gpl.html>
This is free software: you are free to change and redistribute it.
There is NO WARRANTY, to the extent permitted by law.  Type "show
copying"
and "show warranty" for details.
This GDB was configured as "arm-linux-gnueabihf".
For bug reporting instructions, please see:
<http://www.gnu.org/software/gdb/bugs/>...
Reading symbols from /home/debian/bbb_recipe_book/projects/debug/
majortom_gdb...done.
(gdb)
```

6. Note gdb at the end of the output. This indicates that you have started a debug session and can now use GDB commands to control the tool. So, now enter the following code:

```
(gdb) run
```

Boom. Your output should show a bug: the dreaded `segfault` (the segmentation fault). The error also tells us that we attempted to access an invalid memory address, as shown in the following code:

```
Starting program: /home/debian/bbb_recipe_book/projects/debug/
majortom_gdb


Program received signal SIGSEGV, Segmentation fault.
0xb6f45904 in strlen () from /lib/arm-linux-gnueabihf/libc.so.6
(gdb)
```

The good news is that GDB just told us that the problem lies with `strlen`, a standard C library function that determines the length of a string. However, the function requires a nonNULL string in order to run properly. Thus, our NULL value threw off the bug. So, now we can fix it.

7. Now, exit out of GDB with the following code:

    ```
    (gdb) quit
    ```

8. Then, open your C file again as follows:

    ```
    ~/projects/debug# sudo nano majortom_gdb.c
    ```

    In line 13, change `NULL` to the `"Ground Control to Major Tom"` string with double quotes, as shown in the following code:

    ```
    const char *a = "Ground Control to Major Tom";
    ```

9. Now, save, close, and press *Ctrl + x*; when prompted type `y` for yes and then press return (*Enter*)key.

10. Recompile the file as follows:

    ```
    # gcc majortom_gdb.c -g -o majortom_gdb
    ```

11. Then, run the compiled file in GDB again, as shown in the following code:

    ```
    # gdb ./majortom_gdb
    ```

12. Now, let's begin the debug session with the following code:

    ```
    (gdb) run
    ```

If all goes as planned, your code should no longer `segfault`, but show the output similar to the following code:

```
Starting program: /home/debian/bbb_recipe_book/projects/debug/
majortom_gdb
The number of characters in Major Tom string a = 27
[Inferior 1 (process 6020) exited normally]
(gdb)
```

This enlightens us to the fact that our string `"Ground Control to Major Tom"` contains 27 characters.

13. Finally, exit GDB normally by entering the following code:

    ```
    quit
    ```

See? Nothing to it. C code. Crash. Debug. Fix C code. All on a very little Linux box.

See also

In *Chapter 7, Applied Recipes – Sound, Picture, and Video*, we will run a more advanced recipe, where we will compile a SIP/VOIP package for the purpose of exploring sound and video. The compilation will include debugging examples with further use of GDB.

Debug an application remotely from Eclipse and GDB server

You are about to dive into the arcane, but necessary world of remote debugging/cross-compiling. In this chapter, we will specifically take a look at a recipe for setting up remote debugging using the GDB server.

We will set up a specific kind of environment on your client desktop, another kind of environment on your BBB, and use an IDE as a way to ease the potential collision between these two worlds.

Wait a minute! Didn't we just do a debug recipe directly on BeagleBone Black using GDB? And can't we just develop and compile right on BeagleBone Black? Yes and yes.

But your BeagleBone Black is not quite powerful enough to serve as a serious development box. Ideally, what we want to do is hand off that work to a fancier, faster, desktop box. Otherwise, you will spend many unnecessary hours testing, compiling, debugging, and watching reruns of *Doctor Who* while waiting for the BBB to complete its tasks.

Why don't we just make something on one box and move it over to another box? Hmm. Not so fast. If you want to create or debug an application on a nonBBB board and output a binary or chunk of code to run it on an ARM Linux board like the BBB's, then you have to have the right toolset. This toolset will juggle between differing board architectures and operating system requirements.

Unfortunately, getting this toolset set up properly can be quite unpleasant. Not only does it take a fair bit of time, the process is also fraught with many opportunities for error. So, be patient and persistent in following this recipe.

Before going into the minutiae, here are the high-level steps to get remote debugging going on BeagleBone Black:

1. Install and set up a virtual machine; you can skip this if your client development box is Linux.

2. Install and set up a cross-compile and debug toolchain.

3. Install and set up the GDB server on your BeagleBone Black.

4. Install and set up Eclipse, our IDE of choice.

Nothing to it, right? Not quite...

How to do it...

Part I: Set up Virtual Machine—Mac OSX

On your client box, we will set up a **virtual machine** (**VM**) with a Linux distribution on board. There are a number of sources for this, but we will use Oracle's free virtual box (once again, if you are already using this book and its recipes with a Linux box as your client machine, installing a VM is not necessary).

 All the steps in this section occur on either your desktop client box or a virtual machine, not on BeagleBone Black.

Download and install the VM from `https://www.virtualbox.org/`. When finished, open the application. Perform the following steps

1. Download a Linux distribution that you will load to Virtual Box's virtual machine environment. We used an i386 net install of Debian Wheezy available from `debian.org` at `https://www.debian.org/releases/wheezy/debian-installer/` (download is available at `http://cdimage.debian.org/debian-cd/7.6.0/i386/iso-cd/debian-7.6.0-i386-netinst.iso`).

[You do not need to have the VM run Debian Wheezy for ARMH as the BBB does, but can use almost any flavor of Linux.]

2. Next, install and set up a Linux environment on the VM. In the open Virtual Box window, click on **New (VM)**.

3. Give the VM a name, something clever like Debian Wheezy.

4. From the drop-down options:

    1. Choose **Linux**

    2. Then choose, **Debian** (32-bit) according to the type of `.iso` you downloaded

5. Then, click on **Continue**.

6. Allocate 1024 MB of memory instead of the default 512 MB. Then, click on the **Next** button.

7. For the hard drive, unless you have another virtual hard disk set up and want to use it, leave it with the default setting: **Create a virtual hard drive now**. Then, click on **Create**.

8. For the hard drive file type, leave the default VDI setting. Then, click on **Continue**.

9. For the storage on the physical hard drive, check whether you prefer the VM to have a fixed drive space allocation (which can be faster once built) or a dynamic storage capacity (which will only expand as needed). I kept mine at dynamically allocated. Click on **Continue**.

10. For the file location and size, click on **Create**. This closes the setup window and returns you to the main dashboard.

11. At the dashboard, you should now see the VM we just created: Debian Wheezy. Before running the VM, we need to configure it some more. So, click on **Settings**.

Follow these settings:

1. **General | Advanced | Shared Clipboard**. Choose **bidirectional** because you will want to share the clipboard data in both the directions between the client box (in our case, Mac OS X) and the Debian VM. You will still need to follow additional steps to get this function working. Navigate to the following:

   System | Storage | Controller IDE—Click on the (**+**) sign (**Add CD/DVD device**) to open a browse directory window. Click on **Choose Disk**.

   Navigate to the folder where you downloaded the `.iso` file of your preferred Linux distro. The filename will be something similar to `debian-x.y.z-i386-netinst.iso` or some variant on the architecture that you chose. Then, click on **Open**.

Your OS should now be loaded. But now, we need to have the OS actually installed in its normal fashion on the virtual drive that you set up. Perform the following steps:

1. On the dashboard, while making sure that your new Debian VM is selected, click on the **Start** button.

2. On your first bootup, you will be presented with a Debian setup window. Choose **INSTALL**.

   You will then be taken through quite a few setup windows, including choosing language, region and keyboard preferences, network options, password and user setup, and other configuration options that I will not elaborate here. Configure as you see fit, while clicking on the **Continue** button until you end up with the hard disk partitioning sequence. Make your choices there according to your preference. In most cases, choosing the default option should be fine.

Keep in mind that an entire OS is being installed on your host machine, so this step will take a while. Also, remember that this new OS is being installed on the Virtual Machine environment and not affecting or modifying your client desktop.

3. Once the Debian installation and setup is completed, you will end up at the Debian GUI login screen. Log in and you will finally arrive at the desktop.

4. Let's open the terminal window in our new Debian environment and perform a basic ping test on BeagleBone Black. We want to make sure that we can communicate with it via our VM as follows:

```
$ ping 192.168.7.2
```

You should get consistent pings.

Adding cut and paste to VM

We now need to implement an additional functionality to the virtual box that will drive you mad if you do not add it: the cut-and-paste function. When you use Mac OS X as your client machine, Virtual Box, like most virtual machine software, does not include cut-and-paste by default. Instead, they have given us a series of 15 steps (yes, 15!). Oracle/Virtual Box refers to this function as Guest Additions. Here we go:

1. Let's begin by installing some external kernel modules on your VM. So, with a terminal window open in the Debian virtual machine on your client desktop, run the following command as a root user:

```
$ sudo -i
~#  apt-get install dkms
```

2. Next, back on your client desktop (Mac OS X), we have to locate a very buried .iso file that contains the code to add the guest additions with its cut and paste feature. In **Finder**, navigate to **Applications | Virtualbox.app | Show Package Contents**.

   This will open all the hidden directories in the package, including our target directory and file.

   Then, navigate to **Contents | MacOS | VBoxGuestAdditions.iso**.

3. Find and copy the VBoxGuestAdditions.iso file to a place where you can find it on your machine.

4. Back in your open Virtual Box, in **Debian Wheezy | Settings | Storage**, click on the small CD icon at the bottom of the screen and select **Choose a Virtual CD/DVD disk file**.

Another way to perform the same thing is from the drop-down menus at the top of the screen (not in the VM/Debian window, but the virtual machine menu options at the very top of your desktop machine. There, you can choose **Devices | CD/DVD devices | IDE (IDE Primary Master) | Choose a Virtual/CD/DVD** disk file.

5. Browse to where you put the VBoxGuestAdditions.iso file and select it. The .iso file should now appear in the CD/DVD drive options. Click on **OK** and restart the VM.

6. With the terminal window open in your Debian VM, run the following two commands:

```
~# apt-get update
~# apt-get upgrade
```

7. Now, confirm that you have the make and GNU C compiler installed, which should already be on the distribution that you installed. Check it with the following code:

```
~# gcc --version
```

8. If you don't get an output that shows the version, but a `command not found` error, you will need to install it as follows:

```
~# apt-get install make gcc
```

9. Reboot your Virtual Box machine.

10. Determine the exact version of your kernel with the following code:

```
~# uname -a
```

11. Install the correct version of the `linux-headers` package. Replace the following version numbers with the version number shown in the prior step:

```
~# apt-get install linux-headers-2.6.26-2-68
```

This may take some time; just wait for the installation to finish and return to your terminal prompt.

12. Restart your VM with the following code:

```
# reboot
```

13. From the screen options, select **Machine** | **options** | **General** and then click on the **Advanced** tab. In the **Shared Clipboard** dropdown, select the **Bidirectional** option.

The cut-and-paste functionality between your client host box (in our case, Mac OS X) and your virtual machine environment should now be enabled.

14. Before moving one though, we need to verify that the cut-and-paste function is working. From your Debian Wheezy virtual machine window, navigate to **Applications** | **Accessories** | **gedit Text Editor** and open a new file, as shown in the following screenshot:

15. From the open file window, enter `Ground Control` and then select **Edit | Copy**. Then, navigate to your client desktop (Mac/Windows machine, and so on), open a simple text editor, and select **Paste**. Hopefully, `Ground Control` will be pasted to the window.

16. We want to check the bidirectional functionality, so now enter `Major Tom` in (Mac/Windows) text editor on the desktop and press *Ctrl + c* (copy). Now, switch back to the VM editor window and then select **Edit | Paste**. `Major Tom` should be pasted successfully to the `gedit` window.

17. Reboot the VM and then log back in as the root user with the following code:

```
# sudo -i
```

18. Add your username to the `sudo` group as follows:

```
# adduser username sudo
```

19. Then, use the `fdisk` command to check whether `sudo` is working properly. The `-v` option will check the version of `fdisk` installed on your VM. You should get a prompt for a user password, as shown in the following code:

```
# sudo fdisk -v
```

The screen output should show the version of `fdisk` that is installed, and there should be no errors about permissions.

20. Install `ssh`. We already use it on the BBB. Now, we need to add it to our VM. SSH gives Eclipse the ability to connect and transfer files to BeagleBone Black using `scp`, a secure network protocol. Install it with the following code:

```
# sudo apt-get install ssh
```

Part II: Installing gdbserver on BeagleBone Black

We need this package on board the BBB so that we can run `gdb` from afar or from another box. Perform the following steps:

1. First, download the Debian installation package of `gdbserver` for `armhf` (the BBB-native architecture) on your VM as follows:

```
# wget http://http.us.debian.org/debian/pool/main/g/gdb/
gdbserver_7.4.1+dfsg-0.1_armhf.deb
```

2. Now, use `scp` to transfer the package to the BBB, as shown in the following code:

```
# scp gdbserver_7.4.1+dfsg-0.1_armhf.deb root@192.168.7.2:~
```

3. You should get a password prompt for the root user on BeagleBone. Log in and install the package as follows:

```
# ssh root@192.168.7.2
root@arm# dpkg -i gdbserver_7.4.1+dfsg-0.1_armhf.deb
```

4. When finished, log out by exiting the SSH session, as shown in the following code:

```
root@arm# exit
```

Part III: Installing and setting up the toolchain

This part and the next one are the hairiest bits of the process; many online tutorials on this subject purport to deliver a working toolchain lashed to an IDE, though few of them actually deliver.

Fortunately for us, engineer and blogger Aaron Clarke's very clear steps at `http://bit. ly/1x7TGUY` provide superb guidelines for a successful toolchain and the Eclipse IDE setup. The vast majority of the credit for the next two parts of the recipe go to Mr. Clarke.

 We chose not to include screenshots of the process because doing so would have made the recipe considerably longer. However, you can find a more graphical version of this recipe online at Aaron Clarke's blog, which includes a version for Debian Jessie at `http://blog.embeddedcoding. com/2015/05/beaglebone-black-development-part-6.html`.

Here we go.

Perform the following steps:

1. At the terminal prompt on your Debian VM, if you are not already logged in as root, do so now with the following command:

```
$ sudo -i
```

2. Create a new directory where you will download the toolchain and then navigate to that directory, as shown in the following code:

```
root@debian:/home/user# mkdir bbb-tools
root@debian:/home/user# cd bbb-tools
```

3. Using `wget`, download the toolchain from the following link to the directory that we just created:

```
# wget -c https://launchpad.net/linaro-toolchain-
binaries/trunk/2013.10/+download/gcc-linaro-arm-linux-
gnueabihf-4.8-2013.10_linux.tar.xz
```

4. Then, untar the file with the following code:

```
# tar xf gcc-linaro-arm-linux-gnueabihf-4.8-2013.10_linux.tar.xz
```

5. Now, run the `echo` command to create the `bbb-vars` file; this will be used to test that our environment is set up properly, as shown in the following code:

```
# echo "export CC=`pwd`/gcc-linaro-arm-linux-
gnueabihf-4.8-2013.10_linux/bin/arm-linux-gnueabihf-" > bbb-vars
```

6. Verify that the command worked. The `bbb-vars` file should appear in the directory as follows:

```
root@debian:/home/user/bbb-tools# ls

bbb-vars
```

7. Set up the environment for a remote test by sourcing the `bbb-vars` file. Take a look at the command preceding the (.) is the file location:

```
root@debian:~# ./home/user/bbb-tools/bbb-vars
```

8. Now, verify that the toolchain version we installed is correct using the following code:

```
root@debian:~# ${CC}gcc --version


arm-linux-gnueabihf-gcc (crosstool-NG linaro-1.13.1-4.8-2013.10
- Linaro GCC 2013.10) 4.8.2 20131014 (prerelease)Copyright (C)
2013 Free Software Foundation, Inc.This is free software; see the
source for copying conditions.  There is NOwarranty; not even for
MERCHANTABILITY or FITNESS FOR A PARTICULAR PURPOSE
```

Part IV: Installing and setting up the Eclipse IDE

Perform the following steps:

1. We will first install Eclipse on our VM with the following code:

```
root@debian:~# sudo apt-get install eclipse eclipse-cdt
```

Then, open Eclipse and set up a workspace by closing the welcome screen and navigating to **Window | Show view | C/C++ Projects**.

2. Create a new C project by navigating to **File | New | C Project**.

3. Give the project a name: `bbb_ground_control`.

4. Select **Project type | Hello World ANSI C Project**.

5. Then, select **Toolchain Cross GCC** and click on **Next**.

6. Enter the basic settings, such as the author name, in the next window.

7. Click on **Next** to bring up the **Select Configurations** window.

8. Now, click on the **Advanced** settings to bring up a **Properties** window.

9. From the left-hand side, navigate to **C/C++ Build | Settings** to bring up **Tool Settings** for the **Debug** configuration.

10. Choose the **Tool Settings** tab, then fill the **Prefix** and **Path** fields in the following manner:

    Prefix: `arm-linux-gnueabihf-`

 Be sure to include the hyphen (-) at the end of the preceding prefix.

    Path: `/home/user/bbb-tools/gcc-linaro-arm-linux-gnueabihf-4.8-2013.10_linux/bin`

11. Then, click on **OK**.

12. This brings up another **C Project** window, which annoyingly asks you to repeat what you just did in the prior step. This may be a bug, but do it anyway:

    Prefix: `arm-linux-gnueabihf-`

    Path: `/home/cah/bbb-tools/gcc-linaro-arm-linux-gnueabihf-4.8-2013.10_linux/bin`

13. Then, click on **Finish**.

14. The sample code runs and you get an error: `Symbol 'EXIT_SUCCESS' could not be resolved`. Aaargh!

    The error says that some C code symbols cannot be resolved by the compiler. Not to worry though. This error can be ignored because according to the Eclipse documentation, it is inaccurate and does not affect the successful operation of the application.

15. Now, we will build the project. On the Eclipse main menu, select **Project | Build All**. Then, open the **Console** window to see the build output messages. You should see the compiler prefix being used for the `gcc` compiler as follows:

```
00:24:52 **** Build of configuration Debug for project bbb_ground_
control ****make all Building file: ../src/bbb_ground_control.
cInvoking: Cross GCC Compilerarm-linux-gnueabihf-gcc -O0 -g3 -Wall
-c -fmessage-length=0 -MMD -MP -MF"src/ bbb_ground_control.d"
-MT"src/ bbb_ground_control.d" -o "src/ bbb_ground_control.o" "../
src/ bbb_ground_control.c"Finished building: ../src/ bbb_ground_
control.c Building target: bbb_ground_control Invoking: Cross
GCC Linkerarm-linux-gnueabihf-gcc  -o " bbb_ground_control "  ./
src/ bbb_ground_control.o   Finished building target: bbb_ground_
control 00:24:52 Build Finished (took 172ms)
```

16. For the Eclipse remote connection setup, on the main menu, click on **Run | Run Configurations**.

17. Select **C/C++ Remote Application**. Click twice on this to open another dialog window.

18. A drop-down option should show **bbb_Hello_World Debug**. Click on the **New** button in the middle of the window to create a project debug run configuration. Click on the **New** button next to **Connection** in the **Main** tab.

19. This brings up the **New Connection** window.

20. Select **Linux** and click on **Next**.

21. This brings up a window with the connection information. Enter BeagleBone Black IP address for **Host name** and name the **Connection name** and **Description** both as `BeagleBone Black`:

    ❑ **Host name**: `192.168.2.7`

    ❑ **Connection name**: `Beaglebone Black`

    ❑ **Description**: `Beaglebone Black`

22. Click on **Next**.

23. In the **New Connection/Files** window, select the `select.ssh` files and then click on **Next**.

24. In the **New Connection/Processes** window, select `processes.shel.linux`. Then, click on **Next**.

25. In the **New Connection/Shells** window, select `ssh.shells`. Then, click on **Next**.

26. In the **New Connection/Ssh Terminals** window, select `ssh.terminals` and click on **Finish**.

27. You will end up back at the **Run Configurations** window. For **Connection**, choose **BeagleBone Black**, not **Local**.

28. Click on **Properties** next to **Connection**. A window will come up, so select **Remote workspace location**.

29. Enter a path to your project on BeagleBone Black. For the sake of simplicity, you should probably follow what we did and input `/root`.

30. Click on **OK**. This takes you back to the **Run Configurations** window.

    In the following steps, we will perform two key things: configure our remote paths on the BBB and give our application permission to execute.

31. At the bottom of the **Run Configurations** screen are two fields. Input the following:

    remote absolute file path for C/C++ application: /root/test_project/bbb_ground_control

    commands to execute before application: chmod +x /root/test_project/bbb_ground_control

> Choose a path on BeagleBone Black where the bbb_ground_control executable file will be placed. In our example, it is /root/test_project/bbb_ground_control, where bbb_ground_control is the name of the binary file that we will compile. The purpose of the chmod +x command is to give our program permission to execute.

32. Click on **Apply**. We are almost there. Be patient and hang on tight.

33. From the terminal window on the VM, we have a couple more things to perform on the BBB itself, which is to mirror what we just input in the two fields in Eclipse. First, log in with the following code:

    ```
    # sudo ssh 192.168.7.2
    ```

34. Answer yes when prompted are you sure.

35. Enter the root password for the BBB: root. You should now be logged in to the BBB.

36. Run the commands to duplicate what we just did in Eclipse, which means that we need to create a new directory, navigate to it and then run the following command to give the application permission to execute:

    ```
    root@beaglebone:~# mkdir test_project
    root@beaglebone:~# cd test_project
    root@beaglebone:~# chmod a+w .
    ```

37. Now, exit the SSH session on BeagleBone Black with the following code:

    ```
    root@beaglebone:~# exit
    ```

38. Back in the **VM Eclipse** window, click on **Run**.

39. Another pop-up window will appear. Enter the user and password as root. Click on them and agree to the next few prompts from the BBB.

    The last few steps are focused on how to set up a remote debug session.

40. In your terminal window, navigate to the project Debug path with the following code:

    ```
    # cd ~/bbb-eclipse-workspace/bbb_ground_control/Debug
    ```

41. Now, we will perform a little obscure but necessary step when you run GDB: create an invisible file called `.gdbinit`. This is an initialization file that resides in the debug directory and automatically loads and parses when you run GDB.

    Typically, you would populate this file with any required commands. However, for our current recipe, the file remains empty, although it needs to remain present for GDB's proper operation.

42. We could use `nano` to create the file because we used this editor in the earlier chapters. However, there is another command that actually generates the file on the fly, saves it, and places it in whatever directory you have entered, as shown in the following code:

    ```
    # touch .gdbinit
    ```

43. Make sure that the file was created with the following code:

    ```
    # ls
    ```

    Hmm. It isn't there!

    To figure out what is happening, this is a case where using different options with a command is vital. With the `ls` command, we want to append the command with the `-a` option. So, try again using the following code:

    ```
    # ls -a
    ```

    The `gdbinit` file should now appear in the directory's lineup.

44. Back in the **Eclipse** window, select **Window | Open Perspective | Other**. Then, select **Debug**. This will shift the window views to a debug-centric UI.

45. From the top menu, select **Run | Debug Configurations**. In the window that opens, select **C/C++ Remote Application | bbb_ground_control Debug.**

    Hold on tight. Almost done.

46. Select the **Debugger** tab. This shows us more tabs because we haven't had our fill of tabs or options yet.

47. Now, select the **Main** tab. Here, we need to populate the two fields: **GDB Debugger** (the executable in the toolchain directory) and the **GDB command file** (the directory where we created the **.gdbinit** file). To facilitate this step, you should be able to browse the relevant directories and grab the right paths as follows:

    GDB Debugger: `/home/user/bbb-tools/gcc-linaro-arm-linux-gnueabihf-4.8-2013.10_linux/bin/arm-linux-gnueabihf-gdb`

    GDB command file: `/home/user/bbb-eclipse-workspace/bbb_ground_control/Debug/.gdbinit`

48. Then, click on **Apply**. I like this part.

49. Now, we finally get to test the whole shebang with **Debug run**. Let me repeat and this time with bugles and proper fanfare: we will test everything we just did and start a Debug session.

    So, at the bottom of the still open window, click on **Debug**. Hold your breath! This will start the remote session with the BBB and finish the cycle just after the `main()` line in your `.c` file.

 You may get another login prompt from your BeagleBone Black. Just do the same drill: `user = root` and `password = root`.

If all went as planned and the gremlins stay home, you should see the following output on your **Eclipse** console screen:

```
Last login: DAY MO DATE TIME YEAR from 192.168.7.1

echo $PWD'>'

chmod +x /root/test_project/bbb_ground_control;gdbserver :2345 /
root/test_project/bbb_ground_control;exit

root@beaglebone:~# echo $PWD'>'

/root>

root@beaglebone:~# chmod +x /root/test_project/bbb_ground_
control;gdbserver :2345  /root/test_project/bbb_ground_
control;exit

Process /root/test_project/bbb_ground_control created; pid = 2910

Listening on port 2345

Remote debugging from host 192.168.7.1
```

50. Since the ultimate goal of all this effort was to actually perform some debugging on a program, now you can really get to work. Make sure your `bbb_ground_control.c` window is selected. Then, at the top, choose **Run**.

51. From the drop-down list, you will see the basket of debug commands now ready for your able, debug-twitchy fingers.

52. If you made it to this point, this recipe has one last set of command ingredients:

```
# Go to actual cabinet on actual shelf

# Take out bottle of single malt scotch

# Pour dram, perhaps two

# Lean back head and drink

# Congratulate Major Tom on a good test flight
```

There's more...

A thorough review of how to debug is beyond the scope of this book. Fortunately, there are ample resources to learn more. Here are a few:

▶ RMS's gdb debugger tutorial is available at `http://www.unknownroad.com/rtfm/gdbtut/gdbtoc.html`

▶ For a deeper understanding of GDB and the `.gdbinit` file, refer to `http://www.dirac.org/linux/gdb/03-Initialization,_Listing,_And_Running.php`

systemd services

First, it wasn't a typo to label this section as systemd in all lowercase letters. It is one of the mandates of Linux that any daemon, which is what systemd is, should be in lowercase. Also, daemons must also come with the lowercase suffix: d.

So what is systemd exactly? Briefly, it is a background process and a system management daemon for managing user space system services. Systemd will become standard plumbing for most major Linux distros and is an integral part of the BBB Debian distribution. It is the first process initiated on bootup in the Linux user space and the last process to terminate on shutdown. Basically, systemd starts the show on your Linux OS and turns out the lights as it's leaving.

Sound familiar? If it does, that's because systemd is the heir to init: Linux's longtime daemon of daemons.

Mastering systemd on your BBB helps us better understand system dependencies because systemd serves as a robust framework for these dependencies. Here are a couple of examples of why you'd want to manipulate systemd processes:

▶ **Bootup**: Since much is happening with your system at bootup, it makes sense to have tighter control and deeper insight into the startup processes. For example, you may want to optimize your system to squeeze out more CPU resources for higher resolution video display. With systemd, it's easier to control that load environment.

▶ **Job scheduling**: You may have created a beautiful prototype for a weather measurement device. However, you had in mind a wireless, battery-driven design, so power consumption is a concern. In this case, you can use systemd to schedule runtimes (systemd Calendar Timers) for the sensors to capture and transmit data and then revert to sleep mode when not needed, thereby prolonging the battery life.

There's more...

Before we move on to the recipes, you'll find a great deal of deeper insight into systemd by taking a look at some of the following referenced material:

- ▸ The definitive (`freedesktop.org`) resource for systemd is available at `http://www.freedesktop.org/wiki/Software/systemd/`
- ▸ The quick reference cheat sheet for systemd commands is available at `http://dynacont.net/documentation/linux/Useful_SystemD_commands/`
- ▸ `man systemd`: This is the command for the very extensive manual for the daemon. It yields more information than you would probably ever want to know about systemd. However, it is there if you want it.
- ▸ If you want the full background on how systemd came to be, one of the creators of the tool provides the full story and context at `http://0pointer.de/blog/projects/systemd.html`

See also

systemd is far from perfect. Many Linux heads gripe about it being too powerful and potentially becoming overly complicated for users. Here is some background on this controversy:

- ▸ A robust slashdot thread provides plenty of rants on the pros and cons at `http://news.slashdot.org/story/14/02/14/166255/ubuntu-to-switch-to-systemd`
- ▸ **Eric Steven Raymond** (**ESR**), an open source guru, is currently on the fence about systemd at `http://interviews.slashdot.org/story/14/03/10/137246/interviews-esr-answers-your-questions`

Despite the disagreements over its long-term impact on Linux, systemd is here to stay at least for the foreseeable future. So, it behooves you to learn some recipes.

Basic commands for systemd services

systemd is modified via a configuration file, rather than a shell script. Before you perform anything too ambitious, we will take a look at how we stop, start, enable, and disable a service.

Our example will reset and reconfigure a key service that will run in your Debian distribution: the `systemd-timedated.service` by default.

How to do it...

Perform the following steps:

1. Navigate to the `systemd` directory (root user) with the following code:

    ```
    # cd /lib/systemd/system
    ```

2. Let's see what services are running, using a command that serves as the control utility for `systemd`, as shown in the following code:

    ```
    # systemctl
    ```

    You should see a long, fat list of services that show their current status on the system. The items appended with the `.service` filename are `systemd` services and controllable via the command line.

3. Run this command to stop the service:

    ```
    systemctl stop systemd-timedated.service
    ```

4. Now, disable the service using the following code:

    ```
    systemctl disable systemd-timedated.service
    ```

5. Then, do the opposite and enable it as follows:

    ```
    Systemctl enable systemd-timedated.service
    ```

6. Although your service may be enabled, you need to actually start it so that the system has access to its routine, as shown in the following code:

    ```
    systemctl start systemd-timedated.service
    ```

7. Finally, check whether the service is running correctly with the following code:

    ```
    systemctl status systemd-timedated.service
    ```

There's more...

A handy list of systemd commands is available as a downloadable PDF or an online reference at `http://www.cheatography.com/tme520/cheat-sheets/systemd/`.

Optimize boot time

You can use systemd to speed up your startup time. This recipe is not a definitive recommendation for which services may be expendable. Instead, it provides the overall method to test the impact of different services on your boot time.

How to do it...

Perform the following steps:

1. Navigate to the `systemd` directory (root user) as follows:

   ```
   # cd /lib/systemd/system
   ```

2. Next, determine how long your overall system is taking to get going with the following code:

   ```
   # systemd-analyze
   ```

3. You can quickly figure out the pokier services. Just point the finger at them with the following command that reveals all the systemd services that are sorted by their boot times:

   ```
   # systemd-analyze blame
   ```

4. From this output, you can immediately pinpoint some of the culprits. We will assume that you're running the current Debian distro, so you'll see things similar to the following command:

   ```
   wicd.service (7205ms)

   apache2.service (3430ms)

   wpa_supplicant.service (1938ms)

   . . .
   ```

5. Some of these may be expendable startup services and worth disabling. Experiment by disabling the different services and see how it affects your boot times. Here is an example:

   ```
   # systemd systemctl disable wicd.service
   ```

Create a systemd service to run at boot time

Remember those ancient days of *Chapter 2, Basic Programming Recipes*, when you were just learning how to send an e-mail with Node.js? No? You skipped that recipe? Well, you may want to do that one before you dive into this one. In this recipe, we'll perform something similar and have the script run at boot up. Instead of having Node.js perform the job, it'll be Python and systemd.

The scenario is that you need to control your BBB remotely via SSH or VNC, but the board is offsite or running headless. As you have learned previously, in order to control the BBB remotely, we have to know the board's IP address. If you're in front of the board, it's easy enough to check the IP at the bottom of your screen via the GUI popup. However, our board is 100 miles away and isn't attached to a display. Systemd (with a healthy dash of Python) comes to the rescue!

Let's take a look at how we can have systemd send us this magical IP-addressed e-mail.

How to do it...

Perform the following steps:

1. Log in as root with the following code:

   ```
   sudo -i
   ```

2. Then, create a new Python file called `email-ip.py` and save it, as shown in the following code:

   ```
   sudo nano email-ip-BBB.py
   ```

3. Here is the Python code (the code is derived from the example code on stackoverflow at http://bit.ly/1kUppmT):

   ```python
   #!/usr/bin/python

   ##Look up your BBB's ip address and email it##

   import socket
   import datetime, time
   import sys

   # Import smtplib for the actual sending function
   import smtplib
   ```

```
# Import the email modules we'll need
from email.mime.text import MIMEText


try:
    b = socket.socket(socket.AF_INET, socket.SOCK_DGRAM)
    b.connect(("8.8.8.8",80))
    bbb1_ip = b.getsockname()[0]
    b.close()
except SocketError:
    print sys.exc_info()[0]
except:
    print error
time.sleep(5)

msg = MIMEText("Beaglebone Black ip address: %s" % bbb1_ip)


From = 'yourname@youremaildomain.com'
To = 'recipientemail@recipientdomain.com'

#include module for date and time
msg['Subject'] = 'BBB ip address at ' + str(datetime.datetime.
now())
msg['From'] = From
msg['To'] = To

# Send the message via our own SMTP server, but don't include the
# envelope header.
s = smtplib.SMTP('smtp.gmail.com', 587)
s.starttls()
s.login('your-name@gmail.com', your-password')
s.sendmail(From, [To], msg.as_string())
s.quit()
```

In our recipe, we've used a Gmail account as the server and user credentials, although you can use any service you prefer. Just replace the Gmail details with your preferred provider.

4. Navigate to the `systemd` directory with the following code:

   # cd /lib/systemd/system

5. Now, create a new service file as follows:

   # nano email-ip.service

6. Copy and paste the following code to the `nano` window. Let's take a look at the systemd code in its entirety first. Then, we'll break down its meaning as follows:

```
[Unit]
Description=Email current IP Address


[Service]
WorkingDirectory=/home/debian/
ExecStart=/usr/bin/python email-ip-bbb.py
SyslogIdentifier=emailip
Restart=on-failure
RestartSec=5



[Install]
WantedBy=multi-user.target
```

7. What does this all mean? First, let's begin with inputting a human-readable name for the systemd service, which describes the properties of the process you'd like to run, as shown in the following code:

```
[Unit]
Description=Email current IP Address
```

8. Next, we will describe where the file is that will be run on bootup with the following code:

```
[Service]
WorkingDirectory=/home/debian/
```

9. Then, we will tell the service about the command or script to be executed for the file:

```
ExecStart=/usr/bin/python email-ip.py
```

10. Now, the system logs should capture the run data, so we have to give the service a unique name for that purpose as follows:

```
SyslogIdentifier=emailip
```

11. We have to prepare for the application exiting with an error, tell it not to despair, and try again with the following code:

```
Restart=on-failure
```

12. Now, not only should the service try again, but keep trying to relaunch, in this case, every 5 seconds, as shown in the following code:

```
RestartSec=5
```

13. Once the service is enabled, we want to give it a run-level target, in our case, tell it to launch as part of a group of processes—the multi-user processes—that trigger near the end of the boot cycle as follows:

```
[Install]
WantedBy=multi-user.target
```

14. Save the file and then enable the service you just created:

```
root@beaglebone:/lib/systemd/system# systemctl enable email-ip.
service
```

15. Now, reboot. If everything went as planned, you should get an e-mail in your inbox that tells you the IP address of your BeagleBone Black. Pretty handy!

5
Basic Programming Recipes with the Linux Kernel

In this chapter, we will cover the following recipes:

- ▸ Kernel application binary interface
- ▸ Installing the latest kernel image
- ▸ Installing and building a custom kernel
- ▸ Interactions with the kernel – sysfs entries and controlling the GPIOs
- ▸ Device Tree and its roots
- ▸ Device Tree / basic build
- ▸ Device Tree / advanced – adding DT overlay to run a custom cape
- ▸ Universal cape overlay
- ▸ Running a script to check DT usage on GPIO pins

Introduction

We will now learn something about the real guts of our platform, the Linux kernel. Of course, understanding all the bits about the kernel is for another very large set of books and discussion. We won't be doing that here!

What we do want to explore is how to update, build, and modify the kernel in ways that will give us tighter control over our hardware and make the development process less opaque. Then, we'll conclude the chapter by working with one of the key differentiators for BeagleBone Black, the Device Tree, which is a clever way to describe the hardware in our system.

The best part is that if you do all the recipes, you'll be forever known as Colonel kernel. Well, lieutenant kernel. All right, maybe private kernel. But it's a start....

Kernel building basics

What is this mysterious kernel thing of which we speak? What does it look like? Where does it live? Well, on one level, it is merely a file. Let's take a peek. Open up a terminal on your BBB and type the following commands:

```
$ cd /boot
```

```
$ ls
```

The command should deliver this output:

```
debian@beaglebone:~$ cd /boot
debian@beaglebone:/boot$ ls
System.map-3.8.13-bone67   dtbs                          uboot
config-3.8.13-bone67       initrd.img-3.8.13-bone67      vmlinuz-3.8.13-bone67
debian@beaglebone:/boot$
```

There it is: the kernel, the file that begins with the name, vmlinuz. However, the file itself—an executable one—does not really do anything until you load it into memory and have it run. That happens, of course, when you have the right boot sequence established, which should be happening by default on your BBB Debian distro.

When the kernel begins running, it performs several key tasks, such as process management, file management, and I/O management. The latter is what we will mainly look at in this chapter as it is the most clearly recognizable—and relevant—function that the kernel performs for physical computing or while building hardware prototypes. For us, I/O means mostly GPIO pins, peripheral devices such as capes and daughterboards, and other add-ons as this is where most of the action is for this book.

See also

Understanding the boot sequence gives you a deeper understanding of the various processes and events occurring on your BBB and can play a key role in development and debugging. The following provide an excellent background on the boot cycle:

- In the context of using ArduPilot, a drone-centric toolset, developer Anuj Deshpande takes you through the steps at `http://diydrones.com/profiles/blogs/booting-up-a-beaglebone-black`

- Although this example from professor Mark Yoder shows an Angstrom distribution boot with an earlier kernel, one of the better tutorials to describe the BBB boot can be found at `http://elinux.org/EBC_Exercise_21a_Boot_Sequence`

- A commonly referenced process map created by Alexander Holler delivers an excellent graphical representation of the boot sequence at `http://ahsoftware.de/Beaglebone_Black_Boot_explained.svg`

Kernel application binary interface

Now, let's do a quick, simple task with a command to find out which kernel we are running. The command can serve as a first-level "diagnostic" tool when we need to troubleshoot errors or incompatibilities with any software we want to add or compile for our system.

Getting ready

This is a simple setup, so all you need to do is connect your board via USB to your host computer and fire it up. Then, open a terminal window.

How to do it...

The steps to do this are simple:

1. Firstly, log in as the root user using the following command:

   ```
   $ sudo -i
   ```

2. Now, run a command that tells us a few important things about the kernel. Let's choose the `-a` option to show all information about the system, as follows:

   ```
   root@beaglebone:~# uname -a
   Linux beaglebone 3.8.13-bone67 #1 SMP Wed Sep 24 01:36:09 UTC 2014 armv7l GNU/Linux
   ```

From this command's output, we discover several items of interest, as follows:

> **The kernel version**: According to our output, the installed version of the Linux kernel is 3.8.13. There are other later, experimental versions (for example, 3.14.x) that many BeagleBone Black developers are currently using. However, version 3.8 is the current stable install.

> **Kernel ABI** : Our version is "bone67", a flavor specific to our board and one that provides an optimized environment to run a basic BBB system. The number "67" is the version number and not significant in itself, but it provides context for when we encounter incompatibilities or errors.

How it works...

So, what is the kernel ABI? Basically, it is an interface layer between the kernel and user space applications. One way of understanding it is by comparing it to an API, a familiar concept to any programmer. When you use an API, you can access the features of an external component, a third-party software feature, or an OS. An ABI is kind of similar to a compiled version of an API.

Think about the software that we built and compiled from source in our prior chapter. Once code is compiled at the kernel level, an application accesses the binary data through the ABI. Just like an API, an ABI defines the structures and methods that your compiled application will use to access an external library, for instance. Except with the kernel ABI, it happens at the lower machine-language level.

Installing the latest kernel image

All the way back in *Chapter 1*, *Setting Up for the First Time*, we used a set of tools that came with our Debian distro. In that case, we used a tool (a bash script) to expand our partition. In this case, we'll use another script from that toolset that runs a routine to update our kernel image. Let's go get it. With developer Robert Nelson's slick scripts (`https://eewiki.net/display/linuxonarm/BeagleBone+Black`), the process to update or build the kernel on Debian for the BBB has become a snap.

Getting ready

As in our preceding recipe, connect your board via USB to your host computer, boot up, and then open a terminal window.

How to do it...

Let's get started! To do this, perform the following steps:

1. Firstly, log in as root with the following command:

   ```
   # sudo -i
   ```

   Following this, check the current version of your kernel through the following command:

   ```
   # uname -a
   Linux beaglebone 3.8.13-bone67 #1 SMP Wed Sep 24 01:36:09 UTC 2014
   armv7l GNU/Linux
   ```

    Write down the version number so that we can refer to it at the end of the recipe.

2. You then need to go to the scripts directory that comes preloaded with your version of Debian for the BBB. You can do this by typing out the following command:

   ```
   $ cd /opt/scripts/tools
   ```

3. Run the following `git` command to update your local files:

   ```
   $ git pull
   ```

4. You have several options for the type of install you prefer: the stable, testing, or custom release. According to your preference, append the command with one of the following options:

   ❑ For the stable release, use the following command:

   ```
   $ ./update_kernel.sh
   ```

   ❑ For the testing release, the following command will be useful:

   ```
   $ ./update_kernel.sh --beta-kernel
   ```

   Running this script installs a version of the kernel that is still in the test phase. Although technically not a release, the testing versions of the kernel can still be quite stable and robust, albeit with some bugs.

   ❑ For the custom release, run the following command (this has to be on `rcn-ee.net`):

   ```
   $ ./update_kernel.sh --kernel v.0.00-bone00
   ```

   For the custom option, you can replace the version number with the exact version you want to run. These versions would be available at Robert C. Nelson's site at `http://www.rcn-ee.net/deb/`.

5. Reboot with your new kernel image and then check that it shows the newer kernel now installed with the following command:

```
debian@beaglebone:~$ uname -a

Linux beaglebone 3.8.13-bone[xx] #1 SMP [day mo date time UTC
year] armv7l GNU/Linux
```

The (xx) box should now reflect an updated version running.

Installing and building a custom kernel

This recipe will build the kernel and modules from scratch and copy them to a deploy or temporary directory.

Getting ready

Connect and power up your board via USB to your host computer; then, open a terminal window.

How to do it...

To perform this recipe, follow these steps:

1. First, log in as the root user and then download the kernel file from Robert C. Nelson's git repo:

```
$ sudo -i

# git clone https://github.com/RobertCNelson/bb-kernel.git
```

2. Navigate to the new directory that git created for you on your BBB with this command:

```
# cd bb-kernel/
```

3. At this point, you have two options for the kernel version you prefer to use: either v3.8.x or the latest experimental v3.14.x. You'll notice that the git command also generates a tmp directory for the build:

   ❑ For the 3.8.x Wheezy branch (this version comes with full cape support) use this command:

   ```
   ~/bb-kernel# git checkout origin/am33x-v3.8 -b tmp
   ```

   ❑ For the v3.14.x Jessie branch (which comes with better USB and Ethernet support but without full cape support) use the following command:

   ```
   ~/bb-kernel# git checkout origin/am33x-v3.14 -b tmp
   ```

4. Now, we will build the kernel with this command:

```
~/bb-kernel# ./build_kernel.sh
```

Be sure to take note of the space between # and . in the command. Otherwise, your command will not be executed. Also, beware that this build cycle may take a while, so be patient for it to finish.

> Since Linux, BeagleBone Black, and the open source community at large move pretty fast, what we deem experimental in this book may be nearly mainstream within a short period of time. For example, note that the current move toward the new Debian 8 Linux kernel "Jessie" (as opposed to the current version 7 nicknamed "Wheezy") is well underway. In 2015, it will likely have moved from the Debian/testing repos to the stable repos and is expected to be part of the BBB shipping firmware.

Interactions with the kernel – sysfs entries and controlling the GPIOs

When first starting out with physical computing and a Linux board, such as the BBB in particular, it is less daunting to use preexisting libraries along with familiar programming tools. This is why we used tools such as Python libraries and BoneScript to gain access to BeagleBone Black's GPIO pins, methods that abstract the kernel layer from the user space layer.

However, it is useful to understand the nature of this abstraction a bit better, particularly when it comes to the GPIO pins. The Linux kernel uses a virtual file system interface—or sysfs—to read and write to the pins. Sysfs easily and effectively exposes drivers for the hardware—buttons, LEDs, sensors, add-ons, and so on. So, you can control them. Manipulating this system gives us insight into how the kernel and hardware can interoperate. In this section, we'll look at how to activate the sysfs interface.

To reiterate, instead of programming with a userland library, this time we want a more direct understanding of what's happening with the platform. So, we will control some pins using a code that transparently accesses the Linux kernel. To do this, it means blinky LED time; except that this time, we will map a pin directly into the filesystem.

> We've referenced it before, but you can never be reminded too many times of the value of a good GPIO reference diagram. Here it is again: `http://elinux.org/Beagleboard:Cape_Expansion_Headers`.

Getting ready

Access to the various pins in the headers on the left- and right-hand sides of the BBB is done through the Linux kernel using its GPIO interfaces. To demonstrate how to give this a spin, we will attach an LED to designated GPIO and GND pins directly on the board's header.

The following are needed:

- ▶ A BBB powered via USB.
- ▶ LED—a cheap LED of the ilk we used in the prior chapters.
- ▶ Resistor—anywhere from 700 (700Ω) to 1k is fine. We will use a 700Ω here (the violet/black/brown/gold bands).
- ▶ Two jumper wires that are easy to connect to the breadboard.
- ▶ A breadboard.

How to do it...

Now that you're ready, let's begin as follows:

1. Ensure that your BBB is powered down.
2. Now, wire up your LED according to the diagram following these instructions:

    ❏ Two jumper wires run from *P8_2* (GND) and *P8_14* on the **P8** header of the BBB onto the breadboard.

    ❏ Insert one end of the resistor (direction does not matter) into the slot corresponding to the *P8_14* jumper wire and the other end a few slots above.

    ❏ Line up the LED's anode (positive/longer) end into the breadboard slot at the upper end of the resistor, while the cathode (shorter/ground) end goes into the slot lined up with the ground wire.

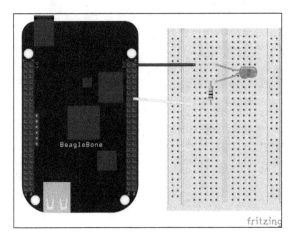

3. You then need to power the BBB back up, logging in as the root user with this command:

```
$ sudo -i
```

4. Navigate to the `gpio` directory using the following command:

```
# cd /sys/class/gpio
```

5. While doing this, take stock of the directory with `ls -l` so that you can compare what you see now with what will occur after the next step. We will add the `-l` option to view the output in a list format, as follows:

```
# ls -l


--w------- 1 root root 4096 Oct 21 10:26 export

lrwxrwxrwx 1 root root    0 Dec 31  1999 gpiochip0 -> ../../
devices/virtual/gpio/gpiochip0

lrwxrwxrwx 1 root root    0 Dec 31  1999 gpiochip32 -> ../../
devices/virtual/gpio/gpiochip32

lrwxrwxrwx 1 root root    0 Dec 31  1999 gpiochip64 -> ../../
devices/virtual/gpio/gpiochip64

lrwxrwxrwx 1 root root    0 Dec 31  1999 gpiochip96 -> ../../
devices/virtual/gpio/gpiochip96

--w------- 1 root root 4096 Oct 21 10:32 unexport
```

6. Once this is done, send an `echo` command as follows:

```
# echo 26 > /sys/class/gpio/export
```

7. Now, take a look at the directory to see how it has changed:

```
# ls   -l


total 0

--w------- 1 root root 4096 Apr 23 16:24 export

lrwxrwxrwx 1 root root    0 Apr 23 16:24 gpio26 -> ../../devices/
virtual/gpio/gpio26

lrwxrwxrwx 1 root root    0 Dec 31  1999 gpiochip0 -> ../../
devices/virtual/gpio/gpiochip0

lrwxrwxrwx 1 root root    0 Dec 31  1999 gpiochip32 -> ../../
devices/virtual/gpio/gpiochip32

lrwxrwxrwx 1 root root    0 Dec 31  1999 gpiochip64 -> ../../
devices/virtual/gpio/gpiochip64
```

```
lrwxrwxrwx 1 root root     0 Dec 31  1999 gpiochip96 -> ../../
devices/virtual/gpio/gpiochip96

--w------- 1 root root 4096 Dec 31  1999 unexport
```

This `echo` command has created a virtual directory, which now allows you to directly interact with the Linux kernel from user space. The kernel's **virtual file system** (**VFS**) is an abstraction of a filesystem and gives you a way to use standard functions for manipulating anything that could be a file on your system. You should also note that pin 26 on which we just ran `echo` corresponds to pin *P8_14* that we wired up on the BBB.

8. Go to the new directory created from the `echo` command and take a look inside using the following command:

    ```
    # cd gpio26
    # ls
    ```

    The output shows the options now available to control the pin as follows:

    ```
    active_low  direction  edge  power  subsystem  uevent  value
    ```

9. Determine the current GPIO value. You should see its initial value as 0 or off, as follows:

    ```
    # cat value
    0
    ```

10. Now, let's light her up by sending the following commands:

    ```
    # echo out > direction
    # echo 1 > value
    ```

    Voila! You should get a sexy, glowing red thing on your BBB.

11. Repeat the same command but change the value back to 0, which should turn the LED back off, with this command:

    ```
    # echo 0 > value
    ```

12. A variation on this is to use another one of the VFS options; in this case, this will be the `high`/`low` direction:

    This turns the LED on:

    ```
    # echo high > direction
    ```

    And then, it turns off:

    ```
    # echo low > direction.
    ```

13. To finish up, it is considered good practice to clean up your pin usage before moving on to some other task. Use the following command lines for this:

```
# cd /sys/class/gpio
# echo 26 > unexport
```

Note that the exported gpio26 has now evaporated:

```
# ls
# export  gpiochip0  gpiochip32  gpiochip64  gpiochip96  unexport
```

You may think that this exercise is just another blinking LED yawn. But really, we did something quite different this time; we reached directly into the kernel from the user space, added a virtual directory to enable control over a pin, and then controlled this pin via the command line. Seeing it work here at a deeper level will bear fruit as we advance toward fancier recipes in later chapters.

There's more...

For more information, refer to the following sources:

Pin states

Understanding pin states can be quite challenging. According to your use case, not only can they be set as input or output pins, but they can also be set as pull-up, pull-down, or floating. For more discussion and background on configuring your pins for these purposes, review *Chapter 3, Physical Computing Recipes Using JavaScript, the BoneScript Library, and Python*, where we discussed GPIO pins.

Other tutorials

For a couple of interesting sysfs methods to turn off the USR LED heartbeat pattern, which many find annoying, follow along with one of these tutorials:

▶ *How to : Disable BeagleBone USR Heartbeat LED lights*: `http://experimentswithlinuxrelatedtech.blogspot.com/2014/12/how-to-disable-beaglebone-usr-heartbeat.html`

▶ Professor Mark Yoder's class, *EBC Exercise 10 Flashing an LED*: `http://elinux.org/EBC_Exercise_10_Flashing_an_LED`

Device Tree and its roots

Linus Torvalds was sad and mad. ARM was making Linus sad and mad. There were too many cooks, too many ingredients, too many new hardware variations in the world of ARM devices. The architecture had become so popular in the embedded computing world that a thicket of third-party devices were being cooked up to work with ARM. Custom hardware drivers and custom kernels were everywhere. This was making the Linux kernel playground increasingly chaotic.

So, Linus roared: go back to the kitchen, cooks, and make a better recipe! So, they did. Or, so the story goes. Thus was born Device Tree....

For beginners, Device Tree can be a bit difficult to wrap one's head around. However, in order to use BeagleBone Black in more interesting projects, an understanding is often critical. Basically, Device Tree is a data structure to describe the hardware that you add on to your board. With Device Tree, the details of a device are available to the board without needing to be hardcoded into the kernel. Prior to its existence, the kernel image—the single binary (`vmlinuz`) that we looked at earlier in the chapter—contained any description needed for the hardware. Beginning with version 3.8 of the Linux kernel for ARM, however, another binary was loaded at boot along with the kernel, **Device Tree Blob** (**DTB**).

BeagleBone Black—with its 3.8 kernel (the shipping version, at least)—is one of the first ARM devices to incorporate the new order of things with **Device Tree** (**DT**). Its benefits for the BBB are many:

- **Upstream dev**: This provides us with the ability to receive and contribute to all the benefits of upstream kernel development.
- **Kernel build simplification**: This avoids the hassle of maintaining a custom kernel.
- **Cape development**: Developers of cape expansion boards enjoy a standardized logic in the kernel. This greatly simplifies life for the cape maker and end user as recompiling the kernel to make the cape function is rarely a requirement.

To reiterate, Device Tree is a binary that describes the system hardware and loads at boot time. Its "tree" nomenclature refers to the fact that it is written in a hierarchical node or tree data structure. The nodes describe the physical device in the system.

The Device Tree overlay

Device Tree is what is used by the kernel during bootup and is common to all modern ARM devices. On BeagleBone Black and its earlier cousins, Device Tree also comes accompanied with a kind of "patch" or overlay. Applied at runtime, Device Tree overlay helps reconfigure hardware resources on the board, such as capes, GPIO pins, LCDs, and so on, and is handled by bone-capemgr (the cape manager).

Although we will do a recipe on the Device Tree overlay (dtbo) in a later section, it might be helpful to browse the following directory to take a look at many of the dtbo files that come with the firmware:

```
# cd /lib/firmware
# ls -l
```

The sample output looks like this:

```
-rw-r--r-- 1 root root   1056 Apr 23 16:57 BB-ADC-00A0.dtbo
-rw-r--r-- 1 root root   2885 Apr 23 16:57 BB-BONE-AUDI-01-00A0.dtbo
-rw-r--r-- 1 root root   2288 May 18  2014 BB-BONE-AUDI-02-00A0.dtbo
-rw-r--r-- 1 root root   2583 May 18  2014 BB-BONE-AUDI-02-00A0.dts
-rw-r--r-- 1 root root   4273 Apr 23 16:57 BB-BONE-BACON-00A0.dtbo
-rw-r--r-- 1 root root   3259 Apr 23 16:57 BB-BONE-BACONE-00A0.dtbo
-rw-r--r-- 1 root root   4536 Apr 23 16:57 BB-BONE-BACONE2-00A0.dtbo
-rw-r--r-- 1 root root   3592 Apr 23 16:57 BB-BONE-CAM-VVDN-00A0.dtbo
```

There's more...

Here are a few other key things to keep in mind about Device Tree and the BBB:

- Many embedded architectures have a wide variety of nondiscoverable hardware, daughterboards, add-ons, and so on
- Depending on the architecture, this hardware is described using either C-code directly within the kernel or a special hardware description language in Device Tree
- Other architectures besides the BBB's ARM also use Device Tree, including PowerPC, OpenRISC, ARC, and Microblaze
- A DTS is compiled into a binary **Device Tree Blob** (**DTB**) data structure and passed at boot time to the kernel
- The bootloader must load both the kernel image and Device Tree Blob in memory before starting the kernel

Device Tree / basic build

On the BBB, there are three essential steps to create and run a Device Tree file:

1. Create a source file (`dts`).
2. Compile it and make a binary (`dtb`)—also known as blob—of the file.
3. Ensure that the kernel knows where to find the new blob.

Let's start with a simple recipe, one that turns off one of the onboard LEDs: specifically, USR0, which is the LED that blinks with the "heartbeat" pattern. There are simpler ways to do this, as we did the same thing with BoneScript in *Chapter 3, Physical Computing Recipes Using JavaScript, the BoneScript Library, and Python*. However, it remains a useful introductory recipe to understand Device Tree's interaction with the kernel.

Getting ready

For the next recipe, simply power up your board via the USB port. Internet connectivity is not required.

How to do it...

You need to perform the following steps:

1. Log in as root with this command:

    ```
    $ sudo -i
    #
    ```

2. Grab the file that we need for this recipe. Going forward in the book, we will more commonly have you use our GitHub repository to get the code instead of downloading a file directly as we did in earlier chapters. Use this command:

    ```
    # git clone https://github.com/HudsonWerks/device-tree.git
    ```

3. Browse the downloaded folder and open up the following file:

    ```
    # cd device-tree
    # nano bspm_USR0_10-00A0.dts
    ```

    Take a look at the code visible in the `nano` window. The intention of this step is for you to review the code structure before we actually move it to its appropriate directory:

    ```
    /*
     * This is a (mostly) template-generated file from BoneScript,
    modified from Kilobaser.com's Device-Tree Overlay Generator
     */
    ```

```
/dts-v1/;
/plugin/;


/{
    compatible = "ti,beaglebone", "ti,beaglebone-black";


    /* identification */
    part_number = "BS_PINMODE_USR0_0x0";


    /* state the resources used */
    exclusive-use =
        "USR0",
        "gpmc_a5";


    /* the LED is set to pulldown or off */
    fragment@0 {
        target = <&am33xx_pinmux>;
        __overlay__ {
            bs_pinmode_USR0_0x0: pinmux_bs_pinmode_USR0_0x0 {
                pinctrl-single,pins = <0x054 0x0>;
            };
        };
    };


    fragment@1 {
        target = <&ocp>;
        __overlay__ {
            bs_pinmode_USR0_0x0_pinmux {
                compatible = "bone-pinmux-helper";
                status = "okay";
                pinctrl-names = "default";
                pinctrl-0 = <&bs_pinmode_USR0_0x0>;
            };
        };
    };
}
```

4. Now, close the window by pressing *CTRL + x*, then type N (for no), and run the following to move the file to its correct directory:

    ```
    # mv bspm_USR0_10-00A0.dts /lib/firmware/
    ```

5. Compile the file using this command, which should finish within seconds:

    ```
    # dtc -O dtb -o /lib/firmware/bspm_USR0_10-00A0.dtbo -b 0 -@ /lib/
    firmware/bspm_USR0_10-00A0.dts
    ```

    The command can basically be broken down in the following fashion:

    ```
    dtc [options] <input file>
    ```

    -O: This capital "O" (not zero) is the output flag that is followed by the type of output desired, which is a `dtb` file or Device Tree Blob (also known as binary) in this case

    -b: This means that you want the file (blob) to be loaded at boot time

    0: This "zero" shows the physical boot ID, which is 0

    -@: This ampersand means that the compiler will generate a symbol node, which makes it possible to dynamically load the Device Tree

    `<file name/source file>`: The command ends with the source file target

6. Assuming you received no error message, confirm that the compile did what you expected and built the `bspm_USR0_10-00A0.dtbo` file using the following command:

    ```
    # ls
    ```

7. Next, we want to enable the overlay file that we just created with the following command:

    ```
    # echo bspm_USR0_10 > /sys/devices/bone_capemgr.*/slots
    ```

    You will now see the heartbeat-flashing USR0 LED turn on immediately. Hallelujah! That darned blink is annoying, isn't it?

Although at the time of writing this book the cape manager is at version 9, we use the wildcard option (*) to ensure that later versions of `bone_capemgr` will still respond to this command.

8. We should now look at what just happened by doing the following:

    ```
    # dmesg | tail -10
    ```

    Your screen output should look similar to this:

    ```
    [   33.848704] IPv6: ADDRCONF(NETDEV_CHANGE): eth0: link becomes
    ready
    ```

```
[  153.829529] bone-capemgr bone_capemgr.9: part_number 'bspm_
USR0_10', version 'N/A'

[  153.829601] bone-capemgr bone_capemgr.9: slot #7: generic
override

[  153.829617] bone-capemgr bone_capemgr.9: bone: Using override
eeprom data at slot 7

[  153.829633] bone-capemgr bone_capemgr.9: slot #7: 'Override
Board Name,00A0,Override Manuf,bspm_USR0_10'

[  153.829723] bone-capemgr bone_capemgr.9: slot #7: Requesting
part number/version based 'bspm_USR0_10-00A0.dtbo

[  153.829738] bone-capemgr bone_capemgr.9: slot #7: Requesting
firmware 'bspm_USR0_10-00A0.dtbo' for board-name 'Override Board
Name', version '00A0'

[  153.834371] bone-capemgr bone_capemgr.9: slot #7: dtbo 'bspm_
USR0_10-00A0.dtbo' loaded; converting to live tree

[  153.834620] bone-capemgr bone_capemgr.9: slot #7: #2 overlays

[  153.835294] bone-capemgr bone_capemgr.9: slot #7: Applied #2
overlays.
```

When we run `dmesg`, it tells us more about the sequence of events, including whether the previous commands were successful. The `-10` option outputs the last ten messages from the kernel. You can make the number higher or lower according to how many messages you want `stdout` to display.

9. Further forensics are useful for a greater insight into the process, so navigate to the following designated directory and run the following:

```
# cd /sys/devices/bone_capemgr.*
# cat slots
0: 54:PF---
1: 55:PF---
2: 56:PF---
3: 57:PF---
4: ff:P-O-L Bone-LT-eMMC-2G,00A0,Texas Instrument,BB-BONE-EMMC-2G
5: ff:P-O-L Bone-Black-HDMI,00A0,Texas Instrument,BB-BONELT-HDMI
7: ff:P-O-L Override Board Name,00A0,Override Manuf,bspm_USR0_10
```

The preceding output tells us something important: that the Device Tree blob that we just built is recognized by the kernel and slotted into position.

Beautiful kernel magic.

Device Tree / advanced – adding DT overlay to run a custom cape

BeagleBone Black introduced the idea of Device Tree overlays that provide even more functionality to DT by modifying the tree in user space, typified in our prior example. With DT overlay, there is no need to reboot.

We saw in our earlier section on sysfs usage the directory/extension `.capemgr`, which refers to cape manager. The BeagleBone kernel uses cape manager as a way to provide dynamic loading and unloading of device tree fragments both at compile time and from user space after the device has booted. We will demonstrate this again here; except this time, we will use DT to enable a custom cape, one which delivers audio I/O functionality to the BBB.

Getting ready

In addition to your usual BBB setup, we will use Audio Cape Rev. B, available from CircuitCo (`http://boardzoo.com/index.php/beaglebone-black/bone-audio.html`). Attach the cape to your BBB's header stack, following the orientation shown in the following pictures:

 If you ran the recipe in the previous chapter to send the IP address of your BBB to your email address, you can run your system remotely and in a headless way.

Be sure to match the header pin rows (**P8** and **P9**) on the audio cape to those of the BeagleBone Black.

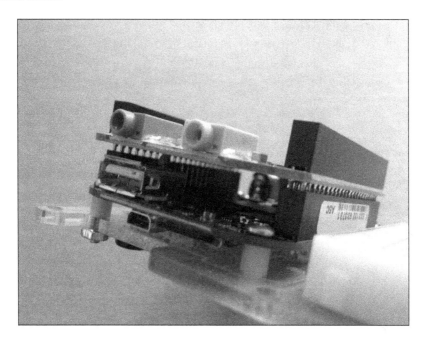

The output jack is green and the input jack is light blue.

In order to do the last part of this recipe, you may also want to either plug a microphone into the input jack on the cape or use a USB mic in the USB port.

How to do it...

Now that you're prepared, let's get started:

1. First, download and unzip the DT overlay from the manufacturer (http://elinux. org/images/1/10/BB-BONE-AUDI-02-00A0.zip). For the fastest method, just download it to your client machine.

2. In a text editor on your client machine, open up a file with the name, BB-BONE-AUDI-02-00A0.dts.

3. On your BBB, log in as root and navigate to the firmware directory:

   # **cd /lib/firmware**

   As an optional step, you can check the contents of the directory. You should see dozens of Device Tree overlay files (.dtbo). Otherwise, you can skip this.

4. Open a `nano` window on the BBB with the following filename:

    ```
    # nano BB-BONE-AUDI-02-00A0.dts
    ```

5. Copy the Device Tree overlay file contents from the text editor window on your client machine into the `nano` window on your BBB by executing the following code:

    ```
    /*
     * Copyright (C) 2012 Texas Instruments Incorporated - http://www.
    ti.com/
     *
     * This program is free software; you can redistribute it and/or
    modify
     * it under the terms of the GNU General Public License version 2
    as
     * published by the Free Software Foundation.
     */
    /dts-v1/;
    /plugin/;

    / {
        compatible = "ti,beaglebone", "ti,beaglebone-black";

        /* identification */
        part-number = "BB-BONE-AUDI-02";
        version = "00A0", "A0";

    ...
    ```

6. Then, compile the Device Tree overlay as follows:

    ```
    dtc -O dtb -o BB-BONE-AUDI-02-00A0.dtbo -b 0 -@ BB-BONE-AUDI-02-
    00A0.dts
    ```

7. Now, we'll open up `nano` to edit the boot file. You can optionally open the same file by browsing your client Mac or PC desktop and drilling down into the `BEAGLE_BONE/` `volume` with the following code:

    ```
    # nano /boot/uEnv.txt
    ```

    ```
    ##Audio Cape (needs HDMI Audio disabled)
    ```

```
cape_disable=capemgr.disable_partno=BB-BONELT-HDMI
```

```
cape_enable=capemgr.enable_partno=BB-BONE-AUDI-02
```

Once opened, we want to uncomment (remove #) from the section labeled `Disable HDMI`, and the following command comes in handy:

```
optargs=capemgr.disable_partno=BB-BONELT-HDMI
```

Take note of two things while modifying the `uEnv.txt` file for this step:

- You only need to disable `BB-BONELT-HDMI`. `BB-BONELT-HDMI` as it will not conflict with the audio cape.
- You may, however, run into a different overlay conflict if you ran other recipes or DT experiments. If so, be sure to also comment out any new lines you might have added for other recipes as these may prevent the `AUDI-02` overlay from loading.

Finally, you need to close and save the `uEnv.txt` file.

8. Now, run the `export` command:

    ```
    # export SLOTS=/sys/devices/bone_capemgr.*/slots
    ```

9. After this, go to the following directory:

    ```
    # cd /sys/devices/bone_capemgr.*
    ```

10. Then, run the `echo` command.

    ```
    # echo BB-BONE-AUDI-02 > slots
    ```

    This command takes the output of `echo`, `BB-BONE-AUDI-02`, and writes it in the slots file, which in turn enables the drivers and device for `AUDI-02` using the Device Tree overlay.

11. Now, reboot the BBB as follows:

    ```
    # reboot
    ```

12. Confirm that the DT overlay loaded properly by going to the designated directory and running the following command:

    ```
    # cd /sys/devices/bone_capemgr.9#
    ```
    ```
    # cat slots
    ```

    ```
    0: 54:PF---
    ```

```
    1:  55:PF---

    2:  56:PF---

    3:  57:PF---

    4:  ff:P-O-L Bone-LT-eMMC-2G,00A0,Texas Instrument,BB-BONE-EMMC-2G

    5:  ff:P-O-- Bone-Black-HDMI,00A0,Texas Instrument,BB-BONELT-HDMI

    6:  ff:P-O-L Bone-Black-HDMIN,00A0,Texas Instrument,BB-BONELT-
   HDMIN

    7:  ff:P-O-L Override Board Name,00A0,Override Manuf,BB-BONE-
   AUDI-02
```

You should see in the last line our AUDI-02 device now enabled.

13. So, let's test the default audio output first. For this, use the following command:

```
# speaker-test
```

You should hear white noise playing. To quit, press *Ctrl + c*.

 Avoid using *Ctrl + z* as the process will likely not end gracefully and prevent you from running additional tests on the cape.

14. Finally, we can optionally test the input and the output. This assumes that you have a microphone plugged into the input jack on the cape or a USB mic via the USB port.

15. First, capture an audio sample using the following command:

```
# arecord -D default:CARD=devicename -r 44100 -c 1 -f S16_LE -t
wav -vv -d 10 example.wav
```

Then, play it back by simply using:

```
# aplay example.wav
```

There's more...

Once you get the cape working, you will probably find that audio levels are too low. So, we need to adjust this with the following commands using an installed audio application called amixer, which is part of **Advanced Linux Sound Architecture** (**ALSA**)'s utilities toolset. ALSA is the multifaceted layer that connects to the kernel and provides audio functionality to user space:

```
$ amixer set PCM 5dB

$ amixer set 'Right PGA Mixer Mic3R' on

$ amixer set 'Left PGA Mixer Mic3L' on
```

Additionally, if you want to plug in a music player or another audio source, you need to switch audio from in to out:

```
$ amixer set 'Right HP Mixer PGAR Bypass' on
$ amixer set 'Left HP Mixer PGAL Bypass' on
```

Finally, use these commands to adjust the gain:

1. To increase volume (for example, to `10%`), run the following:

    ```
    $ amixer set PGA 10%+
    ```

2. To decrease the volume (for example, to `5%`), run the following:

    ```
    $ amixer set PGA 5%-
    ```

3. To toggle mute, run the following:

    ```
    $ amixer set PGA toggle
    ```

See also

There is a wealth of supporting information to satisfy your curiosity and take your understanding of Device Tree to new heights:

- Entire *LINUX KERNEL IN A NUTSHELL* (O'Reilly) is available as a downloadable PDF at `http://free-electrons.com/doc/books/lkn.pdf`

- A general overview of DT with examples can be found at `http://www.circuidipity.com/bbb-dt.htm`

- A discussion about using DT overlays and its relevance to controlling GPIOs can be found at `https://groups.google.com/forum/#!topic/beagleboard/c2LFLEUg6Aw`

- *Enabling Device tree overlay on startup on BeagleBone Black* can be found at `http://hipstercircuits.com/enable-device-tree-overlay-on-startup-on-beaglebone-black/`

- Lots of good tips on DT and overlays are available at `http://hipstercircuits.com/category/device-tree/`

- The canonical reference site for Device Tree is at `http://devicetree.org/Device_Tree_Usage`

- There are 45 slides providing a deeper discussion on Device Tree at `http://free-electrons.com/pub/conferences/2013/elce/petazzoni-device-tree-dummies/petazzoni-device-tree-dummies.pdf`

▸ Take advantage of this great find of a site that helps you easily generate device tree overlays, which provide easy pin muxing—`http://kilobaser.com/blog/2014-07-28-beaglebone-black-devicetreeoverlay-generator`

▸ Linus Torvalds' original rant about the ARM device mess that led to the emergence of Device Tree is at the following site. It doesn't get more geeky than this—`http://article.gmane.org/gmane.linux.ports.arm.omap/55060`

Universal cape overlay

Developer Charles Steinkuehler developed an enormously useful addition to the BeagleBone Black and DT world with his universal cape overlay. Now included by default on the current 3.7 and 3.8 kernels, the code greatly simplifies pin and cape management via simple command-line calls. The toolset can, in some cases, obviate the need to use many types of sysfs calls, some of which you learned earlier in the chapter.

Getting ready

A BBB hooked up and powered via USB.

How to do it...

Perform the following steps:

1. Begin by logging in as the root user and then loading the cape overlay using the following commands:

```
$ sudo -i
# echo cape-universaln > /sys/devices/bone_capemgr.*/slots
```

This command loads all devices and exports `gpio`. The pins currently default to `gpio` inputs. However, with the next set of commands, we can easily change their state.

2. Let's consider the example of the `P8_12` pin and run a command to find out its state:

```
# config-pin -q P8.12
P8_12 Mode: gpio Direction: out Value: 0
```

You will recall from earlier recipes that the `0` value means that the pin is set at low or off.

3. Then, we can easily change its state with the following commands:

```
# config-pin P8.12 hi
# config-pin -q P8.12
P8_12 Mode: gpio Direction: out Value: 1
```

Now, the value will change from 0 (low) to 1 (high). Indeed, this is a much snappier method to manipulate pins than the sysfs approach we discussed earlier.

4. The toolset has additional functionality and options that you can further explore with the following command:

```
# config-pin -h
```

There's more...

▶ The developer's site, `https://github.com/cdsteinkuehler/beaglebone-universal-io`, has extended examples and usage for the overlay

Running a script to check DT usage on GPIO pins

When modifying or working with Device Tree files, we frequently need to check pin usage so that we do not inadvertently try to write to claimed or unsuitable pins.

The following recipe employs two scripts that you can run with Node.js and helps us locate which pins are free. The scripts exist thanks to the coding work of Professor Mark Yoder at Rose-Hulman Institute of Technology.

Getting ready

You do not need anything more than your basic BBB kit for this recipe, which is a board connected to your host computer via USB.

How to do it...

To run this script, you need to follow these steps:

1. You first need to open up the Cloud9 IDE and create a new script called `freeGPIO.js`.

2. If you ran the recipe *Device Tree Basic Build* earlier in this chapter, you will find the file `freeGPIO.js` in the directory that you got from our GitHub repo. This was available by running the following command:

git clone https://github.com/HudsonWerks/device-tree.git

Otherwise, you can cut and paste the same code below into the IDE window. If you run into problems with the cut-and-paste version here, then just grab the same code from the directory file on the GitHub repo.

```
#!/usr/bin/node
// Lists all gpio pins with MUX UNCLAIMED and GPIO UNCLAIMED in
$PINMUX
// Usage:  freeGPIO.js    # List free GPIOs using P8 or P9 pin
number
//
// Approach:
//  1. search PINMUX for all entries with "(MUX UNCLAIMED) (GPIO
UNCLAIMED)"
//  2. An entry looks like "pin 8 (44e10820): (MUX UNCLAIMED)
(GPIO UNCLAIMED)"
//  3. Extract the address (44e10820) and subtract 0x44e10800 to
ge the offset
//  4. Format the offset as 0x020, with leading 0's to give 3
digits
//  5. Search for the address in the muxRegOffset field in b.bone.
pins
//  6. Print the matching key

var PINMUX = "/sys/kernel/debug/pinctrl/44e10800.pinmux/pinmux-
pins",
    b = require('bonescript'),
    exec = require('child_process').exec;

exec('grep "(MUX UNCLAIMED) (GPIO UNCLAIMED)" ' + PINMUX,
            function (error, stdout, stderr) {
                var list,     // Array of unused pins
                    pin,      // pin offset in form 0x020
                    addr,     // pin address, 44e10820
                    keylist = []; // List of all unused
                    header pins, P9_12
```

```
                            if(error)  { console.log('error: '  + error ); }
                            if(stderr) { console.log('stderr: ' +
                            stderr); }

    //                         console.log(stdout);
                            stdout = stdout.substring(0,stdout.length-
                            1);  // Get rid of extra \n
                            list = stdout.split('\n');
    //                         console.log(list);
                            for(var i in list) {
                                // list[i] is of form "pin 8
                                (44e10820): (MUX UNCLAIMED) (GPIO
                                UNCLAIMED)"
                                // Get the address from the 2nd field
                                and remove the ()'s
                                addr = list[i].split('
                                ')[2].substring(1,9);
                                // Find the offset and return as 0x020,
                                that is, zero padded to 3 digits.
                                pin = '0x' + ('000' +
                                 (parseInt(addr,16)-
                                0x44e10800).toString(16)).slice(-3);
    //                             console.log(pin + " " + list[i]);
                                for(var j in b.bone.pins) {
                                    if (b.bone.pins[j].muxRegOffset ===
                                    pin) {
    //                             console.log(b.bone.pins[j].key);
                                    keylist.push(b.bone.pins[j].key);
                                        break;
                                    }
                                }
                            }
                            keylist.sort();
                            console.log(keylist.join(' '));
                        });
```

3. In the Cloud9 IDE, click the Run button.

```
P8_10 P8_11 P8_12 P8_13 P8_14 P8_15 P8_16 P8_17 P8_18 P8_19 P8_26
P8_7 P8_8 P8_9 P9_11 P9_12 P9_13 P9_14 P9_15 P9_16 P9_23 P9_24
P9_26 P9_27 P9_30 P9_41 P9_42 USR0 USR1 USR2 USR3
```

This script gave us a list of pins that are not currently in use by the BBB and can be exploited for other purposes.

Next, we will create and use a second script that we will name `findGPIO.js`,
a script which will identify more information about an unused pin. To get the code,
you can cut and paste the code below into the IDE, or follow the same step described
in the prior step of getting it from our GitHub repo. Look for the file `findGPIO.js` in
the device-tree directory that you downloaded.

```
#!/usr/bin/node
// Program to test looking up information in /usr/share/bone101/
static/bone.js
// Usage: findGPIO.js 7      # Look up info for gpio7 (internal
pin number)
//          findGPIO.js P9_12 # Look up using header pin number
(external)
//          findGPIO.js P9_12 P9_13 ...  # Look up multiple pins
and use one line
//                                      # output for each.
// Returns current pin mux

var PINS = "/sys/kernel/debug/pinctrl/44e10800.pinmux/pins",
    PINMUX =
    "/sys/kernel/debug/pinctrl/44e10800.pinmux/pinmux-
    pins",
    b = require('bonescript'),
    exec = require('child_process').exec;

/*
process.argv.forEach(function(val, index, array) {
  console.log(index + ': ' + val);
});
*/

function pinMux(gpio, flag) {
    var addr = '(' + (0x44e10800 +
                    parseInt(gpio.muxRegOffset, 16)).toString(16)
+ ')';

//    console.log('grep "' + addr + '" ' + PINS);
    exec('grep "' + addr + '" ' + PINS,
            function (error, stdout, stderr) {
                var mux,     // Current mux setting
                out,     // output string
                dir = 'down';    // Direction of pullup
                or pulldown
```

```
            if(error)  { console.log('error: '  + error
            ); }
            if(stderr) { console.log('stderr: ' +
            stderr); }


            stdout = stdout.substring(0,stdout.length-1);  //
Get rid of extra \n
            // console.log(stdout);
            mux = parseInt(stdout.split(" ")[3], 16);
  // Get the mux field
            out = gpio.key + ' (gpio ' + gpio.gpio + ")
            mode: " + (mux & 0x7) +
                    " (" + gpio.options[mux & 0x7] + ")
                    " + gpio.muxRegOffset;
            if(!(mux & 0x8)) {   // Pullup or down is
            enabled
                if(mux & 0x10) {
                    dir = 'up';
                }
                out += ' pull' + dir;
            }
            if(mux & 0x20) {
                out += " Receiver Active";
            }
            if(mux & 0x40) {
                out += " Slew Control Slow";
            }
            console.log(out);
        });
    if(flag) {
        exec('grep "' + addr + '" ' + PINMUX,
            function (error, stdout, stderr) {

                if(error) { console.log('error: ' + error); }
                if(stderr) {console.log('stderr: ' +
                stderr); }

                stdout = stdout.substring(0,stdout.length-
                1);  // Get rid of extra \n
                console.log(stdout);
        });
    }
}
```

```
var gpio,
    flag = process.argv.length < 4,
    i;

for(i=2; i<process.argv.length; i++) {
    gpio = process.argv[i].toUpperCase();
    if (gpio[0] === 'P' | gpio[0] === 'U') {
        if(flag) {
            console.log(b.bone.pins[gpio]);
        }
        pinMux(b.bone.pins[gpio], flag);
    } else {
        console.log("Looking for gpio " + gpio);
        for (var i in b.bone.pins) {
            if (b.bone.pins[i].gpio === parseInt(gpio,10)) {
                if(flag) {
                    console.log(b.bone.pins[i]);
                }
                pinMux(b.bone.pins[i], flag);
            }
        }
    }
}
```

4. To run this script, we do not just click the **RUN** button in the IDE. Instead, we type the following command into the IDE's bash terminal window. Note that we append the command with one of the pins, specifically any of the pins that we saw output as available in the previous script's output (here we used *P8_13*). The output reveals a great deal of information about this pin, as follows:

```
# node findGPIO.js P8_13
```

```
{ name: 'EHRPWM2B',
  gpio: 23,
  mux: 'gpmc_ad9',
  eeprom: 15,
  pwm:
   { module: 'ehrpwm2',
     index: 1,
     muxmode: 4,
```

```
        path: 'ehrpwm.2:1',
        name: 'EHRPWM2B' },
   key: 'P8_13',
   muxRegOffset: '0x024',
   options:
     [ 'gpmc_ad9',
       'lcd_data22',
       'mmc1_dat1',
       'mmc2_dat5',
       'ehrpwm2B',
       'pr1_mii0_col',
       'NA',
       'gpio0_23' ] }
P8_13 (gpio 23) mode: 7 (gpio0_23) 0x024 pulldown Receiver Active
pin 9 (44e10824): (MUX UNCLAIMED) (GPIO UNCLAIMED)
```

Among other items of interest, what we learn from the preceding example is that the *P8_13* pin is one of the PWM cadre—more specifically, `EHRPWM2B`, the type of pin we learned about in *Chapter 3, Physical Computing Recipes Using JavaScript*, the BoneScript Library, and Python, that controls devices like motors.

6
Run Faster, Run Real Time

In this chapter, we will cover the following recipes:

- ▶ Installing a test tool
- ▶ Modifying the kernel using RT-PREEMPT
- ▶ Modifying the kernel using Xenomai
- ▶ Programmable real-time units – an introduction
- ▶ A simple PRU test with an assembler
- ▶ Running an ultrasonic range sensor with the PRUs
- ▶ Using Python with the PRUs

Introduction

Things are getting interesting: no more blinky LEDs from sysfs. It's real time...time to learn about how to make your BeagleBone Black perform real-time tricks.

This is not to say that the BeagleBone Black is pokey. The challenge is that, nowadays, innovators, developers, product designers, and engineers always demand faster, more predictable results, especially in scenarios where small latencies can make the difference between success or crash. Crash in this case meaning bang, crash goes the device, not just a software crash.

So, in this chapter, we will examine recipes that help boost the responsiveness of your BBB under certain conditions. To perform this, we will explore the following topics:

- ▸ Kernel modifications for the purpose of creating real-time environments using:
    - ❑ RT_PREEMPT
    - ❑ Xenomai
- ▸ Programmable real-time units

And now for something completely contradictory: Linux is not real time. It is fast and efficient, but it is not a real-time system.

Harummph! But isn't Linux supposed to be the sexy, better alternative to all those bloated, expensively closed systems out there? It depends.

To begin with, it's important to understand what Linux Mavens—particularly the embedded folks—mean when they refer to real time on their systems. First, it's not just about speedier performance. Although squeezing out faster response times is always a goal—and this can be one of the benefits of enabling a real-time environment—that's not an end in itself. Real time is also about ensuring rock-solid predictability on the system, for example, event-x must occur within a very strict time frame. No other event, thread, or interrupt can take priority or get in the way of a real-time event...no excuses!

You may ask why is this a problem anyway? After all, aren't Linux and our super duper BBB supposed to be super fast? Yes. But all systems experience delays in processing events. We have all seen evidence of this, even in mundane circumstances where not much was happening. For example, from time to time, your cursor doesn't quite move from point A to point B on the screen as quickly as you expect. Alternatively, when you clicked on a taskbar item and the pop-up window didn't appear as lightning fast as it did when you clicked on it five minutes ago.

This kind of latency is typical for all systems, and Linux is not immune to it. In our case, we will refer to this phenomenon as *kernel jitter*. Also, certain scenarios absolutely cannot abide by any kind of jitters. For example, a milling machine can't have "late" commands in its I/O; otherwise, the project could be ruined. Therefore, there has to be a solution that delivers real-time performance.

For the BeagleBone Black, there are in fact three (actually four) choices to make your system real time, sometimes referred to as an RTOS or real-time operating system. The recipes follow in order of least to most real timely:

1. PREEMPT_RT
2. XENOMAI
3. PRUs
4. PRU + Xenomai

Now, we will take a look at how to define real-time categories. There are shades of real time; not all scenarios require nanosecond management or response time. Further, engineers and developers often have their own spin on what they define as real time, which is once again determined by their own scenario requirements. However, for our purposes, we'll define real time using the following spectrum of categories:

- **Soft**: This is where use case requirements for real time are met most of the time. Consider the example of music playback on your system. It's mostly smooth, but hiccups happen sometimes on playback. This standard is typically adequate for most desktop use cases.

- **Life-safety hard**: This specifies that the system must deliver on real-time requirements 100 percent of the time. If it doesn't, it might result in death or injury. None of our recipes—and certainly not our lovely BBB—will deliver this standard of response or reliability. I repeat that our recipes and use cases do not cover these scenarios. Only custom, dedicated systems, and certainly the ones that cost more than USD $45.00 can perform this way.

- **100 percent hard**: This indicates that the system delivers real-time performance 100 percent of the time. This may sound like *Life-safety hard*, but the only thing at stake is nonhuman. The worst thing that can happen is that a product gets botched in a milling machine, or your UAV fell down and went boom. But nobody got hurt, and nobody died.

- **95 percent hard**: This denotes that our system is nearly perfect (with only 5 percent error margin). This is commonly acceptable, for example, when you're capturing data from sensors. There may be some gaps in the data stream, but nothing egregious that throws off your outcomes or analysis. You can just resample for another dataset.

 The preceding definitions are inspired by the paper *How fast is fast enough? Choosing between Xenomai and Linux for real-time applications* (`https://www.osadl.org/fileadmin/dam/rtlws/12/Brown.pdf`).

On the subject of real-time systems, embedded developers like to throw around the term "determinism". They aren't getting philosophical. In a real-time context, they're referring to event and temporally-driven outcomes that are precisely determined. That is, with an event, you have an input and a determined (locked) set of outputs, whereas in the temporal piece for a real time environment, the timing is determined as well.

So, why wouldn't you use real time all the time?

The answer is effort, money, time, and project requirements. And sometimes there are distinct trade-offs when using a real time variant in your kernel or system. For example, an event you mark for real time response may hum along perfectly; however, this can end up being a drag on overall system performance.

The following table is a latency table:

System	Typical instruction/interrupt cycle latency
Linux OS	This specifies 1 second
PREEMPT_RT	This denotes 200 milliseconds
Xenomai	This denotes 20-50 milliseconds
PRU	This specifies 5-10 nanoseconds

Source: *Charles Steinkuehler and his MachineKit (LinuxCNC) milling machine use cases: Typical latency with a Xenomai-patched kernel for the BBB is about 25 uS, with worst case around 70-80 uS.*

 For more information, refer to `http://www.embedded.com/design/operating-systems/4204740/Getting-real--time--about-embedded-GNU-Linux`

Installing a test tool

Before we can convert our BeagleBone Black to a blazing real-time wonder, we need a way to measure latency in the Linux kernel. A popular tool for this purpose is cyclictest. Cylictest measures the amount of time that passes between when a timer expires and when the thread that set the timer actually runs. It uses time snapshots, one just before a specific time interval (t1), then another one just after the timer finishes (t2). We can then compare these two snapshot values to pinpoint excessive latency sources within the kernel.

Getting ready

The usual minimal setup is all you need: a BBB powered over mini USB with Internet connectivity enabled.

How to do it...

Cyclictest isn't available as a prebuilt binary. So, we will have to compile it from source:

1. Log in as root:

    ```
    # sudo -i
    ```

2. Go get the source files for cyclictest:

    ```
    # git clone git://git.kernel.org/pub/scm/linux/kernel/git/
    clrkwllms/rt-tests.git
    ```

3. Navigate to the new directory that `git` creates:

   ```
   # cd rt-tests
   ```

4. Compile that baby:

   ```
   # make all
   ```

5. Make a copy of the binary in the `/usr/bin` directory so you can type `cyclictest` from whatever directory you find yourself:

   ```
   # cp ./cyclictest /usr/bin/
   ```

6. Bang on the tool's documentation to make sure it installed properly:

   ```
   # cyclictest --help
   ```

7. Now, let's run a simple test to see what kind of data that `cyclictest` captures:

   ```
   # cyclictest --smp -p95 -m
   ```

   The sample output should look like the following:

   ```
   # /dev/cpu_dma_latency set to 0us
   policy: fifo: loadavg: 0.00 0.01 0.05 1/221 4471


   T: 0 ( 4464) P:95 I:1000 C:  31326 Min:     39 Act:    58
   Avg:    69 Max:     785
   ```

   This output tells us that our CPU had an average latency of 69 microseconds, which is a decent value. Yet, we also had a maximum latency of 785 microseconds. Ouch! What's happening there? Let's debug (or trace) that.

Alas, we can't do a trace until we've customized the kernel to run a trace routine with cyclictest. So, that's what we'll do in the next section since we also need to modify the kernel to accommodate a new patch.

In the meantime, let's quit the program with *Ctrl + C*.

See also

- FAQ on real time with PREEMPT-RT—`https://rt.wiki.kernel.org/index.php/Frequently_Asked_Questions`
- The home of the developers of cyclictest—`https://rt.wiki.kernel.org/index.php/Cyclictest`
- More details on how to set up and configure cyclictest—`http://people.redhat.com/williams/latency-howto/rt-latency-howto.txt`
- Long, but useful video explaining the deeper functionalities and virtues of cyclictest—`https://www.youtube.com/watch?v=f_u4r6ehZKY`

Modifying the kernel using RT-PREEMPT

To dive into the real time realm, we'll begin by exploring a piece of code that you apply to the Linux kernel directly, one which is often considered the de facto standard for real-time applications, a patch called PREEMPT_RT.

First, nomenclature. In the literature, our patch can be found referred to as CONFIG_ PREEMPT_RT, PREEMPT_RT, RT-Preempt, or simply Linux RT patch. Whew! Can't anyone decide? We'll default to calling it RT-PREEMPT since that is the most common usage.

The RT-PREEMPT patch forces onto our system what is known as native real time pre-emption. This means that the patch is applied directly—or natively—onto the kernel, and allows you to *preempt* the entire kernel's events and processes in favor of targeted events or tasks. It makes sections of the Linux kernel pre-emptible that are ordinarily blocking.

For example, let's say we have two processes. We assign a higher priority to the second process than the first one. The patch enables a time tick interrupt to preempt the first (or any other process) since the second one is given the highest priority. This way, the process fires and finishes exactly on schedule.

RT-PREEMPT also happens to enjoy the least "real timeliness" in this chapter's basket of tricks. Because the patch utilizes a pre-emption process, the kernel stops whatever it is doing and focuses on delivering the real time event. This is good for your real time requirement, but not so good holistically since it often results in an overall system slow down.

This is not to say that RT-PREEMPT is a duffer. Much outstanding work has gone into this code to optimize it, and make it as useful as possible for many scenarios. In fact, RT-PREEMPT is often considered a software standard precisely because it fulfills the majority of real time requirements for devices and systems.

The last thing we will say before moving on to the recipe is that we are only going to give you the method for applying RT-PREEMPT onto Debian Jessie, and intentionally ignore Debian Wheezy. Why? Because much hair-pulling has been occurring over the years to get RT-PREEMPT onto the 3.7-3.8 kernel. And for budding Linux and BBB users, the process could make you go bald. The great news, though, is once you are committed to using the Jessie kernel (3.14.x), it's an easy few steps to get up and running.

Getting ready

All you need is the usual minimal setup: a BBB powered over the USB tether with Internet connectivity enabled.

How to do it...

1. Log in as root user:

   ```
   $ sudo -i
   #
   ```

2. Check the version of Jessie that you are running:

   ```
   # uname -r
   3.14.39-ti-r61
   ```

 Your version may vary and will follow the convention `3.14.XX-ti-rXX`.

3. Run a command that will do a custom search for available real-time Jessie kernels:

   ```
   # sudo apt-cache search linux-image | grep ti-rt
   ```

   Although the version numbers may vary somewhat, your search should have pulled down something like the following into your screen output:

   ```
   linux-image-3.14.38-ti-rt-r60 - Linux kernel, version 3.14.38-ti-
   rt-r60

   linux-image-3.14.39-ti-rt-r61 - Linux kernel, version 3.14.39-ti-
   rt-r61

   linux-image-3.14.40-ti-rt-r62 - Linux kernel, version 3.14.40-ti-
   rt-r62

   ...
   ```

4. Next, from the available list shown from step one, install the real time kernel version that matches your currently installed kernel:

   ```
   # sudo apt-get install linux-image-3.14.XX-ti-rtX
   ```

   And...you are done! RT-PREEMPT is now baked into your kernel.

There's more...

If you are feeling a bit masochistic and just have to try applying RT-PREEMPT onto your Debian Wheezy kernel, you can piece it together from the following resources:

- `https://github.com/beagleboard/kernel/tree/3.8-rt`
- `http://www.osadl.org/Realtime-Preempt-Kernel.kernel-rt.0.html`

Modifying the kernel using Xenomai

Because it's a magic spell handed down from Gandalf the Grey, this recipe will only work by saying it aloud three times fast: Xenomai, Xenomai, Xenomai! All right. It sounds like an incantation. But, unfortunately, it's only a software layer on top of a kernel.

The good news, however, is that adding Xenomai to the kernel mix can magically bring real-time(ish) oomph to our BeagleBone Black. So, what is it exactly? It is a set of patches bringing several useful ingredients:

▸ Real-time support from the hardware interrupt level to user space applications.

▸ A dual-kernel mix composed of the primary Linux kernel and the secondary Xenomai kernel.

▸ A subsystem underneath Linux that does not rely on the kernel to pre-empt designated events (like our previous method).

But why should we use it instead of PREEMPT_RT? With its focus on embedded systems, Xenomai is useful for several reasons:

▸ Lowers system overheads.

▸ **Legacy porting**: Easier to port legacy real-time systems. As a budding BBBer and embedded Linux neophyte, you may not be porting legacy systems anytime soon. But if you were, then Xenomai would be an easier way to do it since you can lash your old system together to the Linux kernel by using Xenomai as a binding interface.

▸ **Highly configurable**: Xenomai can be configured to set thread priorities/timer IRQ, for example, to high or low based on your preference (99 is the highest in Xenomai) with the result that events never get interrupted.

▸ Works better with version 3.8 of the kernel and above.

Getting ready

The usual minimal setup is all you need: a BBB powered over mini USB with Internet connectivity enabled.

How to do it...

Although there are methods (noted later in this section) for installing Xenomai from source, our recipe will illustrate a simple method for getting your kernel modified:

1. In order to run this recipe properly, you will need to start by appending your repositories. Begin by opening up your source list:

```
$ sudo nano /etc/apt/sources.list
```

In the open edit window, paste the following text into the end of the file. Choose the option based on the version of Debian you are using:

Wheezy

```
deb [arch=armhf] http://repos.rcn-ee.com/debian/ wheezy main
#deb-src [arch=armhf] http://repos.rcn-ee.com/debian/ wheezy main
```

Jessie

```
deb [arch=armhf] http://repos.rcn-ee.com/debian/ jessie main
#deb-src [arch=armhf] http://repos.rcn-ee.com/debian/ jessie main
```

2. Save and close the edit window, then update your repositories:

```
$ sudo apt-get update
```

With Debian Wheezy, you may encounter an error of the following ilk:

```
W: GPG error: http://repos.rcn-ee.com wheezy Release: The
following signatures couldn't be verified because the public key
is not available: NO_PUBKEY D284E608A4C46402
```

3. So, run this command to fix it:

```
$ sudo apt-get install rcn-ee-archive-keyring
```

4. Update your repositories again and the error should be gone:

```
$ sudo apt-get update
```

5. Check the version of your installed kernel:

```
$ uname -r
```

6. Next, we will run a search command to find the version of Xenomai that is suitable for our kernel. Make sure you run the command appropriate to Wheezy or Jessie:

Wheezy

```
$ sudo apt-cache search linux-image | grep 3.8.xx-xenomai|
```

Jessie

```
$ sudo apt-cache search linux-image | grep xenomai
```

At the time of writing this chapter, your Debian output will look like the following. Jessie will vary slightly according to your installed version:

```
linux-image-3.8.13-xenomai-r67 - Linux kernel, version
3.8.13-xenomai-r67
linux-image-3.8.13-xenomai-r69 - Linux kernel, version
3.8.13-xenomai-r69
```

```
linux-image-3.8.13-xenomai-r70 - Linux kernel, version
3.8.13-xenomai-r70

linux-image-3.8.13-xenomai-r71 - Linux kernel, version
3.8.13-xenomai-r71

linux-image-3.8.13-xenomai-r72 - Linux kernel, version
3.8.13-xenomai-r72
```

7. Now, we will install the Xenomai kernel. Replace the x with the version of the bone kernel that you have on your board (Take a look at step 6 if you do not remember):

   Wheezy

   ```
   $ sudo apt-get install linux-image-3.8.XX-xenomai-rX
   ```

   Jessie

   ```
   $ sudo apt-get install linux-image-3.14.XX-ti-xenomai-rXX
   ```

8. Install the toolset for running basic Xenomai tests:

   ```
   $ sudo apt-get install xenomai-runtime
   ```

9. Confirm that we installed Xenomai:

   ```
   $ uname -r
   ```

   Wheezy

   ```
   3.8.XX-ti-xenomai-rXX
   ```

   Jessie

   ```
   3.14.XX-ti-xenomai-rXX
   ```

10. Check the version of Xenomai (you may have a later one):

    ```
    $ cat /proc/xenomai/version
    2.6.4
    ```

    It's looking good! You now have a real time Xenomai environment set up on your BBB.

11. To round out the recipe, we want to run a couple of tests to both check that the kernel layer is installed and determine latency. First, log in as root user:

    ```
    $ sudo -i
    #
    ```

12. Run the user-mode latency test:

    ```
    # xeno latency
    ```

Your output should look something like this:

```
RTT|  00:00:01  (periodic user-mode task, 1000 us period, priority
99)

RTH|----lat min|----lat avg|----lat max|-overrun|---msw|---lat
best|--lat worst

RTD|       1.583|      1.999|       6.541|       0|       0|
1.583|       6.541

RTD|       1.583|      2.958|      35.916|       0|       0|
1.583|      35.916

RTD|       0.916|      2.083|      30.624|       0|       0|
0.916|      35.916

RTD|       0.958|      2.041|      15.749|       0|       0|
0.916|      35.916

RTD|       1.124|      2.083|      28.791|       0|       0|
0.916|      35.916

RTD|       1.583|      2.083|      31.541|       0|       0|
0.916|      35.916

RTD|      -0.084|      2.916|      35.791|       0|       0|
-0.084|      35.916

RTD|       0.916|      2.083|      28.041|       0|       0|
-0.084|      35.916
```

13. Finally, run a test to see how the board performs under load. This particular command—xeno-test—requires several options to be included in order for it to run a useful test:

```
# xeno-test -l "dohell -s 192.168.0.5 -m /mnt -l /ltp" -p 100 -g
histo
```

Let's take a closer look at the various parts of this script so we can understand what it does:

```
dohell [ -b <path> ] [ -s <server> ] [ -p <port> ] [ -m <path> ] [
-l <path> | <duration> ]
```

There's more...

If the preceding easy recipe for getting the Xenomai kernel installed does not exactly suit your specific needs, you have a couple of other ways to attack it: Use a prebuilt, downloadable software image called MachineKit or you can install it from source.

MachineKit:

Developer and engineer Charles Steinkuehler has created an essentially turnkey real-time Debian image that requires not much more than downloading and flashing a pre-built kernel to a microSD card or the eMMC. As its name suggests, MachineKit targets machine users (CNCs, 3-D printers) and comes with LinuxCNC, Xenomai and other real time ingredients already loaded. The image can save end users an enormous amount of time in installing and setting up their machines.

- Download the software at `http://elinux.org/`
  `Beagleboard:BeagleBoneBlack_Debian#BBW.2FBBB_.28All_Revs.29_`
  `Machinekit`

- Instructions are at `http://blog.machinekit.io/p/machinekit_16.html`

At his site, you will also find an extensive list of capes designed specifically for controlling 3-D printers and CNCs—`http://blog.machinekit.io/p/hardware-capes.html`

Install from source

There are several excellent tutorials for doing a custom build:

- Professor Mark Yoder's top-notch lesson—`http://elinux.org/EBC_Xenomai`

- *Installing Xenomai on Beaglebone using Debian distribution*—`https://randomlinuxhacks.wordpress.com/2015/02/22/installing-xenomai-on-beaglebone-using-debian-distribution/`

- *Xenomai on the Beaglebone Black in 14 easy steps*—`http://brunosmartins.info/xenomai-on-the-beaglebone-black-in-14-easy-steps/`

See also

To further explore the latency command and its numerous options, check out the guide written by the Xenomai.org team—`http://www.xenomai.org/documentation/xenomai-head/html/latency/`

Another useful tool for testing the Xenomai kernel is *klatency*, a test that requires either compiling Xenomai from source as outlined here, or making kernel configuration changes that are beyond the scope of this recipe. However, in the following *There's more...* section are several methods for installing Xenomai from source.

Programmable real-time units – an introduction

Now it's time for hardware magic, for serious real time, and a shift away from mere software mods on the kernel.

It's time for Programmable Real-Time Units And Industrial Controller Subsystem, also known as PRU-ICSS, or PRUs. How's that for a mouthful? More techno-acronyms are always so helpful and delicious. OK. Let's deconstruct it.

PRUs are specialized chips on the BeagleBone Black that give you real time task control over your system. These two 32-bit microcontrollers are actually separate CPUs from the main CPU and the operating system. That's right: PRUs are separate hardware. This means they are not reliant on the core kernel and are more efficient at accessing I/O pins and driving real time events.

Having onboard PRUs is one of the BBB's big differentiators in the microcomputer market. Real-time hardware control typically requires adding on daughterboards such as FPGAs (another big scary acronym) that boost your system's mojo. Using PRUs requires no overhead on the BBB's main processor, and the hardware can be managed without worrying about interrupts from the OS.

This is a huge distinction and advantage from our prior examples of RT-PREEMPT and Xenomai patches, both of them software solutions for real time challenges.

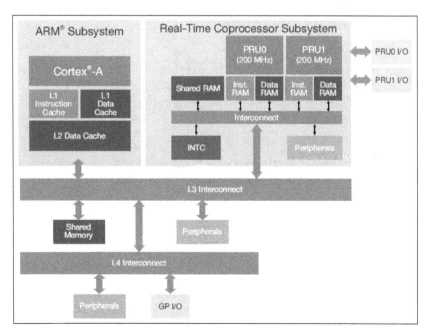

PRUs exist as parallel but distinct processors on the board

To further clarify, the PRU subsystem is not a hardware accelerator that speeds up algorithm computing. However, PRUS do:

- **Reduce latency**: Digital I/Os respond in nanoseconds, not milliseconds like we saw in our software RT scenarios.

- **Extend connectivity and add-ons**: Although the BBB is often positioned as a hobbyist or prototyping platform, PRU capability opens up use cases to professional embedded computing scenarios, unlike other players in the market such as the Raspberry Pi.

- **Manage power**: With the ability to reduce power consumption in real time, far better control over the system—and its uses—becomes possible. For the embedded dev crowd, that's a real boon.

- Deliver 100 percent hard real time.

Texas Instruments—the inventor of the BBB—doesn't actually "support" your use of the board with the PRUs. They provide examples, and even encourage use of the PRUs, but still caveat the whole thing by saying that the code is "for DIYers to use at their own risk." Maybe they're afraid someone will use the PRUs to make a flux capacitor?

On one level, it only takes two things to make the PRUs fly: you enable them, and then you run a C program (or another wrapper with Python) to make use of them.

Easy, right? However, buried within those two seemingly straightforward tasks are some challenges. Because we are manipulating an entirely second set of hardware separate from the main processor, handling PRUs on the BBB is quite a different animal from nearly all the other recipes in this book.

It doesn't help that current documentation—though extensive—is scattered, sometimes useful, but more often poorly written. The good news, though, is that `Beagleboard.org` and the open source community have made considerable progress in simplifying the tasks ahead of us.

Although you could cross-compile the following recipes on another client machine, we will develop them natively on the BBB.

Now let's prep and enable the PRUs.

Earlier methods of interacting with the PRUs were a truckload of hurt. The process required many steps, including creating and compiling a device tree just to run a sample application.

However, cooking with PRUs has been simplified considerably with the recipe below. And happily, you can use everything for both Debian Wheezy and Jessie versions.

Getting ready

The usual minimal setup is all you need: a BBB powered over mini USB with Internet connectivity enabled.

How to do it...

1. Log in as the root user:

   ```
   $ sudo -i
   ```

2. Install driver Library and PRU toolset:

   ```
   # apt-get install am335x-pru-package && ti-pru-cgt-installer
   ```

   The installation includes a number of items required to operate the PRUs from user space:

   ▶ **PASM assembler**: Being rather unique in nature, the PRUs don't speak BoneScript or JavaScript or Python or C. Instead, they communicate using Assembly, and require the PASM assembler to compile and run its code. You may have little experience with Assembly; you may have none. Don't despair: after running the command above the tool comes ready to use.

   ▶ **libprussdrv**: This consists of the driver library and library headers.

3. In a similar vein as we do with GPIO pins, to make use of the PRUs we have to enable them. And interaction with the PRUs requires the use of a Device Tree fragment. With the current Wheezy and Jessie distributions, the DT overlay comes pre-compiled and ready to use on your system, a huge time-saver over earlier versions of the software.

   Before loading a fragment, let us first look at the system's Device Tree slots where it will appear so we can see understand the before-and-after output:

   ```
   # cat /sys/devices/bone_capemgr.9/slots

   0: 54:PF---
   1: 55:PF---
   2: 56:PF---
   3: 57:PF---
   4: ff:P-O-L Bone-LT-eMMC-2G,00A0,Texas Instrument,BB-BONE-EMMC-2G
   5: ff:P-O-L Bone-Black-HDMI,00A0,Texas Instrument,BB-BONELT-HDMI
   7: ff:P-O-L Override Board Name,00A0,Override Manuf,BB-UART4
   ```

   Nothing shows, yet, in the output above that indicates PRU visibility or communication with the kernel. The next command changes that status.

4. Using the `echo` command, load the device tree fragment. This enables the PRU:

```
# echo BB-BONE-PRU-01 >/sys/devices/bone_capemgr.9/slots
```

The command should return you to the prompt without any message or error:

```
#
```

5. With the `cat` command again, check to make sure that the fragment loaded:

```
# cat /sys/devices/bone_capemgr.9/slots
0: 54:PF---
1: 55:PF---
2: 56:PF---
3: 57:PF---
4: ff:P-O-L Bone-LT-eMMC-2G,00A0,Texas Instrument,BB-BONE-EMMC-2G
5: ff:P-O-L Bone-Black-HDMI,00A0,Texas Instrument,BB-BONELT-HDMI
7: ff:P-O-L Override Board Name,00A0,Override Manuf,BB-UART4
8: ff:P-O-L Override Board Name,00A0,Override Manuf,BB-BONE-PRU-01
```

A new overlay should appear in the last slot, namely `BB-BONE-PRU-01`. Your slot number for the PRU may differ according to other drivers and daughterboards you already have loaded.

 If you ran the universal I/O device tree recipe in our prior chapter, you may get the following error: `-bash: echo: write error: File exists` If so, don't despair. All this means is that universal I/O properly loaded your PRU device tree already. So, you're good to go!

6. Run an additional command, `lsmod` , which shows all modules loaded into the kernel. We want to confirm that the `uio_pruss` driver connected properly, since it is the module that opens a gate between user space applications and the PRU, allowing them to speak to one another:

```
# lsmod
Module          Size Used by
uio_pruss        4066 0
g_multi         50407 2
libcomposite     15028 1 g_multi
8192cu         449033 0
omap_rng         4062 0
mt7601Usta            601404   0
```

7. To be safe, we should also run `dmesg` in order to peek at the kernel messages and see if any other errors occurred. Add the options pipe (|) and (`less`) so you don't get one big output dump on the screen.

    ```
    # dmesg | less
    ```

    Scroll through the output by tapping the spacebar at the bottom of the terminal screen until you start seeing output for `bone-capemgr bone_capemgr.9`. Keep advancing to the next screen until you begin to see the following:

    ```
    [ 2268.218496] bone-capemgr bone_capemgr.9: part_number 'BB-BONE-
    PRU-01', version 'N/A'

    [ 2268.218670] bone-capemgr bone_capemgr.9: slot #8: generic
    override

    [ 2268.218713] bone-capemgr bone_capemgr.9: bone: Using override
    eeprom data at slot 8

    [ 2268.218761] bone-capemgr bone_capemgr.9: slot #8: 'Override
    Board Name,00A0,Override Manuf,BB-BONE-PRU-01'

    [ 2268.219031] bone-capemgr bone_capemgr.9: slot #8: Requesting
    part number/version based 'BB-BONE-PRU-01-00A0.dtbo

    [ 2268.219079] bone-capemgr bone_capemgr.9: slot #8: Requesting
    firmware 'BB-BONE-PRU-01-00A0.dtbo' for board-name 'Override Board
    Name', version '00A0'

    [ 2268.219140] bone-capemgr bone_capemgr.9: slot #8: dtbo 'BB-
    BONE-PRU-01-00A0.dtbo' loaded; converting to live tree

    [ 2268.219821] bone-capemgr bone_capemgr.9: slot #8: #2 overlays

    [ 2268.241573] omap_hwmod: pruss: failed to hardreset

    [ 2268.248299] bone-capemgr bone_capemgr.9: slot #8: Applied #2
    overlays.
    ```

8. Before moving on to an actual test application, we should add an additional ingredient to make our preceding `echo` command stick. Although this step is optional, you should still go through the process of doing it so that when we reboot we will not lose the loaded DT fragment. So, let us set up our environment to load the fragment on boot:

    ```
    # nano /etc/default/capemgr
    ```

9. In the open edit window, you should see the following:

    ```
    # Default settings for capemgr. This file is sourced by /bin/sh
    from
    ```
    ```
    # /etc/init.d/capemgr.sh
    ```

```
# Options to pass to capemgr
CAPE=
```

Append it to the following:

```
# Default settings for capemgr. This file is sourced by /bin/sh
from
# /etc/init.d/capemgr.sh


# Options to pass to capemgr
CAPE=BB-BONE-PRU-01
```

10. Reboot your BBB, log in as root user, and check that the fragment loaded:

```
# cat /sys/devices/bone_capemgr.9/slots
0: 54:PF---
1: 55:PF---
2: 56:PF---
3: 57:PF---
4: ff:P-O-L Bone-LT-eMMC-2G,00A0,Texas Instrument,BB-BONE-EMMC-2G
5: ff:P-O-L Bone-Black-HDMI,00A0,Texas Instrument,BB-BONELT-HDMI
7: ff:P-O-L Override Board Name,00A0,Override Manuf,BB-UART4
8: ff:P-O-L Override Board Name,00A0,Override Manuf,BB-BONE-PRU-01
```

All right, now we can move on to an actual test of the PRU.

A simple PRU test with an assembler

Although there are many complex and far more sophisticated tests for the PRUs, our intention is to create a very minimal test recipe that you can observe from user space.

To do this, we will use a C program that runs directly on our BBB's ARM processor. From Linux user space, it will give a big hug to the PRU, upload an assembler code binary, run it, then pass and fetch information between the ARM and the PRU.

The basic steps are:

1. Create a program in assembly language for the dedicated hardware (the PRU)

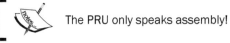

[The PRU only speaks assembly!]

2. Create a program in C for the main CPU (BBB's ARM)

> This program reaches over and handshakes the assembler code on the other PRU.

3. Run a PRU test with the combined (compiled) magic of the first two steps.

Getting ready

The usual minimal setup is all you need: a BBB powered over mini USB with Internet connectivity. You will also need to have executed the preceding recipe on prepping and enabling the PRUs.

> Be sure that you are properly connected online so that the BBB time clock accurately reflects the current time. Otherwise, you may run into errors in compiling the binary file.

How to do it...

1. We begin by logging in as root and cloning a repository on Github containing the files:

```
$ sudo -i
# git clone https://github.com/HudsonWerks/bbb-pru.git
```

> The example files in the repo are based on code from developer Douglas G. Henke (http://mythopoeic.org/bbb-pru-minimal/).

2. Browse to the sample files directory:

```
# cd /bbb-pru/simple-tests
```

> You should see three files—major-tom-pru.c, major-tom-pru.p, Makefile—and a README.

3. The Makefile will run the PRU assembler application and generate a binary from the combination of the .p file and the .c:

```
# make
```

The output should look as follows:

```
pasm -b major-tom-pru.p


PRU Assembler Version 0.86
Copyright (C) 2005-2013 by Texas Instruments Inc.


Pass 2 : 0 Error(s), 0 Warning(s)


Writing Code Image of 6 word(s)


cc -Wall -Werror  -c -o major-tom-pru.o major-tom-pru.c
cc  major-tom-pru.o -lpthread -lprussdrv -o major-tom-pru
```

4. The compiled binary created by assembler is what we now use to run a test program on the PRU (be sure you include the sudo):

```
# sudo ./major-tom-pru
```

Your output should look like the following:

```
waiting for interrupt from PRU0...
PRU test program completed. Major Tom's blast off event number 1
```

It should take approximately 3 seconds between the first line and the second. The blast off (event) number will increase each time you run it.

In the `major-tom-pru.p` file, try changing the `DELAYCOUNT` default number (currently set to 3 seconds) to another number. Then, run `make` again, and run the new `major-tom-pru` binary again. You should be able to see differences in the duration according to any new values that you set.

Hooray! You have now finished tackling one of the more arcane and advanced features of the BeagleBone Black. Now, let's do it again in the next section...

See also

At the beginning of this recipe, we also installed a command line version of Texas Instrument's **PRU Code Generation Tools** (`ti-pru-cgt-installer`). The install comes not only with the assembler package, but C code compile tools, as well. This toolset makes it possible to more easily develop PRU programs in C instead of assembly code. You can download the extensive manual at `http://software-dl.ti.com/codegen/non-esd/downloads/download.htm`.

Running an ultrasonic range sensor with the PRUs

The fast twitch eye muscle on a robot is only as good as its processor. And with many robotic projects where mobility and motion is part of the design, the speed and reliability of the twitch can be the difference between a successful foray or a smash and crash.

Which is where nanosecond response time and reliability—a PRU specialty—is crucial. To that end, let us look at a more ambitious recipe that cooks up a way to use the PRUs with one of those cheap and ubiquitous ultrasonic range sensors, the kind that are commonly found on basic robotic devices. The sensor uses sound to send a ping, similar to what a submarine does to measure the time between sending and receiving a signal for determining distance from an object.

Getting ready

The requirements are as follows:

- BBB powered over 5V power supply. If you only power the board via the USB tether, you will deliver very unreliable power to the sensor, so be sure you maintain a 5V supply.
- Internet connectivity.
- HC-SR04 sensor.
- Breadboard.
- Jumper pins.
- Resistors—1x 1k and 1x 2k.

How to do it...

Perform the following steps to run an ultrasonic range center:

1. Hook up your breadboard and BBB according to the diagram below. Make note of two crucial items:

   - **Resistors**: As you should recall, the BBB can only accept a maximum of 3.3V on its pins. Therefore, the wiring design requires two resistors, a 1k and a 2k. In tandem, they serve to step down the voltage from the sensor's **Echo** pin (5V) being sent back to the BBB.
   - Confirm that you have both resistors in place; otherwise, you may damage your beloved BBB!

    ❏ **Power**: The range sensor needs a 5V supply. Anything less will yield unpredictable results.

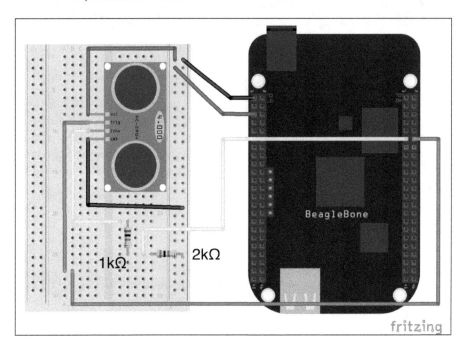

The following table displays the wiring configuration:

Pin purpose	Pin number	
GND	P9_1	Or P9_2
VCC/VDD_5V	P9_5	Or P9_6
Trigger	P8_12	
Echo	P8_11	With 1k and 2k ohm resistors

Be sure to double and triple-check your work. Otherwise, you could end up frying your board.

2. Log in as root:

```
$ sudo -i
#
```

3. Clone the files that we will be using from GitHub:

```
# git clone https://github.com/HudsonWerks/Range-Sensor-PRU.git
```

4. Browse to the new directory:

   ```
   # cd Range-Sensor-PRU
   ```

   Take a look inside the directory to get a sense of what kind of files we will be using:

   > `rangepru.dts`: Device Tree source file from which we will build a Device Tree overlay, or driver for our test application
   >
   > `rangepru.c`: Contains the application code written in C
   >
   > `rangepru.p`: Contains the assembly code which will be run against our C file to build the binary
   >
   > `Makefile`: Builds a binary that we will ultimately use to run our range sensor test with the PRUs

5. We need to add a custom device tree overlay to the mix. The overlay serves as a driver for the sensor and maps to the GPIOs we are using. In the current directory, we will modify the `.dts` file to include the target GPIOs seen in our fritzing diagram:

   ```
   # sudo nano rangepru.dts
   ```

6. In the open edit window, scroll down to the following section:

   ```
   exclusive-use =
       "<TRIGGER PIN HERE>", "<ECHO PIN HERE>",
       "GPIO44", "GPIO45";
   ```

   Change it to the following:

   ```
   exclusive-use =
       "P8_12", "P8_11",
       "GPIO44", "GPIO45";
   ```

   Save your changes and close the `nano` window (*Ctrl + X*, then type `y` for yes, and press Return (*Enter*) key).

7. Next, we need to compile a Device Tree overlay file (`dtbo`) with the DT compiler, adding all appropriate flags.

   ```
   dtc -O dtb -o rangepru-00A0.dtbo -b 0 -@ rangepru.dts
   ```

    See *Chapter 4, Exploring GNU/Linux Recipes Using Bash, Autotools, Debugger, and systemd*, for a refresher on Device Tree, the compiler and its options.

8. Now we need to copy the compiled output file—rangepru-00A0.dtbo—to the directory where the overlays are referenced:

   ```
   # cp rangepru-00A0.dtbo /lib/firmware
   ```

9. Although we put the overlay in its proper directory, we have to load it, just like a driver has to load in order to recognize a new piece of attached hardware. So, run the following:

```
# echo rangepru > /sys/devices/bone_capemgr.*/slots
```

10. Take a look at the slots and see that the overlay is ready for action:

```
# cat /sys/devices/bone_capemgr.9/slots
```

Your output should look similar to this:

```
0: 54:PF---
1: 55:PF---
2: 56:PF---
3: 57:PF---
4: ff:P-O-L Bone-LT-eMMC-2G,00A0,Texas Instrument,BB-BONE-EMMC-2G
5: ff:P-O-L Bone-Black-HDMI,00A0,Texas Instrument,BB-BONELT-HDMI
7: ff:P-O-L Override Board Name,00A0,Override Manuf,rangepru
```

11. Confirm the overlay took hold:

```
# dmesg
```

Your output should look similar to this:

```
[ 1462.225670] bone-capemgr bone_capemgr.9: part_number
'rangepru', version 'N/A'

[ 1462.225742] bone-capemgr bone_capemgr.9: slot #7: generic
override

[ 1462.225758] bone-capemgr bone_capemgr.9: bone: Using override
eeprom data at slot 7

[ 1462.225773] bone-capemgr bone_capemgr.9: slot #7: 'Override
Board Name,00A0,Override Manuf,rangepru'

[ 1462.225856] bone-capemgr bone_capemgr.9: slot #7: Requesting
part number/version based 'rangepru-00A0.dtbo

[ 1462.225870] bone-capemgr bone_capemgr.9: slot #7: Requesting
firmware 'rangepru-00A0.dtbo' for board-name 'Override Board
Name', version '00A0'

[ 1462.230469] bone-capemgr bone_capemgr.9: slot #7: dtbo
'rangepru-00A0.dtbo' loaded; converting to live tree
```

12. We should also check that the PRU module is loaded as expected:

```
# lsmod
```

Your output should look similar to this. You should see the `uio-prussdrv` driver:

Module	Size	Used by
uio_pruss	4058	0
g_multi	50519	2
libcomposite	15032	1 g_multi
8192cu	449177	0
cpufreq_userspace	2013	0
evdev	7244	2
omap_rng	4054	0

Whew! That was the first part of the recipe completed. Okay, let us now move right along to creating the actual file we will use to capture data from the ultrasonic range sensor.

13. Using the `Makefile` script, we will run two actions: one will create an Assembly code binary to interact with the PRUs from the file `rangepru.p`; the other will generate a compiled C program from the file `rangepru.c` that serves as both an interface to the assembly binary while taking the sensor data and displaying it in a human-readable fashion.

```
# make
```

 Using `sudo nano make`, it might be useful to look under the hood for a moment to see what the script is doing.

14. The magical `make` command creates a new executable file—rangepru—in our directory. We will now run it to monitor and output data being captured by our ultrasonic range sensor:

```
# ./rangepru
```

If all is well in BBB-land, you should be getting screen output that looks akin to this. Carefully move the sensor around to watch the distance change (note, your numbers will vary according to the distance your sensor is from an object:

```
>> Initializing PRU
>> Executing range-sensor code
  1: Distance = 70.21 cm
  2: Distance = 71.95 cm
```

```
 3: Distance = 71.95 cm

 4: Distance = 7.68 cm

 5: Distance = 64.27 cm

 6: Distance = 4.09 cm

 7: Distance = 5.20 cm

 8: Distance = 53.25 cm

 9: Distance = 6.62 cm

10: Distance = 2.28 cm

11: Distance = 2.34 cm

12: Distance = 10.13 cm

>> PRU Disabled.
```

Outstanding! You have now successfully hooked up a sensor that is ubiquitous in robot building, and taught it how to dance with your BBB and its fancy PRUs.

Using Python with the PRUs

Contrary to popular geek belief, ancient Egyptians did not write on PyPRUSS. But if they'd known Python, they might have.

Actually, the oldest thing about PyPRUSS— a Python library for the PRUs—is that it was primarily focused on the earlier Angstrom firmware for the BBB, a distribution now looking increasingly mummified. Which is not to say that PyPRUSS does not still remain a great userland touchstone for Pythonistas and PRU-ophiles.

In fact, even though there is no pre-compiled binary in the Debian repositories for PyPRUSS, it takes all of 90 seconds to compile and install from source, and begin running Python on the PRUs quickly.

Getting ready

The usual minimal setup is all you need: a BBB powered over mini USB with Internet connectivity. You will also need to have done the first recipe in this section on prepping and enabling the PRUs.

How to do it...

1. Log in as root:

   ```
   $ sudo -i
   ```

2. Grab the source files:

   ```
   # git clone https://github.com/HudsonWerks/pypruss.git
   ```

3. Navigate to the directory we just created:

   ```
   # cd pypruss
   ```

4. Run the script for installing the PyPRUSS library:

   ```
   # python setup.py install
   ```

5. Make sure your library is mapped properly:

   ```
   # export LD_LIBRARY_PATH=/usr/local/lib
   ```

6. Browse the example directory:

   ```
   # cd examples
   ```

7. Take a look at what is available in that directory:

   ```
   # ls
   ```

8. Now, we will run some examples. We begin with everyone's favorite blinky thing:

   ```
   # cd blinkled
   ```

9. Next, compile an assembly binary file:

   ```
   # make
   ```

10. Run the Python file:

    ```
    # python blinkled.py
    ```

    Oops! You may have gotten an error. If you didn't, just skip the next step. But if you did, then it probably looked like this:

    ```
    ERROR: could not insert 'uio_pruss': Numerical result out of range
    modprobe failed
    : No such file or directory
    Traceback (most recent call last):
      File "blinkled.py", line 7, in <module>
        pypruss.modprobe() # This only has to be called once pr boot
    SystemError: error return without exception set
    ```

    Errors always shows us something important: that `uio_pruss` has to be loaded before the PRUs can be pinged, just like we saw in our previous recipe.

11. Thus, we will load that fragment:

    ```
    # echo BB-BONE-PRU-01 >/sys/devices/bone_capemgr.9/slots
    ```

12. Now, try running the python script again:

```
# python blinkled.py
```

Assuming all goes well now, you should then see three of the user LEDs blink 10 times in rapid, seizure-inducing succession.

See also

There are various resources for learning more about PRUs. There is quite a bit to learn about how to use the PRUs on the BBB, most of it well beyond the scope of this book. However, we have compiled a list of useful background information, tutorials, and projects to further your exploration of these unique real time subsystems.

- PRU wiki with the most up-to-date information—`http://elinux.org/Ti_AM33XX_PRUSSv2`

- Beagleboard's official overview of PRUs. More detail than you'll likely need, but good context, and a helpful table of commands for PASM—`https://github.com/beagleboard/am335x_pru_package/blob/master/Documentation/01-AM335x_PRU_ICSS_Overview.pdf`

- Texas Instruments' official overview of PRUs—`http://processors.wiki.ti.com/index.php/Programmable_Realtime_Unit_Software_Development`

- PRU C project—from device tree to program execution, an extensive and useful thread on PRU usage—`https://groups.google.com/forum/#!category-topic/beagleboard/pru/VW361VUkCcI`

- An assortment of PRU-centric projects—`http://processors.wiki.ti.com/index.php/PRU_Projects`

- Another take on setting up and running PRUs—`http://www.embeddedrelated.com/showarticle/586.php`

- An early, some consider seminal post on using PRUs with the BB White, not the Black—`http://boxysean.com/blog/2012/08/12/first-steps-with-the-beaglebone-pru/`

- Debuggers and editors:
  - VisualPRU, a sexy, browser-based editor and debugger for the PRUs—`https://github.com/mmcdan/visualpru`
  - PRUdebug, a functional CLI-centric app for debugging your PRU code—`http://sourceforge.net/projects/prudebug/`

▶ **BeagleRT**: Most projects on the subject of using RT on the BBB focus on driving motors for machine tools or other industrial applications. BeagleRT, however, is a fascinating project that uses Xenomai and PRUs on the BBB in the service of creating hackable **Digital Musical Instruments** (**DMIs**). This novel use case for an ultra-low-latency sensor/audio platform requires a high level of machine responsiveness to fulfill a performer's expectations and performance techniques, thus the need for predictable timing from the board:

   ❑ Project overview—`http://www.eecs.qmul.ac.uk/~andrewm/hackable.html`

   ❑ Open source code—`https://code.soundsoftware.ac.uk/projects/beaglert`

▶ **PRU speak**: An implementation of the BotSpeak robotics language for the PRU. This project enables dynamic control of the BeagleBone Black's PRU from the Linux user space on ARM:

   ❑ `http://botspeak.org/supported-platforms/beaglebone/`

   ❑ `https://github.com/deepakkarki/pruspeak`

▶ **PRUCAPE**: Texas Instruments designed a low-cost cape to facilitate usage of the PRUs

   ❑ Good verbiage on its purpose and usage—`http://linuxgizmos.com/beaglebone-cape-eases-access-to-the-sitara-socs-pru/`

   ❑ You can purchase it here—`http://www.ti.com/tool/PRUCAPE#buy`

7
Applied Recipes – Sound, Picture, and Video

In this chapter, we will cover the following recipes:

- ▶ Wiring up a mini amp and speakers
- ▶ Creating a high-quality audio platform with Volumio
- ▶ Using videos and displays in projects
- ▶ Testing a mini LCD cape
- ▶ Making a video chat client prototype using Linphone

Introduction

We need to get a little dirtier. So far, we played it safe with physical computing recipes. But how far can you go by just plugging in some wires into a breadboard? To make the BBB a really useful tool, we have to heat up the iron—the soldering iron—and make some nice, shiny joints. Many great add-ons, such as PCBs, sensors, headers, and peripheral devices arrive at your doorstep unsoldered, full of fiddly bits, or just downright unsuitable out of the box. So, soldering is a must on the microcomputing landscape.

However, this is only one part of the picture for this chapter on picture, sound, and video. We will also explore different advanced methods to add a range of capes, PCB add-ons, and some USB devices for more complex recipes using digital sound, pictures, and video and look at the following:

- Wiring up a mini sound amplifier and speakers
- Creating a high-quality audio platform with Volumio
- Using videos and displays in projects that include these devices:
  - OLED PCB
  - Mini LCD cape
- Making a video chat client

Here's the truth about BeagleBone Black: when it comes to audio and video, the BBB is not for the faint-hearted. Other than a single USB port (which is obligatory for all kinds of reasons beyond just audio or video add-ons), the BBB is a tough system to learn for hardware and Linux newcomers. There is no onboard camera port; you have to piggyback on USB or buy a dedicated cape. There is no onboard audio I/O pin, USB device, or dedicated cape required either. So, if you are looking for a quick and easy, media-rich development box, then dare I say it: Raspberry Pi might be a better choice.

As a result of this difference, the BBB is often criticized for not being better at Rich Media. However, the difference is intentional; RPi's engineers intended to make an educational, hobbyist board with a desktop-like experience to encompass Rich Media use cases. On the other hand, the BBB's engineers designed their platform to create advanced prototypes for embedded applications where high-end graphics and sound are not commonly required.

With these caveats, BeagleBone Black still remains more than up to the challenge of delivering sound and picture in many, very useful scenarios, including streaming music and videos.

Bringing audio onto BeagleBone Black

The absence of onboard audio output or input is a real pain when it comes to the BBB. Yet, there are several methods of attacking this challenge. Firstly, you can go cheap and easy with a simple USB sound dongle; two varieties are shown in the following picture attached to a powered USB port:

Secondly, you can add a dedicated audio cape (as we did in *Chapter 5, Basic Programming Recipes with the Linux Kernel*). Thirdly, you can do it the hard(ish) way using a dedicated PCB and by piggybacking on the GPIO pins. Why bother with the latter? This is because using USB is often inadequate for certain applications. When you require faster, more RT-style performance, running audio packets across USB can be disappointing. We also want to stretch our limbs and add some complexity so that you have more types of technologies to draw upon in future projects and prototypes.

Wiring up a mini amp and speakers

To get some rocking audio going, we thought about wiring a BeagleBone Black up to a personal favorite device of ours: a c. 1960 Gruntal amplifier and radio:

We then thought better of it and decided to go with something a wee bit smaller for our recipe: the TPA2016 PCB, which contains a Texas Instruments chipset and is packaged as a final product by Adafruit:

It doesn't pack quite the volume as an ancient tube-based amp, but this surface-mount PCB amp is a heck of a lot handier and easier to use than our antique beauty. Also, it delivers nearly 3W of power for our tunes, plenty of volume for many situations. Additionally, its I2C interface allows us to control audio gain via software instead of using jumpers, switches, or other physical hardware.

In this recipe, you will learn how to set up and test the device on a breadboard with speakers and BeagleBone Black. Afterwards, in a later recipe, we'll use it as part of our kit to set up a listening library on the BBB.

I2C background and usage

I2C (pronounced "eye-squared-C" or "eye-two-see") is a hardware bus intended for motherboards and daughterboards to communicate easily. It is frequently leveraged in embedded applications and typically used in accelerometers, magnetometers, and other sensors, as well as other add-ons requiring low voltage. In our case, we will use it to run a very small audio amplifier.

Other than its power leads, the bus only uses two wires to communicate: SCL and SDA. The first one is the clock line, SCL, which is used to sync any data passing over the bus. The second line, SDA, carries the actual data. I2C also utilizes a simple master/slave relationship between devices, with the bus allowing the roles to be interchangeable. I2C is also good at noise filtering, which is a relevant feature for our recipe.

Working with I2C pins on the BBB is pretty straightforward. There are three I2C buses implemented on the BBB, but only one of these is easy to use:

- **I2C0**: This is used for some onboard components, such as HDMI, EEPROM, and power management. If we disable it, it will interfere with these components, so it is typically not used unless needed.

- **I2C1**: This is available for use but requires enabling.

- **I2C2**: This is usable out of the box (Expansion port **P9**; refer to table 11 in the SRM). These are the pins that we will use.

I2S bus

I2C should not be confused with **Integrated Interchip Sound** (**I2S**), another serial bus available on the BBB. Unlike I2C, which is bidirectional, I2S only handles data in one direction. Coincidentally, I2S is typically used as an interface to communicate PCM audio data between devices, commonly with a **Digital to Analog Converter** (**DAC**) audio device, though we will not use it in our audio recipes. There are several helpful tutorials on making a DAC, interface with I2S and connecting it to the BBB, such as the one at `http://bit.ly/1HQMc1N`.

Getting ready

Here are the materials we need:

- **PCB amp kit**: This can be TPA2016 or similar. Adafruit has several choices, which you can access at `https://www.adafruit.com/search?q=amplifier`.

- **Speakers**: You can use any set of speakers that take mono or stereo mini connector cables.

- **Audio input jack**: Either one of the following two methods will work:

    - **3.5mm Stereo Headphone Jack (breadboard-ready)**: This is very cheap and available at Sparkfun (`https://www.sparkfun.com/products/8032`) or Adafruit (`https://www.adafruit.com/product/1699`) for around USD $1.00.

    - **3.5mm stereo plug to "pigtail" cable**: This is basically a simple stereo mini cable using a standard plug on one end and a left and right speaker with wire-stripped "tinned" leads on the other. The leads break out, so you can plug them into a breadboard easily. It is cheap and available at Adafruit (`https://www.adafruit.com/product/1700`) for USD $1.95.

- **Mp3 or portable music player**: This can be an iPod or smartphone with 3.5mm audio jack output and containing sample music or audio files.

- **2-plug (male) audio cable**: A standard 3.5mm cable that you likely already have around the house.

- **Soldering iron**

- **Lead-free solder**

- **Mini Philips head screwdriver**

- **Jumper wires**

- **Breadboard**

How to do it...

To prep the PCB amp, we followed some of the guidance provided by Adafruit's tutorial to work with their board (`https://learn.adafruit.com/adafruit-tpa2016-2-8w-agc-stereo-audio-amplifier`). Perform the following steps:

1. Your tasks begin with soldering an 8-pin header strip to the 8-holed side of the PCB amp and then soldering the speaker terminal blocks into the marked slots along the opposite side of the board. This is shown for you in the following image:

This recipe is not a general how-to on soldering. If you have never soldered a wire or joint on a PCB, consult the following excellent tutorials:

How to Solder—Through-hole Soldering: `https://learn.sparkfun.com/tutorials/how-to-solder---through-hole-soldering/`

NYU's ITP soldering lesson: `https://itp.nyu.edu/physcomp/Labs/Soldering`

Adafruit's excellent guide to soldering: `https://learn.adafruit.com/adafruit-guide-excellent-soldering`

Instructable secrets of good soldering: `http://www.instructables.com/id/How-to-solder-the-secrets-of-good-soldering/`

After this, you can begin by inserting the long pins of a header strip with 8 pins into the breadboard, short pins sticking up, as shown in the following picture:

As it is important to get your PCB amp mounted on an even plane, the easiest way to do this is by using the leftover pins to support the board on the opposite edge. To clarify, these pins will not be soldered; they are only there for temporary support.

You then need to solder up the headers on the PCB amp, as you can see on the left-hand side in this picture. We used lead-free solder; so, when finished, the joints will look dull instead of the typically shiny cast from a well-poured leaded joint.

2. Solder the speaker terminal blocks to the PCB amp. Verify that your connections are solid. You may notice that the blocks don't sit neatly parallel to one another. This appears to be due to a slight design imperfection in the PCB amp, but there's nothing to worry about functionally.

3. Snip off the white connector that comes already attached to the ends of the speaker wires:

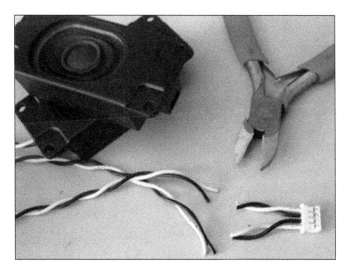

Following this, with a wire stripper, cut away the wire ends, as you can see in the following image:

4. Next, attach the finished PCB amp to a breadboard. Then, insert the speaker wires into the speaker terminal blocks. The black wires go into the (-) ground connectors, and the white wires into the (+) power connectors. Use a small Philips head screwdriver to first release tension in the block. Finish by tightening it after the wires are inserted. The end result is shown in this image:

5. Since we plan to use sound in this recipe—which is what an audio amplifier is good for—we need to also add some means for sound input. You can use either the breadboard-ready headphone jack, which you will see in the next picture, or the pigtail cable, as described at the beginning of this recipe.

6. Hook up your audio player to the other end of the audio cable. In our case, we used an old iPod that we had in a drawer. If you refer closely to the following image, it shows how all the parts should fit together before you have hooked it up to your BBB:

7. Choose an audio track on your player and press **Play**. Now that we know we have solid audio output with all hardware soldered, snipped, breadboarded, and wired properly, we will run an audio test using Python.

8. Now, we want to wire the amp up to our BeagleBone Black, following the Fritzing diagram. Although it looks like a thicket of mini jumper wires, the scheme is really simple. In fact, you will notice that on the BBB's GPIO pins, there are only two pins in use other than power and ground.

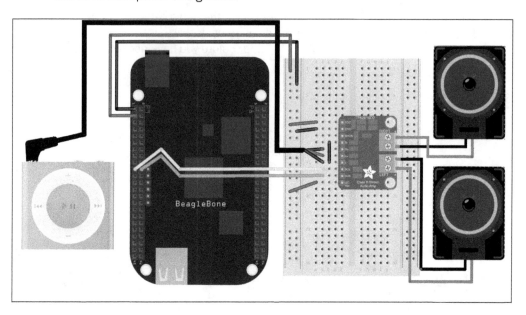

In case there is any uncertainty from the diagram, here is a table clarifying how to wire it up:

FUNCTION	BeagleBone Black	TPA2016 amplifier	Breadboard component
Power	P9_5 (5V) or P9_3 (3.3V)—5V for full capacity of the amp	VDD	
Ground	P9_1	GND	
I2C	P9_19 (SCL)	SCL	
I2C	P9_20 (SDA)	SDA	
Audio input—left speaker		L+	L+ on 3.5mm headphone jack
Audio input—right speaker		R+	R+ on 3.5mm headphone jack
Audio ground		L- to R-	
Audio ground		R-	R- on 3.5mm headphone jack

9. Let's get programming! To start, open up the BoneScript IDE and create a new `.py` file called `audio-amp-test1.py`.

10. Download the Python script from our Github repo with following command:

    ```
    $ git clone https://github.com/HudsonWerks/audio-amplifier.git
    ```

11. Browser to the audio-amplifier directory created and open up the python script in a `nano` window:

    ```
    $ $ cd audio-amplifier
    $ sudo nano audio-amp-test1.py
    ```

12. Now, copy and paste the code into the Cloud9 IDE window.

13. Restart a music track on your media player that, in our case, is an iPod. You should be able to hear the track playing through the speakers.

14. Now, click on the **Run** button on the Cloud9 IDE to test the script. Audio levels should shift up and down as you input the (+) or (-) sign at the command prompt.

Success (we hope)! Give yourself a high-five for getting dirtier with your board and adding some PCB add-ons to the mix.

Creating a high-quality audio platform with Volumio

Volumio is a wonderful open source alternative to the iTunes straightjacket. For audiophile geeks who happen to be microcomputer or electronic geeks (you know who you are!) and RPi enthusiasts in particular, Volumio is well-known for its fastidiousness at serving up high-quality audio, be it web-based radio or high-resolution audio files. The system has now been ported to the BBB from its earlier incarnation as RaspyFi.

Essentially, Volumio leverages a Linux music server called **Music Player Daemon** (**MPD**). MPD provides a client environment with a web-centric GUI (sans plugins) and a robust networking architecture to serve your audio files.

One of the many appealing aspects of Volumio Is that it is (nearly) file-agnostic, so you can play virtually any audio file type within the environment. For now, this includes FLAC, WAV, MP3, AAC, ALAC, M4A, and **playlist** (**PLS**) files.

Each new version of Volumio seems to leap forward in stability and ease of use. However, it does come with caveats as no open source tool is ever "finished." Volumio, in some respects, typifies the pleasures and perils of open source tools and bending them to your will on microcomputers. There's no out of the box perfection. Some of the recipes in this chapter use a number of "prepackaged" toolsets to get you where you want to be faster, and Volumio is still, technically, a beta release.

For example, other than a perfunctory setting up and installing procedure, developers do not have a nice handy set of obvious instructions. Instead, you have to spend a fair amount of time perusing their forum (`volumio.org/forum/`) to find answers to common questions.

Examples include: how do I SSH into Volumio? What's the password for remote login? How do I add a new internet radio station? Why is my external hard drive, which is chock-full with music files, not recognized by Volumio? How do I gracefully shut down my BBB if Volumio crashes? These are burning questions, indeed. Thankfully, you bought this book, so the answers to these questions are right here.

Getting ready

To get Volumio up and running, you need the following:

- **A USB-powered hub**: As we need several USB devices to get the system operating reliably, you will need to add a powered hub to your configuration.

- **A keyboard**: Plug one into the USB hub. We will use it for terminal access in case we lose or cannot get a remote SSH session and want to do a graceful shutdown of the system. However, we only need it temporarily and can disconnect it later.

- **An LCD Monitor**: You need one of these plugged into the HDMI port. As with the keyboard, the monitor is only necessary for first boot and system tweaking.

- **Connectivity**: We will first use an Ethernet cable plugged into the BBB for setup. After we've got a confirmed ping and stable setup, we will remove the cable and use a USB Wi-Fi dongle in our powered hub to establish a wireless environment.

- **Audio out**: For output audio in this recipe, you can use three different methods—easy, intermediate, or advanced, which are as follows:
  - **Easy method—the USB audio dongle**: There are numerous flavors of these devices in the wild. Unless you feel compelled to use an expensive one, they can be purchased cheaply; the kind pictured at the beginning of this chapter came for roughly USD $10.00. You should use a powered hub to supply power to the dongle instead of through the BBB's USB port.

❏ **Intermediate method—the RevB audio cape**: Although slightly more complex, using the audio cape that we already used in *Chapter 4, Exploring GNU/Linux Recipes Using Bash, Autotools, Debugger, and systemd,* is a more robust and elegant setup than using the USB audio dongle. Refer to the same chapter for cape setup and audio testing.

❏ **Advanced method—the PCB audio amplifier (daughterboard)**: If you were with us in the previous section, we just did a recipe with this, and now, we can use it for real. Refer to the recipe mentioned before to set up this configuration, including the images and the Fritzing diagram.

For audiophiles, one of the attractive features of Volumio is that it supports the use of DAC boxes. Although sexy, useful, and powerful, DAC boxes can be quite expensive. We don't have one, so we're not including the hookup methodology in this recipe. At Volumio's support forum (`http://volumio.org/forum/`), you will find ample discussion around using DAC boxes.

- ▸ **Speakers**: Connect the speakers that you used in the prior recipe or use the audio out jack on a USB audio dongle.
- ▸ **Speaker cable**: You can use mono or stereo jacks
- ▸ **Media storage**: Audio files can be served from a variety of storage devices, such as USB, NAS, and so on. Since we had it on hand, we used a powered USB hard drive.

How to do it...

Now that you're ready, let's begin:

1. Start by downloading the Volumio BeagleBone Black disk image on your client machine (not your BBB). The current version is available at `http://volumio.org/get-started/`.

   Following the download, extract the downloaded archive. You should end up with a `.img` file on your local box.

2. Insert an SD card reader with a minimum 4 GB microSD card installed. As Volumio claims to require a very minimal install (piggybacking on Debian Wheezy), you may be able to get away with a smaller amount of storage than 4 GB.

3. Flash the `.img` file to your SD card. As we are using a Mac box, we will use our trusty tool, *PiFiller*, which we used and explained in prior chapters. On a Windows box, you can use *Win32DiskImager*.

4. Confirm that you have adequate storage remaining on your SD card. To do this, run the check from a terminal window on your client machine with the following command:

   ```
   $ df -ah
   ```

   Your output should show somewhere around 22 percent capacity used.

5. From the preceding *Getting ready* section, you should have all the required hardware connected. Remove the SD card from your client machine, insert it in the BBB, and boot.

   I have seen some flaky performances on first boot, so you may need to reboot again to get the login screen to appear. If you have used Volumio on Raspberry Pi, you will find booting up on the BBB considerably faster.

6. You now need to set up terminal access, first directly on the BBB and then remotely.

   Technically, neither is a requirement to run Volumio as there's a lovely web-based GUI to control the tool; we'll get to that next. However, you will inevitably need to troubleshoot various issues, and terminal access is really the best way to do so. So, first type the following command on the BBB:

   ```
   # user: root

   pw: Volumio
   ```

   You should now see the following screen output; date and version may vary, of course:

   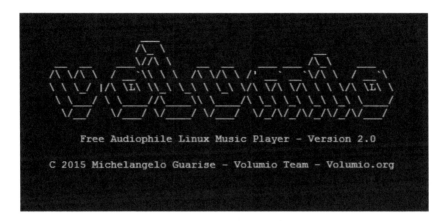

7. Now, repeat the previous step on your client desktop box for SSH access with the same user (`root`) and password (`volumio`) credentials:

   ```
   $ ssh volumio@xxx.xxx.xx.xxx
   ```

   If you have any problems logging in and you are on your own local LAN, you can also do the following:

   ```
   $ ssh root@volumio.local
   ```

8. Check that you have a solid internet connection (from either your SSH remote session or directly on the BBB) by typing in:

   ```
   # ping www.google.com
   ```

   Your screen output should show stable ping responses. If it does not, you may need to reboot and repeat steps 7 through 10.

   To quit the `ping` command, remember to press *Ctrl + C* on your keyboard.

9. We are not quite ready to play your fabulous music library, but we can do a test to get a quick feel-good hit. So, open up a browser on your desktop client and type in the address, `http://volumio.local`.

   Voila! A fancy GUI with all kinds of knobs, buttons, and sliders appears!

 One of the appealing things about Volumio is that its main controller is a web-based open source UI and not a bloated proprietary piece of software. This means that with a touch of HTML and a dash of jQuery, you can mod your own controller UI.

10. In the GUI, click on **Browse | WEBRADIO**. You will see a list of streaming radio stations that came preloaded with the install. Let's choose one that has a reliably consistent streaming URL: "the Beeb", which is also known as *BBC World Radio*.

    After clicking twice on the link, the mellifluous sounds of a British newscaster will pour from your speakers.

 You may find that many of the preloaded WEBRADIO stations have outdated or nonfunctioning links, leading you to believe that your installation is not working properly. However, this is not the case; you simply need to fix or update the links manually.

11. Under the **Playback** tab, you will see a volume control akin to an iPod's "click wheel." Fiddle with it a bit, and you will notice that the volume level of the output doesn't change. Frustrating, right? This means that adjusting sound levels requires another tweak.

12. If you connected your system to DAC, ignore this step as you will have hardware controls to adjust the volume. Otherwise, go to **MENU | SETTINGS**, click on the dropdown for **Volume Control**, and select **Software**.

13. Following this, reboot using a terminal command or via the GUI underneath the **MENU | SYSTEM** tab.

14. Once rebooted, let's push the recipe a bit further by grabbing a couple of files remotely and loading them into Volumio. We will use the familiar `wget` command:

```
# wget http://hudsonwerks.com/beaglebone-black-recipes/downloads/
volumio-sample-media.tar.gz
```

15. Untar the archived files with the following command:

```
# tar -zxvf volumio-sample-media.tar.gz
```

16. Use this command line to put the files in the correct Volumio directory:

    ```
    # mv Space-Oddity-Hadfield-CLIP.m4a /var/lib/mpd/music/USB
    ```

    Then, run the following:

    ```
    # mv wbgo_jazzFM_NJ.pls /var/lib/mpd/music/WEBRADIO/
    ```

17. The media library now needs to be updated to reflect the new additions. So, via the Volumio web GUI on your desktop client, go to `http://volumio.local`.

18. Then, navigate to **MENU | LIBRARY** and click on the **UPDATE LIBRARY** button. At this point, if you have the media from this simple recipe, the update will take only a few seconds.

19. It's time to test our files; we will begin by using the `m4a` file. Again, on the web GUI, go to the **Browse | USB** tab. Then, click on **Space-Oddity-Hadfield-CLIP** twice.

    You should hear a brief sample of a remix of David Bowie's song, "Major Tom", from the album, *Space Oddity*. In this case, it will be sung by US astronaut Chris Hadfield on board the International Space Station. It is a remake of a classic, but the astronaut does a great job of it.

 We would have preferred using the whole track, but we limited the length of the clip to conform to the Fair Use legal restrictions. For a longer version of the song, the video is available online at `https://youtu.be/KaOC9danxNo`.

20. Now, let's test our newly downloaded web radio station playlist. On the web interface, go to **Browse | WEBRADIO**. Then, click on **wbgo_jazzFM_NJ**.

21. With a nearly finished setup, we can cut the Ethernet cord and run Volumio via Wi-Fi. Go to **Menu | Network** and input your network's name and password in the appropriate fields. Then, click on **Save Changes**, and Volumio will reset the web interface.

22. Next, remove the Ethernet cable. If you do not already have it open, type in the Volumio server address, `http://volumio.local`, again on your desktop client browser.

    You should be able to control Volumio fluidly now without the Ethernet connection.

23. Assuming you have a smartphone, pull it out and open up a browser to the same address that you just entered on your desktop: `volumio.local`.

    Voila! You are now freed from the desktop and have remote control of your media library from any smartphone:

    Although the Volumio interface can be a bit crowded on small smartphone screens, you should see a tighter, highly usable design on tablet clients.

24. Next, we need to check the version of Volumio. Doing this will output the compatible file types that the software can play:

    ```
    # mpd --version
    ```

The screen output should yield not only the usual copyright boilerplate, but an extensive list of the audio file types that are playable with Volumio. Check that your music library's file types are in the list, particularly in the very lengthy `[ffmpeg]` section.

25. Next, you need to update the MPD database so that it catalogues all files on your attached storage drive. You can use the Volumio GUI for this; navigate to **MENU | Library | Update MDB database**. You can also do the same thing with the following command line:

```
# sudo service mpd restart
```

Depending on the size of your library and regardless of the method you use, the database update may take a while. So, get a cold drink, a sandwich, or go for a jog—a long one.

If all went as planned, your music library should now be catalogued. Go to **Library**, select the *your USB* music directory, and verify that everything's visible.

26. We also have a potential bug fix. Depending on your version of Volumio, this is where you may encounter some quirks. Because of a lingering bug in the in the last few versions of the MPD server environment (which is not Volumio's fault), many file types compatible with FFMPEG are disabled by default.

This means that the GUI-based *update MDB database* function that we just executed may capture some of the metadata for a music file, including its name, but not the actual media data itself. So, let's fix this in the command line as follows:

```
# nano /etc/mpd.conf
```

Scroll down to the `FFMEG = disable` line and change `disable` to `enable`. Following this, save the `mpd.conf` file and close it.

27. Now, let's test our media files via the GUI; go to **Browse | USB**, select your *album* or *music track*, and choose a favorite music file. (Note that it doesn't have to be a David Bowie track).

With all this done, we are left with one thing to do: turn it up to 11!

There's more...

Here is some supplementary information about playlists, which you can use to extend this recipe. As in most music library environments, Volumio uses playlists (`.pls` files) as a means to categorize or organize your media into custom play sequences. Here are two basic methods of adding playlists to Volumio:

▶ **The drag and drop method**: With any `.pls` files you may have, simply drag and drop the file into your WEBRADIO folder.

▶ **Manual method**: You may have already found that some of the default web radio stations listed don't work. There is a good chance that the problem is not your in hardware; it's more likely that the station's URL has changed, which is one of the vagaries of web radio. So, you will need to tweak the address in the playlist file. Here's what we do:

1. Open up a `.pls` file in a text editor. You can do this on your BBB or locally on your media library drive. The drive is connected to the server as a shared drive, so you should see it appear on your client box desktop. Here is what you should see when you open the file:

```
[playlist]
File1=http://xxx.yyy.zzz:port
Title1=station name
Length1=-1
Numberofentries=1
Version=2
```

2. We will typically modify two items in this file. First, we will use the following command to modify the web radio address:

```
File1=http://xxx.yyy.zzz:port
```

In this line, insert the URL of the stream you are adding; the port setting is optional. Here's an example:

```
File1=http:/ http://xstream1.somafm.com:8000
```

Then, we want the name of the station to appear in the Volumio player while the audio is streaming:

```
Title1=station name
```

For example, if we wanted to call our station Space Station Soma, we would run the following line:

```
Title1=Space Station Soma
```

See also

The following are some key links to gain more information about Volumio, which also illustrate many ways to troubleshoot issues:

- ▸ The very active Volumio support forum is available at `http://volumio.org/forum/`
- ▸ M4A file support is available at `http://volumio.org/forum/m4a-support-t14.html`
- ▸ To fix Wi-Fi drop off / freezing issues, navigate to `http://volumio.org/forum/volumio-for-feeback-thread-t781-70.html`

Using videos and displays in projects

It's one thing to just plug an HDMI monitor into the mini HDMI port on your BBB and get a picture. In many cases, this is may be all you care about for a project. However, for bona fide embedded or mobile scenarios where you need a display, using the HDMI option can be overkill; your needs are low power, small form factor, and just enough display to convey basic information.

In this section, we will take a look at two other options for display: a mini OLED display available as a breadboard-able PCB and a custom BBB cape designed with a very small LCD panel.

Hooking up a mini OLED

In this recipe, we will take a look at a very small 1.3 inch OLED display with a resolution of 128 x 64 pixels. It has a monochrome screen, which means that we will not be watching Lawrence of Arabia on this device. Instead, we will explore some methods for basic control and input and take a preliminary peek at typical design choices for embedded devices.

The nice thing about experimenting with a device like this is that we can make use of another set of pins available on BeagleBone Black: the **Serial Peripheral Interface** or **SPI** pins. The BBB packs two SPI ports, and we will use one of these. Some of the advantages of this interface include higher throughout and lower power consumption than I2C, which we used in an earlier recipe in this chapter.

 To be clear, this recipe will not result in an alternative desktop display. Instead, it is the basis for building a more robust—albeit considerably smaller—low-powered display option for your customized prototyping requirements and tests. To demo the screen, we will run Python scripts as they are an easier entrée into the hardware.

Getting ready

You'll need the following items:

- **OLED PCB**: We will use the SSD1306 driver chip version, which is available (mostly) preassembled at Adafruit (`https://www.adafruit.com/product/938`). The board requires only a minor soldering job to attach the pins and costs around USD $25.00.

- **The BBB, both powered and remote SSH called, via the USB cable**: Let's go headless... no cheating! There's also a practical reason to eschew an external monitor in this recipe: we will be disabling the HDMI port, so you would lose the signal anyway.

- **6x jumper wires**

- **A breadboard**

Adafruit's OLED comes with its own tutorial and Python example scripts. Although we will rely on the Adafruit Python BBIO library, we will actually use an additional Python library developed by Guy Carpenter and modified by Ethan Zonca along with our own custom example code.

How to do it...

Now that you're ready, let's get started:

1. Wire up your board and breadboard in the following manner:

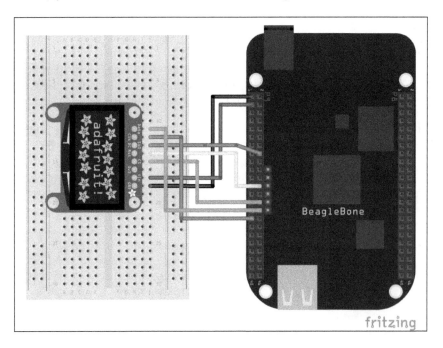

To be clear, here is the hookup in table form:

OLED Screen	BBB pin	Function
GND	GND: P9_1	Ground
VIN	VDD_3V3: P9_3	Power
CS	CSO: P9_28	Slave connector
RST	GPIO: P9_24	Reset display
DC	GPIO: P9_16	
CLK	P9_31	Clock
Data	P9_30	

2. In order to use SPI pins, we need to enable a Device Tree overlay, which is easy to do as it is already compiled on the system and most efficient to load at bootup. So, first call SSH into your BBB, open a terminal window, and then browse to the following directory:

    ```
    $ cd /boot
    ```

3. Now, open the file, uEnv.txt:

    ```
    $ sudo nano uEnv.txt
    ```

4. Then, add the following lines at the very end of the document:

    ```
    ##This line added to enable device tree overlay for SPIDEV
    optargs=capemgr.enable_partno=BB-SPIDEV1
    ```

5. Save and close the file, and then reboot your BBB as follows:

    ```
    # reboot
    ```

6. Log back in as the root user and confirm that the /dev/spidev1.0 and /dev/spidev1.1 files are visible, indicating that the SPI drivers are available for access:

    ```
    $ sudo -i
    # ls -l /dev/spidev*
    ```

    You should get an output similar to this:

    ```
    crw-rw---T 1 root spi 153, 1 Mar  1 20:46 /dev/spidev1.0
    crw-rw---T 1 root spi 153, 0 Mar  1 20:46 /dev/spidev1.1
    ```

7. Next, we need to install a number of Python libraries and their dependencies. Some of them may already be available on your system, but run the following commands just to be certain:

```
# apt-get update
```

```
# apt-get install build-essential python-dev python-pip python-imaging python-smbus python-dateutil
```

```
# pip install spidev
```

```
# pip install pil
```

```
# pip install Adafruit_BBIO
```

 You could run all the pip install commands off one line; however, for clarity's sake, we will show each individual package install.

8. Next, we want to actually do something with the display and all these libraries. So, download a GitHub repo with sample code:

```
# git clone https://github.com/HudsonWerks/OLED-SSD1306.git
```

9. Browse to a subdirectory of example in the directory of code we just downloaded and take a look at what is inside:

```
# /OLED-SSD1306/samples
```

```
# ls
```

10. Before looking at what is inside the code, let's run the main example to see if all of the hardware wiring is correct:

```
# python oled-test1.py
```

If all went well, you will see text cycling on the screen with messages from *ground control*.

11. We want to take a brief look at the Python code, so we will now run the following command:

```
# nano oled-test1.py
```

12. Finally, open up the Cloud9 IDE (http://192.168.7.2:3000/ide.html), create a new .py file called oled-test1.py, and then copy and paste the code from your nano window into the IDE file window. From here, you can begin customizing the code, starting with the messages displayed on the screen.

13. Once appended, save the file and click on the **RUN** button in the IDE. An updated scrolling text message will appear on your OLED display.

Before running a Python script in the Cloud9 IDE, remember to save the document each time. Otherwise, the IDE may run a cached version that does not contain your new changes.

There's more...

The following is some supporting information:

- You can dig deeper into the nuances of modifying the SPIdev pins at `http://elinux.org/BeagleBone_Black_Enable_SPIDEV`

- You can also experiment with py-gaugette, a Python alternative to the Adafruit Python library to control SPI (and other GPIO pins), including a thorough explanation of using higher-quality fonts with the display at `http://guy.carpenter.id.au/gaugette/2014/01/28/spi-ssd1306-oled-for-beaglebone-black/`

Testing a mini LCD cape

In this section, we will cook up an introductory recipe to use the mini LCD display cape designed by CircuitCo.

With a mere 1.8 inches of screen territory, you might wonder what kind of scenarios would be relevant for an add-on such as this. You might also think that the design is a bit odd as the PCB board space dwarfs the actual screen size. Keep in mind a couple of things, though, when deciding to purchase the cape and testing it:

- The BBB is an embedded computing-centric development environment, not desktop-centric as RPi is. As such, an add-on similar to this mini display cape addresses the needs of typical use cases for an embedded device. These are situations that commonly require extremely low power and minimal display, if any.

- The need for fast prototyping, durability, and testing drive the design of a cape such as this results in an overall form factor much larger than the screen itself. Looking more closely at the cape, we discover a number of exciting things:

  - **Open source design**: The cape design and its components are all open sourced, with the core element—the display itself—referenced and clearly sourced so that you can make your own mods once you've got your prototype device ready to fly or amble. Here are the design files and schematic (`http://elinux.org/CircuitCo:MiniDisplay_Cape`) and the component vendor's URL for the display (`https://www.crystalfontz.com/product/CFAF128128B0145T`).

- ❑ **Low cost**: At the preceding referenced source, you will see that in a high-quantity purchase of the display (not the finished cape), the price dramatically drops per unit. So, you can model a low-cost scenario for multiple final production units of your device without incurring the finishing and design costs of a third-party supplier, such as CircuitCo.

Getting ready

In this recipe, we will cook a bit more professionally so that our environment looks more like a true embedded device. Thus, our kit is minimal:

- ▸ **A mini LCD cape**: Resolution 128 x 128 (purchased from `http://boardzoo.com/index.php` for around $USD 30.00).
- ▸ Let's go headless again and wireless, which means we will need the following:
  - ❑ **A USB cable**: We will just power up via a mini USB cable.
  - ❑ **A Wi-Fi dongle**: Insert this directly into the Ethernet port on your BBB. Remote SSH calling sans an annoying Ethernet cable is the goal. Although many users would suggest you to not use a dongle without a powered USB, my tests have delivered stable connectivity without any external hub, making the whole recipe and setup much cleaner.

Note that this code is a variation of Professor Mark Yoder's code (`https://github.com/MarkAYoder/BeagleBoard-exercises/tree/master/miniDisplay`), which is, in turn, a modification of the CircuitCo example code (`http://elinux.org/images/e/e4/Minidisplay-example.tar.gz`).

How to do it...

With everything prepared, what are you waiting for?

1. First, carefully insert the cape into the header pin slots on the BBB. As the cape board has a recessed side to accommodate the BBB's Ethernet port, it is difficult to get the orientation wrong:

The cape fully inserted into the pins.

 You may be a little tentative getting the pins footed properly as the pins are a very tight fit. Once inserted, removing the cape is a bit tricky due to the snugness, so it's best to ease it out slowly from the board headers.

2. With the cape fully inserted, power up your BBB via USB.

    You then need to log in via SSH and then as `root`, with the following code:

    ```
    debian@beaglebone:~$ sudo -i
    root@beaglebone:~#
    ```

3. Now that you're logged in and ready, you need to download and compile some sample code for the display. This code is a slight modification of an open source archived version:

    ```
    # wget https://github.com/HudsonWerks/minidisplay-cape.git
    ```

4. Finally, navigate to the new directory created and compile the test application:

    ```
    # cd minidisplay-cape
    # make
    ```

5. The cape will need a Device Tree Overlay; however, before we take action on this, let's take a look at what cape manager shows us about what is currently loaded using the following command:

```
# cat /sys/devices/bone_capemgr.*/slots
```

```
0: 54:PF---
```

```
1: 55:PF---
```

```
2: 56:PF---
```

```
3: 57:PF---
```

```
4: ff:P-O-L Bone-LT-eMMC-2G,00A0,Texas Instrument,BB-BONE-EMMC-2G
```

```
5: ff:P-O-L Bone-Black-HDMI,00A0,Texas Instrument,BB-BONELT-HDMI
```

6. Next, we will run the following command to load Device Tree so that the cape is recognized. This is made considerably easier with the inclusion of universal Device Tree Overlay with the latest versions of the BBB firmware:

```
# config-pin overlay BB-SPIDEV0
```

7. Check that the overlay loaded as expected by executing the following command:

```
# cat /sys/devices/bone_capemgr.*/slots
```

```
Your output should look similar to this with the last item in the
slot list your loaded overlay:
```

```
0: 54:PF---
```

```
1: 55:PF---
```

```
2: 56:PF---
```

```
3: 57:PF---
```

```
4: ff:P-O-L Bone-LT-eMMC-2G,00A0,Texas Instrument,BB-BONE-EMMC-2G
```

```
5: ff:P-O-L Bone-Black-HDMI,00A0,Texas Instrument,BB-BONELT-HDMI
```

```
7: ff:P-O-L Override Board Name,00A0,Override Manuf,BB-SPIDEV0
```

8. Now, run the test application:

```
# ./minidisplay-test
```

If all goes as planned, the display will begin with a color bar test screen and then end with an image showing Major Tom's view of Earth from the **International Space Station** (**ISS**).

Making a video chat client prototype using Linphone

In this recipe, we will first compile and install Linphone, a well-known open source chat client, with the assumption that we'll use both audio and video. After compiling and running, we will test and optimize the package.

Getting ready

Since we will run a more power intensive, graphics-and GUI-centric environment for the next several recipes, you will need to set up your BeagleBone Black board accordingly:

- **LCD**: Attach an HDMI LCD to the micro HDMI port or an LCD cape if you have one. As we will be running an x-session, headless is not possible.

- **A powered USB hub**: We will use a bushel of peripherals, so plug the powered hub into the USB port and make the BBB happy.

- **Keyboard and mouse**: The packages we will install do not like VNC sessions, so you will need to include a USB keyboard and mouse in your powered USB hub.

- **USB webcam**: As we are doing video chat sessions, we have to have a camera and microphone; a USB webcam is the fastest option.

How to do it...

Once ready, it's time to begin the recipe. Please note that this is split into two parts, and you need to complete them in order. The objective is to first go through the process of installing a pre-compiled version of the software. Then, based on that outcome, see how we can improve the functionality of the tool by compiling it from source files.

Part I – compiling and installing a Linphone binary from the repository

To begin this recipe, you will firstly need to compile and install the Linphone binary from the repository as follows:

1. **Installing Linphone**: This is the easy part; you can actually install the Linphone binary via `apt-get`, as follows:

   ```
   $ sudo apt-get update
   $ sudo apt-get install linphone
   ```

With this, you'll end up with the latest precompiled binary of Linphone on your BBB. So, let's check the version that we get using the following command:

```
$ dpkg -p linphone
```

Take note of the version from the screen output as we will refer to it later.

2. **Setting up an SIP account**: Open up the application under **Internet | Linphone**. You will be greeted with a GUI-based wizard, which includes setting up an SIP telephone number on the application. SIP is a signaling protocol that works with Voice Over IP (VOIP) telecommunications. Numerous free SIP servers are available (just Google "free SIP account"). Here, we will make it easy and use the free one offered by Linphone.org, the developers of the tool.

3. **Doing a desktop install**: We also want to install the binary on your desktop client so that we can test a two-way call connection with the BBB. Downloadable binaries for other platforms (Mac or Windows versions) are available at `http://www.linphone.org/technical-corner/linphone/downloads`. Follow the on screen wizard to set up an account as you just did in the previous step.

4. **Making a video call**: Once you've authenticated your new SIP telephone number and configured your account on Linphone, you can make a video call.

You probably ran into problems while running the application. Did it run slowly? Did it take up most of your CPU's resources? Could you make a connection to the desktop client and run a video chat session? When it comes to CPU hogs, such as video and audio, the BBB does not shine. However, we have a plan for this; thus, take a look at the next part of this recipe.

Part II – compiling and installing Linphone from source

Now, we will compile and install Linphone from source to note how the two versions compare.

Getting ready

If you completed the first part of this recipe, uninstall the prebuilt binary of Linphone before creating a new one and installing it from source. So, remove it completely by running:

```
~$ sudo dpkg --purge linphone
```

How to do it...

Let's get to it:

1. Begin by updating and upgrading your packages and then set up a directory to keep the source files with the following commands:

```
$ sudo apt-get update && sudo apt-get upgrade
$ mkdir packages
$ cd packages
```

To be sure we have certain basic packages, install the following:

```
$ sudo apt-get install automake autoconf gnu-standards gettext
build-essential pkg-config git libtool antlr3 libantlr3c-dev
intltool
```

2. Next, we will get the essential packages by executing the following commands:

```
$ git clone git://git.linphone.org/polarssl
```

```
$ git clone git://git.linphone.org/belle-sip
```

```
$ git clone git://git.linphone.org/linphone --recursive
```

3. Then, we will install the latest Oracle JDK. This is a tricky but necessary set of steps because another package that we need to compile—**antlr**—is dependent on the correct installation of the JDK.

4. To start, we should first look at the version of the JDK that comes preloaded on the current Debian BBB distribution (note that your version may vary). The following command will be useful for this:

```
$ java -version
```

```
java version "1.6.0_32"
```

The output should look something similar to this:

```
OpenJDK Runtime Environment (IcedTea6 1.13.4) (6b32-1.13.4-
1~deb7u1)
```

```
OpenJDK Zero VM (build 23.25-b01, mixed mode)
```

5. Let's move along to installing the new SDK. To do this, we will switch from pure command line interaction over to the BBB's desktop GUI. Open up the Chrome web browser in your applications menu in the lower-left corner. Browse the following Oracle site and download the current JDK for ARM devices, the **hardfloat** version, into your /home directory. You will need to agree to the licensing terms to get the file, which is why we cannot use **wget** or **git** to grab the file:

http://www.oracle.com/technetwork/java/javase/downloads/jdk8-arm-downloads-2187472.html

When trying to download via your browser, you may encounter the error, **Failed. Insufficient permissions**. This tells us that when using the GUI's file browser window, we do not have write privileges to the /home directory by default. Change permissions this way:

```
$ sudo chown <user> /home
```

After running this command, you should no longer have read/write problems, and you will be able to download the Java archive without error.

6. With the permissions to access the file, go to your /home/user directory as follows:

```
$ cd /home/user
```

You should see the .gz file there.

For a sanity check, we will confirm that we are in the right directory with the output as follows:

```
$ pwd
/home/user
```

 As a reminder, user will likely be debian, unless you change it to another name.

We can then confirm that our downloaded file is in the right place:

```
$ ls

Desktop  bin jdk-0a0-linux-arm-vfp-hflt.tar.gz  packages
```

7. You then need to unpack the Java TAR file in your /home directory with TAR. Note that you should be sure to replace the proper file name of the current version available with the following XX file names:

```
/home$ tar -zxvf jdk-8uXX-linux-arm-vfp-hflt.tar.gz
```

We can verify that our untar command did its job and created the new Java directory using:

```
$ ls

Desktop  bin  jdk-8u6-linux-arm-vfp-hflt.tar.gz  jdk1.8.0_XX
packages
```

8. Next, we set up PATH and JAVA_HOME so that the compiled Linphone binary will know where to find the working directory for Java. We will do this by adding PATH information to the .bashrc file:

```
$ sudo nano ~/.bashrc
```

9. In the open nano window and at the end of the file, paste the following:

```
export PATH="/home/debian/jdk1.8.0_07/bin:$PATH"

export JAVA_HOME="/home/debian/jdk1.8.0_07"
```

Reminder!

Here, /debian is the username and may be different in your case based on any earlier changes you may have made; the JDK version shown here should be replaced with the version that you downloaded and unarchived earlier.

You should then save and close the file by pressing *Ctrl + X*; when prompted, type *Y* for yes, and then press the return key (*Enter*).

Following this, reboot your BBB.

10. In the terminal, confirm that the version of the SDK you just installed is now being referenced properly through the following command:

```
$ java -version
```

Cross your fingers, and you will see an output similar to this:

```
Java version "x.y.z_00"
Java(TM) SE Runtime Environment (build x.y.z_00-xyx)
Java HotSpot(TM) Client VM (build 00.0-xyz, mixed mode)
```

If so, hurray! We can move on! If not, you need to repeat the preceding steps to install the JDK.

11. Next, we need to install the `belle-sip` and `linphone` dependencies, as follows:

```
$ sudo aptitude install libswscale-dev libavcodec-dev libv4l-dev
libglew1.6-dev libxml2-dev libgsm1-dev libsqlite3-dev libupnp-dev
libsdl1.2-dev
```

12. This next step is not difficult, but it will slow down the recipe as we need to both get another library (**libvpx**) and compile it from source files. This library, which we get from Google, installs a neon-optimized version of `libvpx` (an HTTP and web file management library). Use the following command for this:

```
$ git clone https://chromium.googlesource.com/webm/libvpx -b
v1.3.0
```

You can then change the directory via:

```
$ cd libvpx
```

13. Following this, run `configure` with the following options:

```
$ CC=cc AR=ar AS=as LD=gcc CXX=g++ ./configure --enable-vp8
--target=armv7-linux-gcc --disable-examples --disable-docs
--enable-error-concealment --enable-realtime-only --enable-
spatial-resampling --enable-multithread --disable-vp9 --enable-pic
```

14. Now, run `make` with the following option and then run `install`. These two commands will take several minutes to complete:

```
$ make -j2
$ sudo make install
```

15. Now, we will go after an audio codec known to efficiently deliver high-quality audio, called **speex**. We will compile it with NEON optimizations enabled. Go to your packages directory and then run `git clone`, as follows:

```
$ cd packages
$ git clone git://git.linphone.org/speex
```

Change the directory and begin the compile process by running the following command:

```
$ cd speex && ./autogen.sh
```

You then need to run configure with the following options:

```
$ ./configure --enable-armv7neon-asm --with-pic --enable-fixed-point --disable-oggtest CFLAGS="-mfpu=neon" --disable-ogg
```

Now, go ahead with the following option and run `make install`. You will note that you can combine these two commands with the double ampersand (`&&`):

```
$ make -j2 && sudo make install
```

16. Next, compile and install `belle-sip` as follows:

```
$ cd packages/belle-sip

$ ./autogen.sh

$ ./configure

$ make && sudo make install
```

17. Then, compile and install `linphone` using the following command:

```
$ ./autogen.sh


$ ./configure --disable-x11 --enable-gtk_ui=no --disable-xv --enable-sdl


$ make V=1 CFLAGS="-Wno-error" && sudo make install
```

We used the `wno-error` flag here because the `mediastreamer` dependency would otherwise keep alerting us about unused functions.

18. We need to relink with:

    ```
    $ export LD_LIBRARY_PATH=/usr/local/lib
    ```

    You can verify that linphone passes the tests via:

    ```
    $ cd tester && ./liblinphone_tester
    ```

19. We are nearly finished. We will now set up the video output by forcing the video display to use a **Simple Direct Media Layer** (**SDL**) output, which will optimize video playback. We will do this by launching a command-line tool that comes with Linphone, called `linphonec`:

    ```
    $ linphonec
    ```

    At the prompt, type the following:

    ```
    > quit
    ```

20. Simply executing this command transparently generates a file called `linphonerc`, which we now need to edit as follows:

    ```
    $ sudo nano ~/.linphonerc
    ```

21. With this file window open, find the `[video]` section and type or replace the following at the end of the section:

    ```
    displaytype=MSVideoOut
    ```

22. We are now ready to launch Linphone. When you launch the application for the first time, you may encounter the following error or something similar:

    ```
    liblinphone.so.6: cannot open shared object file
    ```

    If so, you need to reset the location of the Linphone libraries as the error indicates that you have installed the package in a "nonstandard" directory on your BeagleBone Black board.

23. This command will help Linphone relink the shared library location:

    ```
    $ export LD_LIBRARY_PATH=_the_path_to_your_linphone_libs
    ```

24. You can now launch Linphone from its command-line tool as follows:

    ```
    $ linphonec
    ```

    In the terminal window, Linphone will launch and allow you to configure the settings in the next two steps.

25. **Setting up an SIP account**: Unlike the GUI-based wizard that you experienced with the initial prepackaged install, setting up and registering is a bit more minimal. As you have already registered an SIP account, you can just register your SIP address with the following command:

    ```
    > linphone / register <sip-address> <sip domain> <password>
    ```

26. **Making a video call**: To test your connection, make a call to your client box, which should already have an installed and registered version of Linphone from the first part of this recipe:

    ```
    > linphone / call <sip-address-of-client-box>
    ```

Well done! It's not an easy install, but it's a good, intermediate recipe that yields a robust, sophisticated tool running on your BBB.

8
The Internet of Things

In this chapter, we will cover the following recipes:

- ▶ Location-based recipes – hooking up GPS
- ▶ Location-based recipes – Bluetooth LE and Beacons
- ▶ Using sensors and data with ThingSpeak
- ▶ Making things smarter – building a wireless digital picture frame

Introduction

The Internet of Things is a large basketful of things. It is in fact so large that no one can see its edges yet. It is an evolving and quickly expanding repo of products, concepts, fledgling business ventures, prototypes, middleware, ersatz systems, and hardware.

Some define IoT as connecting things that are not normally connected, thus making them a bit more useful than they were as unconnected devices.

We will not show you how to turn off the lights in your house using the BBB, or how to autoraise the garage door when you drive onto your street. There are a bunch of tutorials that do that already. Instead, we will take a look at some of the recipes that provide some fundamental elements for building IoT-centric prototypes or demos.

Location-based recipes – hooking up GPS

A common question in the IoT realm: where is that darn thing? That Internet of Things thing? Being able to track and pinpoint the location of a device is one of the most typical features of many IoT use cases. So, we will first take a look at a recipe on how to use everyone's favorite location tech: GPS. Then, we will explore one of the newer innovations that has spun out of Bluetooth 4.0, beacons, a technology for capturing more precise location-based data than GPS.

The UART background

In the galaxy of embedded systems, developers use dozens of different serial protocols. More common and familiar to most consumers are components such as USB and Ethernet. Then, there are protocols familiar to engineers, such as SPI and I2C, which we have already explored in this book. For this recipe, we will use yet another flavor of serial, UART, an asynchronous or clock-less protocol. This comes in handy in a variety of scenarios to connect IoT-centric devices.

Universal asynchronous receiver/transmitter (**UART**) is a common circuit block used for managing serial data and hardware. As UART does not require a clock signal, it uses fewer wires and pins. In fact, UART uses only two serial wires: RX to receive packets and TX to transmit them.

The framework for this recipe comes from AdaFruit's tutorial for the RPi. However, the difference between these two boards are nontrivial, so this recipe needs quite a few more ingredients than the RPi version.

Getting ready

You will need the following components for this recipe:

- **GPS PCB**: You can probably find cheaper versions, but we will use AdaFruit's well-regarded and ubiquitous PCB (`http://www.adafruit.com/product/746 at around USD $40.00`).

- **Antenna**: Again, Adafruit's suggested SMA to the uFL adapter antenna is the simplest and cheap at USD $3.00 (`https://www.adafruit.com/product/851`)

- **5V power**: Powering via the 5V DC in lieu of simply connecting via the mini USB is advisable. The GPS modules consume a good bit of power, a fact apparent to all of us, given how the GPS functionality is a well-known drain on our smartphones.

- **Internet connectivity via Wi-Fi or Ethernet**.

- **Breadboard**.

- **4x jumper wires**.

How to do it...

For the GPS setup, the steps are as follows:

1. Insert the PCB pins into the breadboard and wire the pins according to the following fritzing diagram:

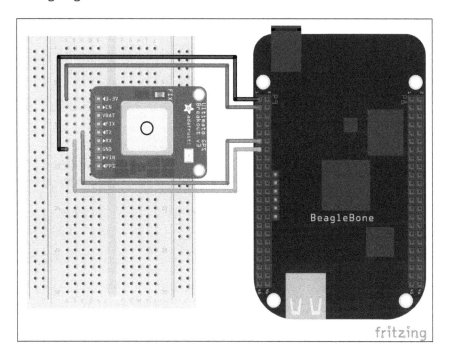

P9_11 (blue wire): This denotes RX on BBB and TX on GPS PCB. At first, it may seem confusing to not wire TX to TX, and so on. However, once you understand the pin's function, the logic is clear: a transmit (TX) pin pairs with a pin that can receive data (RX), whereas a receive pin pairs with a pin that transmits data.

P9_13 (green wire): This specifies TX on BBB and RX on GPS PCB

P9_1: This indicates GND

P9_3: This specifies 3.3V

2. Now, carefully attach the antenna to the board's uFL connector.
3. Next, power your BBB. Here's where it gets a bit tricky.

    When your BBB starts, you will immediately see the **Fix** button on the GPS board that will begin to flash quickly, approximately 1x per second. We will come back to check the integrity of the module's satellite connection in a later step.

4. In order to gain access to the UART pins on the BBB, we have to enable them using a Device Tree overlay. Until recently, this was a multistep process. However, now that the BeagleBone Universal I/O package comes preloaded on the current versions of the firmware, enabling the pins (in the case, UART4) in a snap. Let's begin by logging in as root with the following command:

```
$ sudo -i
```

5. Then, run the relevant Universal I/O command and check whether it went to the right place, as shown in the following code:

```
# config-pin overlay BB-UART4
# cat /sys/devices/bone_capemgr.*/slots
```

6. Now, reboot your BBB and check whether the device is present in the device list by using the following command:

```
$ ls -l /dev/ttyO*
crw-rw---- 1 root tty      247, 0 Mar  1 20:46 /dev/ttyO0
crw-rw---T 1 root dialout 247, 4 Jul 13 02:12 /dev/ttyO4
```

7. Finally, check whether it is loading properly with the following command:

```
$ dmesg
```

This is how the output should look:

```
[  188.335168] bone-capemgr bone_capemgr.9: part_number 'BB-
UART4', version 'N/A'

[  188.335235] bone-capemgr bone_capemgr.9: slot #7: generic
override

[  188.335250] bone-capemgr bone_capemgr.9: bone: Using override
eeprom data at slot 7

[  188.335266] bone-capemgr bone_capemgr.9: slot #7: 'Override
Board Name,00A0,Override Manuf,BB-UART4'

[  188.335355] bone-capemgr bone_capemgr.9: slot #7: Requesting
part number/version based 'BB-UART4-00A0.dtbo

[  188.335370] bone-capemgr bone_capemgr.9: slot #7: Requesting
firmware 'BB-UART4-00A0.dtbo' for board-name 'Override Board
Name', version '00A0'

[  188.335400] bone-capemgr bone_capemgr.9: slot #7: dtbo 'BB-
UART4-00A0.dtbo' loaded; converting to live tree

[  188.335673] bone-capemgr bone_capemgr.9: slot #7: #2 overlays

[  188.343353] 481a8000.serial: ttyO4 at MMIO 0x481a8000 (irq =
45) is a OMAP UART4

[  188.343792] bone-capemgr bone_capemgr.9: slot #7: Applied #2
overlays.
```

Tips to get a GPS Fix

Your best method to get the GPS module connected is to take it outdoors. However, as this is not a likely option when you develop a project, putting it against or even just outside a window will often suffice. If it is cloudy, and if you don't have a reasonably clear sky view from your module's antenna, do not expect a quick connection. Be patient. When a fix is made, the flashing LED will cycle very slowly at about 15-second intervals.

Even if GPS modules do not have a fix, be aware that they will still send data. This can be confusing because you may run some of the following commands and think that your connection is fine, but you just keep getting junk (blank) data. However, to reiterate, the flashing LED needs to have slowed down to 15-second intervals to verify that you have a fix.

8. Although the output is not pretty, the following command is a useful first step in making sure that your devices are hooked up because it will show the raw NMEA data coming out of the GPS:

```
$ cat /dev/ttyO4
```

NMEA - The National Marine Electronics Associations' GPS language protocol standard.

9. Verify that your wiring is correct and that the module is generating data properly (irrespective of a satellite fix) as follows:

```
$ sudo screen /dev/ttyO4 9600
```

The output should immediately begin and look something similar to this:

```
$GPGGA,163356.000,4044.0318,N,07400.1854,W,1,5,2.65,4.0,M,-34.2,M,,*67

$GPGSA,A,3,13,06,10,26,02,,,,,,,,2.82,2.65,0.95*04

$GPRMC,163356.000,A,4044.0318,N,07400.1854,W,2.05,68.70,031214,,,A*46

$GPVTG,68.70,T,,M,2.05,N,3.81,K,A*09

$GPGGA,163357.000,4044.0322,N,07400.1853,W,1,5,2.65,3.7,M,-34.2,M,,*68

$GPGSA,A,3,13,06,10,26,02,,,,,,,
```

10. Now, quit the program using one of the the following methods:

Ctrl + a, enter or copy and paste :`quit` with the colon to the highlighted box at the bottom, or press *Ctrl + a + k + y*.

Installing the GPS toolset

1. The next set of ingredients in the recipe consists of installing and testing a common toolset to parse GPS on Linux. As always, before installing something new, it is good practice to update your repos with the following command:

```
$ sudo apt-get update
```

2. Install the tools, including `gpsd`, a service daemon to monitor your GPS receiver. The package exposes all the data on location, course, and velocity on the TCP port 2947 of your BBB and efficiently parses the NMEA text that pours out of the GPS receiver, as shown in the following command:

```
$ sudo apt-get install gpsd gpsd-clients python-gps
```

For the preceding code, `gpsd-clients` installs some test clients, and `python-gps` installs the required Python library to communicate with `gpsd` via Python scripts.

 After the installation, you may find it useful to run `man gpsd` and review the package's well-written and informative manual. It not only provides the details around what you just installed, but it also provides the general GPS-related content.

3. If the planets or communication satellites are aligned, you can run this command from the newly installed toolset and begin to display the GPS data:

```
$ sudo gpsmon /dev/ttyO4
```

You should see a terminal GUI that looks similar to the following screenshot:

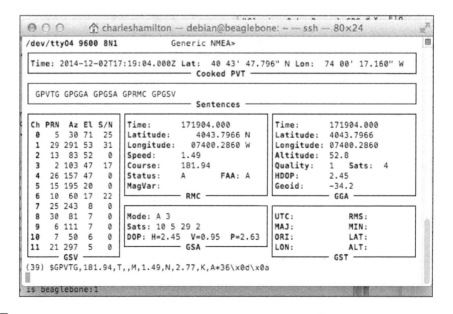

4. To quit, press *Ctrl + C* or enter `q` and then return (*Enter*) key.

5. Now, we will test the other principal tool that you just installed with the following command:

```
$ sudo cgps -s
```

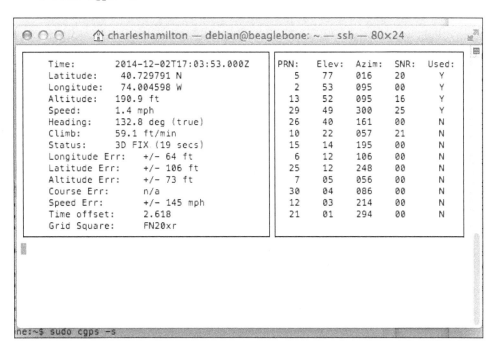

The output includes the current date and time in UTC, the latitude and longitude, and the approximate altitude.

Troubleshooting—Part 1

You may run into problems here. Commonly, on a first time set up and running, `cgps` may time out, close by itself, and lead you to believe that there is a problem with your setup. If so, the next steps can lead you back on the path to GPS nirvana:

1. We will begin by stopping all the running instances of GPS, as shown in the following code:

```
$ sudo killall gpsd
```

2. Now, let's get rid of any sockets that the `gpsd` commands may have left behind with the following command:

```
$ sudo rm /var/run/gpsd.sock
```

There is a systemd bug that we will typically need to address. Here is how we fix it:

3. Open the systemd GPSD service using the following command:

```
$ sudo nano /lib/systemd/system/gpsd.service
```

4. Paste this command to the window with the following script:

```
[Unit]
Description=GPS (Global Positioning System) Daemon
Requires=gpsd.socket

[Service]
ExecStart=/usr/sbin/gpsd -n -N /dev/ttyO4

[Install]
Also=gpsd.socket
```

5. Then, restart the systemd service as follows:

```
$ sudo service gpsd start
```

6. You should now be able run either of the following services again:

```
$ sudo gpsmon /dev/ttyO4
```

Alternatively, you can run the following command:

```
$ sudo cgps -s
```

Troubleshooting—Part 2

Sometimes, the preceding fixes don't fix it. Here are several more suggestions for troubleshooting purposes:

1. Set up a control socket for GPS with the following command:

```
$ sudo gpsd -N -D3 -F /var/run/gpsd.sock
```

> The explanation of the command-line flags or options are as follows:
>
> - -N: This tells gpsd to immediately post the GPS data. Although this is useful for testing purposes, it can also drain power, so leave it off if your use case is battery-powered.
> - -F: This creates a control socket for device addition and removal. The option requires a valid pathname on your local filesystem, which is why our command is appended with /var/run/gpsd.sock.

2. We may also need to install a package that lets us examine any port conflict that could be occurring, as shown in the following command:

   ```
   $ sudo apt-get install lsof
   ```

3. This installed utility will open and display the system files, including disk files, named pipes, network sockets, and devices opened by all the processes. There are multiple uses for the tool. However, we only want to determine whether the GPS module is speaking correctly to the port 2947 and if there are any conflicts. So, we will run the following command:

   ```
   $ sudo lsof -i :2947
   ```

   This is how the output should look:

   ```
   COMMAND   PID    USER    FD    TYPE DEVICE SIZE/OFF NODE NAME
   systemd    1     root    24u   IPv4  6907     0t0   TCP
   localhost:gpsd (LISTEN)
   gpsd     5960 nobody     4u    IPv4  6907     0t0   TCP
   localhost:gpsd (LISTEN)
   ```

4. You may also want to check whether any instances of the GPS are running and then kill them with the following command:

   ```
   $ ps aux |grep gps
   $ sudo killall gpsd
   ```

For a final bit of cooking with the GPS board, we want to run a Python script and display the data in tidy, parsed output. The code was originally written for the RPi, but it is useable on the BBB as well.

1. Go get it with the following command:

   ```
   $ git clone https://github.com/HudsonWerks/gps-tests.git
   ```

2. Now, browse to the new directory that we just created and take a look at the file that we will use with the following code:

   ```
   $ cd gps-tests
   $ sudo nano GPStest1.py
   ```

3. Let's peruse the script a bit to understand some of its key parts:

The script requires a number of Python libraries:

```
import os
from gps import *
from time import *
import time
import threading
```

Keep in mind that getting a fix and then obtaining a good GPS data can take several moments before the system settles into a comfortable flow, as shown in the following code:

```
#It may take a second or two to get good data
#print gpsd.fix.latitude,', ',gpsd.fix.longitude,'
Time: ',gpsd.utc
```

If you find the output overwhelming, you can always modify the print commands to simplify the display as follows:

```
print
print ' GPS reading'
print '----------------------------------------'
print 'latitude      ' , gpsd.fix.latitude
print 'longitude     ' , gpsd.fix.longitude
print 'time utc      ' , gpsd.utc,' + ', gpsd.fix.time
print 'altitude (m)' , gpsd.fix.altitude
print 'eps           ' , gpsd.fix.eps
print 'epx           ' , gpsd.fix.epx
print 'epv           ' , gpsd.fix.epv
print 'ept           ' , gpsd.fix.ept
print 'speed (m/s) ' , gpsd.fix.speed
print 'climb         ' , gpsd.fix.climb
print 'track         ' , gpsd.fix.track
print 'mode          ' , gpsd.fix.mode
print
print 'sats          ' , gpsd.satellites
time.sleep(5)
```

4. Now close the script and run the following command:

```
$ python GPStest1.py
```

In a few seconds, the nicely formatted GPS data will be displayed in your terminal window.

There's more...

- ▸ Sparkfun's tutorial on GPS is definitely worth the read at `https://learn.sparkfun.com/tutorials/gps-basics/all`

- ▸ For further GPSD troubleshooting, refer to `http://www.catb.org/gpsd/troubleshooting.html`

Location-based recipes – Bluetooth LE and Beacons

In the past, you may have had the opportunity to use Bluetooth devices in your projects. However, in all probability, that would have been an earlier version of BT, now commonly referred to as "classic" Bluetooth. Before we jump into an actual recipe on how to use these small radio devices, we should take a look at some of the significant differences between the classic version of Bluetooth and the **Bluetooth Low Energy** (**BLE**) spec because they are very different animals. Although they are both available as part of the 4.0 spec, we will work only with the BLE piece for our recipe.

Classic Bluetooth

With the classic version of the stack, one device basically connects to another device, data is exchanged serially, and the data does not persist. For example, when you set up a BT headset, the audio comes piping into your ears, and the data goes on after the throughput. Furthermore, the connection does not reveal or show anything about what's happening in the middle of that pipe with the data itself.

Bluetooth Low Energy

Although more challenging to work with and still nascent with its documentation, BLE (sometimes referred to as Bluetooth Smart) is a far more robust environment for managing data, particularly in the world of IoT. Several key elements distinguish it from its earlier kin:

- ▸ **Central device versus peripheral device rubric**: In a BLE ecosystem, there will be a broadcast (peripheral) device that sends out data and a (central) device or devices that reads from this broadcast. The device relationship is analogous to a community bulletin board with a bunch of readers or a client/server relationship. However, in BLE-land, the normal assumptions are flipped: the server is a very low-powered device, whereas the client is typically a more sophisticated device, such as a smartphone, a laptop, a tablet, or other wireless device.

- ▸ **Not one-to-one**: BLE allows multiple simultaneous connections to the same server or peripheral device.

- **Low power**: The connections between devices are very short in BLE. This results in extremely low power usage. Devices can operate with simple lithium coin cell batteries.

- **Broad services and characteristics schema**: The data presented by a peripheral is structured as services, which are then subdivided into characteristics. Services are akin to the notices on a bulletin board, whereas characteristics are similar to the individual paragraphs of these notices.

   You can easily hook up to different services and characteristics with a few lines of code. For example, you can interact with a battery service and easily determine the power levels remaining for a device. Alternatively, your use case may be related to health or fitness, which means that you can leverage the onboard health service that includes a characteristic (such as heartbeat data).

Beacons and iBeacons

Where GPS leaves off, Beacons begin. This emerging BLE technology is quickly becoming the next big thing in location sensing. Although proven, powerful, and ubiquitous, GPS can only determine the coordinates of an object within 20-30 feet. However, the BLE Beacon technology is commonly referred to as hyperlocal in its sensitivity because it is accurate within a range of 100 meters down to inches. Thus far, most of the interest around the Beacon technology is focused on how marketers and advertisers want to use it in order to send you targeted offers... Yuck!

This is largely due to the fact that Apple's marketing-centric version of the protocol called iBeacons has been the most commonly referenced and easiest type to get running quickly. However, the intrinsic BLE Beacon stack, iBeacon or otherwise, is very exciting for several reasons:

- It delivers low cost radio signaling
- It provides fairly rapid and simple development requirements
- It requires very low power with its use of BLE
- It broadcasts far more precise location data than GPS

For IoT-like scenarios, both indoor and outdoor, Beacons provide much promise far beyond annoying marketing messages. Also, you can actually buy premade beacons for very little money, sometimes for only a few dollars (USD).

It may seem like overkill to be using a full-blown microcomputer, such as the BBB, to serve as a Beacon. However, our intention is to create our own BBB version so that we have more flexibility in understanding and building the constituent parts of a Beacon network. Doing this as an open source recipe allows you to pull the levers yourself.

A further point to clarify here is that BLE Beacons do not actually send content that a user receives on their smartphone app. The beacon simply provides the rudimentary data to a mobile app, which allows that app to determine its location in a venue or outdoor spot and in turn sends the user location-specific data. Alternatively, it can capture and make use of that data in other ways.

Furthermore, iBeacons do not track users based on any kind of profiling requirements; the interaction can be—and generally is—completely anonymous, so concerns about privacy are negligible.

With Beacons, there are several data fields that you typically want to watch. This helps in differentiating one beacon from another. For instance, let's say that we are in the Museum of Natural History in New York City that has a beacon network. Here are the relevant data fields:

- **UUID**: Services are identified by unique numbers known as UUIDs (Universal Unique Identifier), which you may be familiar with from other projects. Therefore, the museum would have its own unique UUID string.

- **The major field (ID)**: Inputting a specific value in this field can specify a more general location, for example, a particular floor in the museum.

- **The minor field (ID)**: Inputting a value in this field will specify a particular gallery on a specific floor.

- **TX Power**: This is used to try to estimate the distance based on the signal strength of the Wi-Fi connection (the RSSI value) in a particular room.

The major and minor IDs can be used to trigger certain behaviors in your application when it discovers one of your beacons. All of these fields come together to make pinpointing locations extremely accurate.

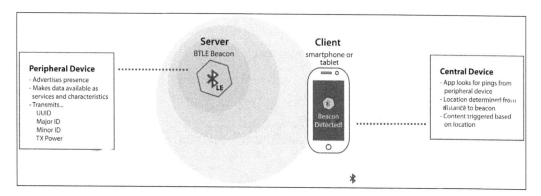

Getting ready

The BBB is powered up via USB and connected online either via Wi-Fi or Ethernet with two additional items:

▸ USB Bluetooth LE (BLE), also known as Bluetooth 4.0 adapter—we will use a Targus dongle (product ID ACB10US1). This uses the Broadcom BCM20702 chipset. There are far cheaper ones that should work fine on the BBB that cost around USD $10.00-15.00. Here is a list of compatible Bluetooth dongles for the Raspberry Pi (`http://elinux.org/RPi_USB_Bluetooth_adapters`). Many of those listed will likely work with the BBB, although they have not all been tested for compatibility.

▸ Smartphone with Bluetooth LE—iPhones starting from 4S to any of the current models are BLE-compliant. On the Android side, there are exceptions. By default, the current models of an Android phone runs on 4.3 or higher BLE. However, any Android phones that cannot run on version 4.3 or higher will not work with this set of recipes.

How to do it...

Part 1—Setting up your smartphone

As mentioned earlier in the chapter, we need to install some apps on our smartphone in order to make this recipe meaningful and demonstrate the BBB's beacon-ness.

For the iPhone, we installed and tested two different free apps from the App Store, one is called Locate (by Radius Networks) and the other is called Beacon Tool. (The developers must gotten up very early in the morning to come up with those names...).

Locate has a few more functionalities than Beacon Tool because it lets us set the major and minor values for the Beacon.

Part 2—Setting up a simple IoT test environment

You can test and track the iBeacon using a web service. There are several businesses in this space. We used a platform called EvoThings, which is a free, open source platform.

Evothings allows you to use a simple IDE on your desktop and then demonstrate an iBeacon app on a smartphone with a Beacon-enabled BBB in the middle of the mix. Perform the following steps:

1. Download and install Evothings Studio (`http://evothings.com/`). The installation requires a Workbench desktop and a mobile app, all of which is explained on their website.

2. After downloading Evothings Studio, you will find a Mac OS X and a Windows version on the desktop. Install your preferred client.

3. For the mobile app, install and start the Evothings client app on your mobile device. Android and iOS are available at their respective online stores.

There are numerous demos and examples that come with Evothings. Although they tend to be focused on how to use an Arduino as a beacon, the code is very flexible (and open source), so everything is customizable for other platforms. For our first quick example, in your desktop Evothings Workbench, open the following file in a text editor:

`Evothings_Studio/examples/ibeacon-scan/index.js`

Then, scan about halfway down the page to find the following code:

```
// Add your own manufacturer UUIDs to this list.
{uuid:'B9407F30-F5F8-466E-AFF9-25556B57FE6D'},
{uuid:'F7826DA6-4FA2-4E98-8024-BC5B71E0893E'},
{uuid:'8DEEFBB9-F738-4297-8040-96668BB44281'},
{uuid:'A0B13730-3A9A-11E3-AA6E-0800200C9A66'},
```

Now, add your generated UUID from the earlier step to line up with the following syntax:

```
{uuid:'3784B5B0-2DA7-11E4-8C21-0800200C9A66'},
```

 Other than their own identity, iBeacons do not push notifications to the central (receiving) devices. However, a mobile app on your phone can use signals received from iBeacons to trigger their own push notifications.

Part 3: Setting up the BBB

Let's start with the essential package on how to control and interact with Bluetooth devices (LE or otherwise) and the Linux Bluetooth stack BlueZ. On the current Debian distro that comes with any newly purchased BBB, BlueZ should be already installed. Perform the following steps:

1. First, update and upgrade the BBB with the following command:

```
$ sudo apt-get update
```

2. Then, we will verify that BlueZ is installed using the following command:

```
$ bluetoothd -v
```

If you see a version number appear, skip to step 4; otherwise, proceed to the next step.

3. Now, install BlueZ with the following command:

```
$ sudo apt-get install bluez
```

You may want to install BlueZ from its source. Here is the code for it:

```
sudo mkdir bluez
cd bluez
sudo wget www.kernel.org/pub/linux/bluetooth/bluez-
x.xx.tar.xz
```

Check for the current version of BlueZ before running `wget`.

4. Then, connect the dongle to the USB port and verify that it is recognized with the following command:

```
$ lsusb
```

5. Now, we want to set up Bluetooth communications between the BBB and any other BLE devices that require using a series of BlueZ commands. To do this, we will use the `hciconfig` tool and begin by taking a look at the address of the USB adapter as follows:

```
$ hcitool dev

Devices:

hci0    00:19:0E:15:DE:87
```

6. The preceding output shows one device present with the ID `0` that is prepended with `hci`; this is part of the protocol's naming convention. We will take this ID and append it to the command, include the (`-a`) option to output information about all the devices present, and check the dongle's ready state, as shown in the following code:

```
$ hciconfig -a hci0
```

Your screen should show the following code:

```
hci0:   Type: BR/EDR   Bus: USB
    BD Address: 00:19:0E:15:DE:87   ACL MTU: 1021:8   SCO MTU:
    64:1
    DOWN
    RX bytes:1267 acl:0 sco:0 events:47 errors:0
    TX bytes:747 acl:0 sco:0 commands:47 errors:0
    Features: 0xbf 0xfe 0xcf 0xfe 0xdb 0xff 0x7b 0x87
    Packet type: DM1 DM3 DM5 DH1 DH3 DH5 HV1 HV2 HV3
    Link policy: RSWITCH SNIFF
    Link mode: SLAVE ACCEPT
```

7. Ensure that it says DOWN, which is not what we want. So, up, up, and away we go:

```
$ sudo hciconfig hci0 up
```

8. Then, verify that the command worked by repeating our earlier step. Your stdout should look similar to the following command:

```
$ hciconfig -a hci0
hci0:   Type: BR/EDR  Bus: USB
BD Address: 00:19:0E:15:DE:87  ACL MTU: 1021:8  SCO MTU: 64:1
UP RUNNING
RX bytes:990 acl:0 sco:0 events:44 errors:0
TX bytes:738 acl:0 sco:0 commands:44 errors:0
Features: 0xbf 0xfe 0xcf 0xfe 0xdb 0xff 0x7b 0x87
Packet type: DM1 DM3 DM5 DH1 DH3 DH5 HV1 HV2 HV3
Link policy: RSWITCH SNIFF
Link mode: SLAVE ACCEPT
Name: 'BCM20702A'
Class: 0x000000
Service Classes: Unspecified
Device Class: Miscellaneous,
HCI Version: 4.0 (0x6)  Revision: 0x1000
LMP Version: 4.0 (0x6)  Subversion: 0x220e
Manufacturer: Broadcom Corporation (15)
```

9. Now, we will set up the dongle to begin what is known as advertising in the BLE parlance. We will perform this in the low energy (le) mode using the flag 3; this sets the connection mode:

```
$ sudo hciconfig hci0 leadv 3
```

> A further word about nomenclature in the iBeacon/BLE landscape is that you will often see references to the word *advertising* when you develop with BLE. The term is used generically to refer to a packet of data that is being sent from a BT device to make its presence known; it has nothing to do with Apple's original advertising/marketing-centric purposes for iBeacon.

10. By default, the BLE dongle will scan for other devices. However, we want to turn this function off because it can interfere with advertising as follows:

```
$ sudo hciconfig hci0 noscan
```

11. The last command adds the UUID, as shown in the following command:

```
$ sudo hcitool -i hci0 cmd 0x08 0x0008 1E 02 01 1A 1A FF 4C 00 02
15 37 84 B5 B0 2D A7 11 E4 8C 21 08 00 20 0C 9A 66 00 00 00 00 C8
```

The instant you send the preceding command, you should see a notification/popup on your smartphone. With the iLocate app on the iPhone, it should say **Entered region: BBB beacon 1**.

(This assumes that a smartphone app is already installed and set up to recognize the BBB beacon UUID).

Congratulations! You are now able to broadcast hyperlocal data without the need for a big GPS satellite.

There's more...

The following references provide more detail on BTLE:

- **Classic versus BTLE discussion**: This gives you an excellent drill-down into the nature of BLE's distinctiveness from Bluetooth Classic at http://makezine. com/2014/06/16/the-bluetooth-le-doc-a-thon-at-itp-camp/

- **BTLE documentation**: This provides various examples from a Doc-a-thon at https://github.com/tigoe/BLEDocs/wiki

- **Estimote teardown**: Make magazine takes apart an Estimote iBeacon, a commercial, mostly closed product at http://makezine.com/2014/01/03/reverse-engineering-the-estimote/

- **Tile**: Information on this new, very cheap, and small Beacon can be found at http://tiletogether.tumblr.com/post/98897004442/tile-is-coming-to-android#notes

- Troubleshoot your Bluetooth installation (https://wiki.archlinux.org/index.php/bluetooth)

- **Bubble app**: This app that strives to simplify the process of setting up and interacting with iBeacon content by using tags to connect websites to things in the real world. Learn more at http://discoverbubble.com/

Using sensors and data with ThingSpeak

Having some facility to hook up sensors is almost de rigueur when you talk about the Internet of Things. Furthermore, learning how to get your arms around the large datasets that typically pour out of these sensors has become a crucial piece of the IoT puzzle. In the next section, we will take a look at a recipe that introduces one method for managing this data.

We will be piggybacking on a recipe from *Chapter 3, Physical Computing Recipes Using JavaScript, the BoneScript Library, and Python*, and will use the TMP36 temperature sensor in particular. However, this time, you will learn how to use the data coming out of the sensor and display it in a more accessible IoT-style manner.

Getting ready

The following materials will be needed:

- BBB powered via 5V supply.
- Ethernet or Wi-Fi connectivity.
- Breadboard.
- 3x jumper wires.
- The TMP36 temperature sensor—this is the same sensor as the one we used in *Chapter 3, Physical Computing Recipes Using JavaScript, the BoneScript Library, and Python*. As a reminder, this low-cost sensor is readily available from numerous sources, including suppliers such as Sparkfun (`https://www.sparkfun.com/products/10988`).

How to do it...

Perform the following steps to use sensors and data with ThingSpeak:

1. If BBB is not already off, turn it off.

2. Using the following fritzing diagram, wire your powered down BBB:

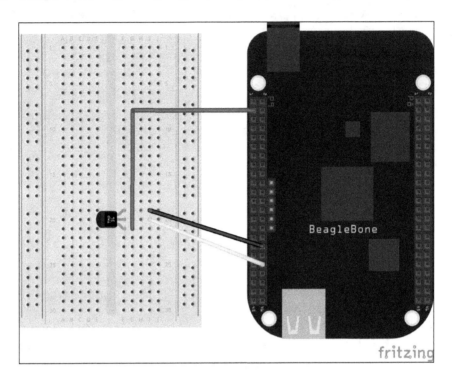

You may remember this configuration from *Chapter 3, Physical Computing Recipes Using JavaScript, the BoneScript Library, and Python* as the wiring is exactly the same: GND uses the analog ground *P9_34* (GNDA_ADC), 3V PWR at *P9_3*, and the sensor pin at *P9_38*.

3. Power your BBB and log in via SSH.

4. Sign up for a new account at ThingSpeak (`https://thingspeak.com/`), a free cloud service for data publishing and creating IoT-style products.

5. Follow the prompts on the ThingSpeak site on how to set up a channel for your account. Just for fun, let's name the channel as `Ground Control Temperature`.

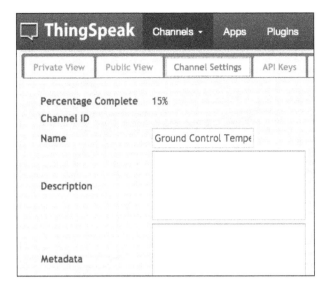

6. At the bottom of the same **Channel Settings** screen, create a second field called `Field Label 2`, as shown in the following screenshot:

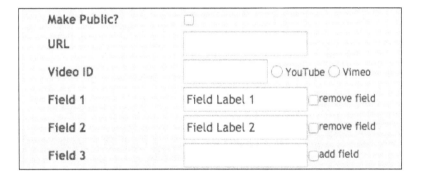

7. You can now see the blank slate charts that have been created for the channel that will receive data from the BBB's sensor:

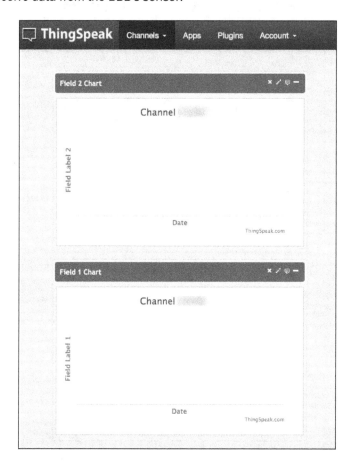

8. From your GitHub repo, download the BoneScript (Node.js) code for this recipe to your BBB with the following command:

```
$ git clone https://github.com/HudsonWerks/tmp36-sensor-
thingspeak.git
```

The repo also includes a Python script example; however, we will only review the node version of the recipe here.

9. Navigate to the new directory that we just created and open the Node.js file with the following command:

```
$ cd tmp36-sensor-thingspeak
$ sudo nano tmp36-thingspeak.js
```

10. In a browser on your client desktop, open the Cloud9 IDE and create a new JavaScript file. Then, copy and paste the code from the open `nano` window on your BBB to the Cloud9 file.

11. Before trying to send data to ThingSpeak, we should first verify that our sensor, wiring, and basic code are functioning properly. Now, in your Cloud9 window, click on the **RUN** button. If all goes well, the console output in the IDE should show readings similar to the following code:

```
debugger listening on port 15454
Sensor reading started.
Output at 10-sec intervals.
Temperature at Ground Control for Tue, 11 Aug 2015 19:20:21 GMT
Fahrenheit: 64.4
Celsius: 18

_____

Temperature at Ground Control for Tue, 11 Aug 2015 19:20:31 GMT
Fahrenheit: 63.86
Celsius: 17.7
```

If you are not getting readings from the sensor, go back and check your wiring.

12. Next, we will hook up our code to the ThingSpeak channel that we set up in the first part of this recipe using the generated API. Back on the ThingSpeak **Channels** tab, drill down to the new channel you created and search for the **API Keys** tab option. Select this tab and then copy (*Ctrl + C*) the **Write API Key** generated, as shown in the following screenshot:

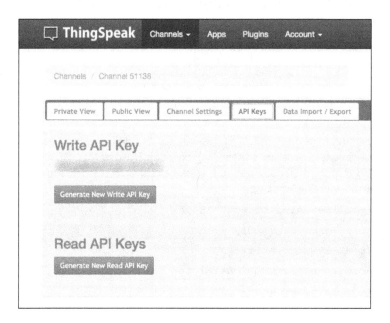

13. Back in the Cloud9 window, on line 30 of the `tmp36` code window, paste your ThingSpeak Write API key to the designated part of the code as follows:

```
//Post temperature data to ThingSpeak

request.post('http://api.thingspeak.com:80/update',{form:{api_
key: 'THINGSPEAK_WRITE_API_KEY_HERE', field1: temp_f, field2:
temp_c}});
```

14. Now, it's time to see your temperature readings that is displayed on the ThingSpeak cloud service. So, as you again click on **RUN** in the IDE, your Cloud9 console should be outputting temperature readings as before. Within a few moments, back on the ThingSpeak channel, data points should be appearing at 10-second intervals on the screen, plotting the fluctuations of **Ground Control Temperature** of your room, as shown in the following screenshot:

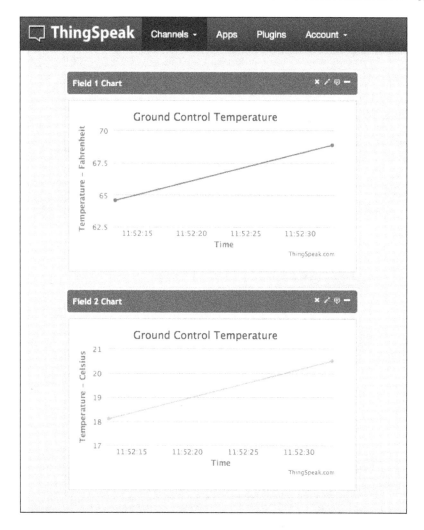

15. Last but not least, we want to make the sensor data visible through yet another method, this time using Twitter. As Twitter is free and readily available on your smartphone, it serves as a useful channel to funnel IoT data. ThingSpeak simplifies the process considerably by having a web hook that lets you plug into a Twitter account.

    If you do not have a Twitter account, set one up now. And even if you do have one, create a new development account that is separate from your primary feed. Otherwise, your followers may not appreciate getting your temperature sensor tweets.

16. On the ThingSpeak site, select **Apps** from the menu and then **ThingTweet**.

17. Under the **ThingTweet App**, select **Link Twitter Account**. This will redirect you to Twitter so you can authorize ThingSpeak access to your account. If you want to proceed with the rest of this recipe, you will need to give permission for authorization.

    Once you have confirmed the right Twitter account, Twitter will send you back to ThingSpeak.

18. After the authorization process, the ThingSpeak app generates a ThingTweet **API Key** that we will need to use in our code, as shown in the following screenshot:

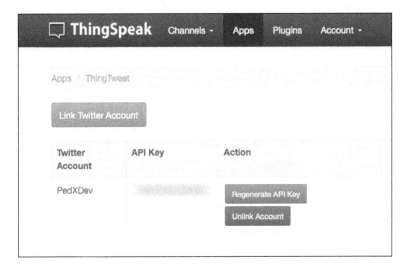

19. Copy and paste this new **API Key** to line 33 of the code in the Cloud9 window, where it says `THINGTWEET_TWITTER_API_KEY_HERE` and the two CHANNEL-IDs to the designated spots in the code:

```
request.post('https://api.thingspeak.com/apps/thingtweet/1/
statuses/update', {form:{api_key: 'THINGTWEET_TWITTER_API_
KEY_HERE', status: "The current Ground Control temperature is
%%channel_CHANNEL-ID_field_1%% F, %%channel_CHANNEL-ID_field_2%%
C"}});
}
```

All the parameters from the Twitter API statuses/update are possible, including geolocation. You can learn more about the ThingSpeak API and its Twitter app on their site at `https://thingspeak.com/docs/thingtweet/`.

20. Last but not least, click on **RUN** in the IDE. Let's keep our fingers crossed because your BBB's Ground Control Temperature will begin to send temperature updates to your Twitter account.

Three cheers for Ground Control Temperature!

See also

You will soon learn that there is a vast array of new ventures playing in the IoT cloud services sandbox. As most of them are nascent businesses in a newly emerging industry, it is difficult to predict who will emerge as go-to platforms in the future. However, a handful of players are worth mentioning for their ease of use or their strong positioning on the marketplace:

- **Cloud deployment**: Deploying software updates to multiple remote devices will become an increasing challenge as the IoT continues to grow. Two players, Resin. io (`https://www.resin.io/`) and Docker (`https://www.docker.com/`), are leading the charge in creating a platform for containerizing your applications, making it easy to deploy packages to all your devices over the cloud.

- Data display and hosting: Many businesses in the IoT space are trying to make it easier for you to manage and display your IoT data in a slicker package and simultaneously host with them. Here are a couple of them:

  - Initial state (`https://www.initialstate.com/`)
  - Ubidots (`http://ubidots.com/`)

- Messaging and alerts: Dweet.io/Freeboard (`http://dweet.io/`)

- Connecting to web services through open APIs: Ship.iot (`https://shipiot.net`)

- Toolsets to hook up IoT devices including the following sample:

  - IBM's Nodered.js (`http://nodered.org/`)
  - Adafruit I/O (`https://www.adafruit.com/io`)

Making things smarter – building a wireless digital picture frame

Taking mundane objects and connecting them to one another is one of the key intentions of the whole IoT phenomenon. In our next recipe, we will create a digital picture frame. However, ours is is not the typical off-the-shelf version where you load images from an SD card. Instead, we will use a combination of web services that are commonly used in IoT together with a wireless image player to update the digital picture frame dynamically and seamlessly from a smartphone.

Getting ready

The materials needed are as follows:

▸ A smartphone with internet connectivity

▸ The BBB powered by 5V

▸ A Wi-Fi dongle

▸ An LCD (5 inches or larger)

You will also need to set up two web service accounts:

▸ **Dropbox**: The free plan is adequate (http://www.dropbox.com)

▸ **IFTTT**: This is a free service (http://www.ifttt.com)

Using IFTTT

For this recipe, we will incorporate the **If This Then That** (**IFTTT**) web service. Although not perfect, IFTTT is a fun, rapid development tool for prototyping IoT scenarios and use cases. There are other ways to perform what I will outline later; you could hook up other popular third-party apps, such as Instagram, Flickr, and Twitter. However, I prefer to keep the additional installations at a minimum and establish more of a least common denominator environment that provides a simpler development path.

For long-term serious product builds, IFTTT is not a good choice because it is too "black box", too opaque in its functionality to rely on for final designs. However, for rapid protoyping and idea generating, it is highly useful. With IFTTT, you can iterate quickly and nimbly using a host of different web services that will always lead to new ideas and directions for your development.

How to do it...

Part one: The smartphone setup

Perform the following steps:

1. On your smartphone, shoot a photograph with a camera app.
2. Save the photo to a custom album on your phone that you need to create. Name it `NowPix`.
3. Set up the IFTTT trigger on your phone to send the saved album file to Dropbox.

Setting up and testing the Dropbox script on the BBB

Perform the following steps:

1. If you do not already have a Dropbox account, sign up for a free account at `https://www.dropbox.com/home`.

2. Download and install a custom bash script called Dropbox Uploader. This is a wonderfully useful open source tool created by developer Andrea Fabrizi. The script provides an easy method to interact directly with the Dropbox's API authentication process, so providing your username and password is not necessary.

3. Now, make sure that you are in your home directory:

   ```
   $ cd
   ```

4. Then, clone the Dropbox Uploader code using the following command:

   ```
   $ git clone https://github.com/andreafabrizi/Dropbox-Uploader/
   ```

5. Make sure that the directory was created, as shown in the following command:

   ```
   $ cd Dropbox-Uploader
   ```

6. Set permissions with the following command:

   ```
   $chmod +x dropbox_uploader.sh
   $./dropbox_uploader.sh
   ```

7. Then, run the script as follows:

   ```
   ~/Dropbox-Uploader$ ./dropbox_uploader.sh
   ```

   You should see the screen output with a set of instructions:

   ```
   This is the first time you run this script.
   ```

Back to your desktop client

Before responding to the terminal prompts, you will now need to set up a Dropbox App via your desktop client (PC or Mac). This app will hook to the Dropbox Uploader script.

Perform the following steps:

1. Open the following URL on the desktop in your browser and log in using your Dropbox account at `https://www2.dropbox.com/developers/apps`.

2. Click on **Create App** and then select the **Dropbox API** app.

3. Select **Files and Datastores.** The rest of the fields should be filled out in the following manner:

    Can your app be limited to its own folder?

    `No`

    What type of files does your app need access to?

    `Specific file types—My app only needs access to certain file types, like text or photos.`

    Last question, what type of files will your app use?

    `Images`

4. Give the app a name in the last text field. Mine is called `NowPix` to remain consistent with the directory/album name that we set up on the iPhone. Then, finish by clicking on the **Create App** button.

5. Now, generate an App key.

Back to the BBB

The next series of steps continue with the verification/authentication process using Dropbox. Perform the following steps:

1. In the open terminal window and at the appropriate prompt, paste the App Key generated in the previous step and follow the onscreen prompts.

2. When your new app is successfully created, enter the App Key, App Secret, and the permission type shown in the confirmation page as follows:

    `# App Key: YOUR_API_KEY_HERE`

3. Hit the return (*Enter*) key after you input the appropriate data, given the next several terminal prompts.

Now, App Secret has been generated. Cut and paste that string from the Dropbox to the terminal window, as shown in the following code:

```
# App secret abcdefghijklmnop1234

Permission type, App folder or Full Dropbox [a/f]:

App folder (f)

App key is abcdefghijklmnop1234, App secret isabcdefghijklmnop1234
and Access level is Full Dropbox. Looks ok? [y/n]:

[y/n]: y
```

Hit return and you are finished at least with the installation.

> If you accidentally input the wrong App Key and App Secret (which I did since I have several Dropbox apps), you can reset the access by running the following script:
>
> ```
> $ ./dropbox_uploader.sh unlink
> ```

Testing and running the script

We now need to verify that the script operates as expected: downloading images from Dropbox and placing them in a specified directory.

1. First, we will verify that the content of our IFTTT directory on the Dropbox can be accessed and read properly, so we will list the images that are there:

   ```
   $ cd Dropbox-Uploader
   $ ./dropbox_uploader.sh list /IFTTT/iOS_Photos/NowPix
   ```

2. Go get the actual images and download them to your directory using the following command:

   ```
   $ ./dropbox_uploader.sh download -s /Apps/NowPix /home/debian/
   NowPix
   ```

   We added the -s option that skips the already existing files when you download/upload; otherwise, the default parameter is to overwrite the files in the target directory.

3. Verify that you did, in fact, get the images with the following command:

   ```
   $ cd NowPix
   $ ls
   ```

4. Assuming that your script executed properly and the images were downloaded to the right directory, we now need to set up a process in order for the script to run transparently so that you don't have to run it each time you want to download images. To perform this, we will set up a `cron` job that automatically runs the script at specified intervals. We will begin this part by opening `crontab` in our default editor with the following command:

```
$ crontab -e
```

The `-e` option tells the shell to open our default editor, which in our case is `nano`.

> You should take note of these comments from the original script developer:
>
> ## Running as `cron` job
>
> Dropbox Uploader relies on a different configuration file for each system user. The default configuration file location is `HOME_DIRECTORY/.dropbox_uploader`. This means that if you do the setup with your user and then try to run a `cron` job as root, it will not work.
>
> So, when you run this script using `cron`, keep the following things in mind:
>
> Remember to set up the script that the user used to run the `cron` job.
>
> Always use the `-f` option to specify the full configuration file path because sometimes in the `cron` environment, the home folder path is not detected correctly.
>
> For security reasons, I recommend you to not share the same configuration file with different users.

5. Add the following code to the end of the file that opens on your screen:

```
*/3 * * * * /home/debian/Dropbox-Uploader/dropbox_uploader.sh -s
download /IFTTT/iOS_Photos/NowPix /home/debian/
```

The number 3 is the frequency in which the `cron` job will run, which in our case is every 3 minutes. We have it set for such a high frequency only for testing purposes. When we are finished with our testing, you should change this number to a higher one, perhaps every few hours or longer, depending on how often you plan to add photos to your `NowPix` digital picture frame.

The rest of the line with all the asterisks corresponds to the following layout for a `cron` job:

```
minute (0-59), hour (0-23, 0 = midnight), day (1-31), month (1-
12), weekday (0-6, 0 = Sunday), command
```

6. With `cron`, it is a good idea to verify that the job has run as expected. You can perform this easily with the following command that checks an e-mail file that `crontab` automatically runs once a `cron` job has been set up:

```
$ tail -f /var/mail/debian
```

You should see a log of the system e-mails that `crontab` will send, including the output from the `downloader.sh` script. This output should mirror the kind of output you saw when you were running the earlier bash script in the terminal window.

7. Next, we need to install and set up a package that will open and cycle the images that we will download on the BBB. For this, we will use `feh`, a lightweight and powerful image viewer, as shown in the following code:

```
$ sudo apt-get update
$ sudo apt-get install feh
```

8. `feh` requires `-x` so that you can run the app remotely via vnc as follows:

```
$ feh -x
```

9. Now, we can view all our photos taken on our smartphone as a slide show:

```
$ feh -FD10 /home/debian/NowPix
```

FD is the command to run a slideshow, whereas the number after FD is an adjustable play duration for the image.

The program must also point to the directory with the images that will run as a slideshow. Use the *Esc* button on your desktop to exit from the slideshow.

You may see another permissions-related error when you try to execute the `feh` program. The error may say something similar to the following code:

```
Invalid MIT-MAGIC-COOKIE-1
```

If so, run the following command to delete the `.Xauthority` file:

```
$ rm .Xauthority*
```

10. Next, we will create a systemd service (remember that?!) that runs the command to load the images and display them in a loop on bootup. So, log in as root, as shown in the following code:

```
$ sudo -i
```

11. Navigate to the systemd directory with the following code:

```
# cd /lib/systemd/system
```

12. Now, create a new service file as follows:

    ```
    # sudo nano nowpix.service
    ```

13. Then, paste the following code to the editor window:

    ```
    [Unit]
    Description=Run NowPix images using Feh on boot

    [Service]
    Type=simple
    ExecStart=/usr/bin/feh -FD10 /home/debian/NowPix
    Environment=DISPLAY=:0
    SyslogIdentifier=fehslideshow
    Restart=on-failure
    RestartSec=5

    [Install]
    WantedBy=multi-user.target
    ```

14. Start the systemd service with the following code:

    ```
    # systemctl start nowpix.service
    ```

15. Finally, run the following command that enables the service to start at bootup:

    ```
    # systemctl enable nowpix.service
    ```

16. Now, reboot your BBB. If all is well, you should now have pictures cycling on your screen updated from your new photos on your smartphone.

See also

Crontabs is a bigger subject to learn and useful in many scenarios, where you want to time events on your BBB. For more information, refer to:

▶ https://help.ubuntu.com/community/CronHowto
▶ http://www.unixgeeks.org/security/newbie/unix/cron-1.html

9
The Black in Outer Space

In this chapter, we will cover the following recipes:

- Grabbing the International Space Station flyover data and visualizing it
- Tracking using RTL-SDR
- Airplane tracking with RTL-SDR
- Satellite tracking using GPredict and RTL-SDR
- Satellite tracking using the SatNogs Network client / ground station and RTL-SDR
- Adding other interfaces – ISS tracking and text to speech

Introduction

There are thousands of satellite "birds" up there. Buzzing around at all hours of the day and night—whether commercial, military, or educational—these satellites send and receive data from professional and amateur ground stations around the globe. And as satellites get cheaper, the number of them has proliferated, leading to an increasing problem for potential catastrophic collisions in space.

Tracking all that activity is a challenge. So, why not employ your own BBB in this endeavor?

Amateur satellite watchers have been around nearly since the dawn of Sputnik, an activity that fell under the rubric of ham radio, or HamSat. Nowadays, there is a host of interesting tools available that play nicely on Linux as well as microcomputers, such as BeagleBone Black.

For your smartphone alone, you can find dozens of free, downloadable tracking apps. Given their basic purpose—telling you when a satellite might pass nearby or passively receiving basic monitoring data—they deliver quick hits of excitement. However, these apps are limited in functionality, flexibility, and purpose. What we want to do is stretch what's possible to track a satellite, bringing this information and data down to Earth in a more pliable form so that you can explore other useful and creative purposes for it.

So, to begin our satellite tracking adventures, we will begin with easy recipes. Then, we will continue with more advanced scenarios and robust tools that will give you greater control over the variety of data that you capture and simultaneously amp up user experience.

Grabbing the International Space Station flyover data and visualizing it

The easiest scenario of all begins by piggybacking on preexisting web services and then making the interaction a little more interesting by combining it with some tasks executed by BeagleBone Black.

IFTTT for the ISS

We used the IFTTT web service in our previous chapter to provide part of the machinery to send photos captured on our smartphone. Here, we will use it to help us track the **International Space Station** (**ISS**), but we will take the interaction a bit further.

Getting ready

The materials needed are as follows:

▸ The BBB, headless or connected to an external monitor and tethered over USB with Ethernet (or Wi-Fi, if you choose)

▸ A smartphone with cell or Internet connectivity

How to do it...

Perform the following steps:

1. The easiest, most basic way to get the ISS's flyover data is by signing up for SMS alerts from NASA's website at `http://spotthestation.nasa.gov/index.cfm`.

   The first few times you get the alert, it is a thrill to know when you can potentially go outside and watch the space station fly over your head. Here is a typical message showing the directional data points:

Subject:SpotTheStation

Time: Tue Apr 21 8:18 PM, Visible: 4 min, Max Height: 80 degrees, Appears: NW, Disappears: SE

Soon, however, you may want to do more with this information. To do this, the next steps will build on recipe of pulling images into a rotating "screensaver" cycle using the `feh` package from *Chapter 8, The Internet of Things*. However this time, we will use fresh space imagery. Additionally, we will add ingredients to grab flyover data and display it.

So, let's slightly modify the steps and code from the earlier chapter.

2. From your smartphone, go to the IFTTT Space Channel (`https://ifttt.com/space`) and activate the version according to whether you use an Android or iPhone.

3. Once you've done this, IFTTT suggests useful trigger pairings, "This channel goes well with...". Choose **Google Drive** as the pairing.

4. Activate the following two triggers:

   Add NASA's Image of the Day to my Dropbox

   Log each time the ISS passes overhead to a Google Docs spreadsheet

   Now, we will tweak our Dropbox Uploader script and `cron` jobs from the last chapter. As a reminder, the `cron` job looks for a new image file in Dropbox at specified intervals and cycles it into a `feh` image playback queue on your screen, while the Dropbox Uploader script actually downloads new images into a specified directory on your BBB.

   So, if you successfully executed the recipe for NowPix in Chapter 8, *The Internet of Things*, proceed to the next steps. Otherwise, return to Chapter 8, *The Internet of Things*, and follow the steps to download and display the images.

5. Create a `Space` directory on your BBB that mirrors your `Space` directory created by IFTTT on your Dropbox account using the following command:

   ```
   $ mkdir Space
   ```

6. Now, confirm that the content of your IFTTT directory on Dropbox can be accessed and read properly; list the images that are there. This is why we put a dummy image here in an earlier step, as follows:

   ```
   $ cd Dropbox-Uploader
   $ ./dropbox_uploader.sh list /IFTTT/Space
   ```

   Your terminal output should look similar to this:

   ```
   > Listing "/IFTTT/Space"... DONE
     [F] sample_image_name_here.jpg
   ```

7. Download the actual images to your BBB's directory with the following command:

```
$ ./dropbox_uploader.sh download -s /IFTTT/Space /home/debian/
Space
```

Your terminal output should look similar to this:

```
> Download "/IFTTT/Space"... DONE
 [F] sample_image_name_here.jpg
```

8. Check that you did, in fact, get the images through the following code:

```
$ cd NowPix
$ ls
```

9. Set up a `cron` job (refer to the prior chapter for more information on running a `cron` job) to run the downloader script, as follows:

```
$ crontab -e
```

10. Append the open file with the following line:

```
*/3 * * * * /home/debian/Dropbox-Uploader/dropbox_uploader.sh -s
download /IFTTT/Soace /home/debian/Space
```

Next, we want to have our space images display on screen whenever a new one is added. This will use `feh`, the package we explored in *Chapter 8, The Internet of Things*. So, if you successfully executed the recipe for NowPix in previous chapter, proceed to the next step. Otherwise, return to *Chapter 8, The Internet of Things* and follow these steps to use `feh`.

11. Modify the `feh` script accordingly:

```
$ feh -FD10 /home/debian/Space
```

12. Next, we want our BBB to parse the flyover time data—both archived and near future—and turn it into nice, visual displays. So, at this point, we will depart from the earlier steps and add a powerful data visualization library used in Python, `matplotlib`. We will also add the `basemap` library, which extends the functionality of `matplotlib` by adding a toolkit to plot 2D data on maps in Python.

So now, install the Python libraries as follows:

```
$ sudo apt-get install python-matplotlib
$ sudo apt-get install python-mpltoolkits.basemap
```

13. Create a python file that will serve as our test ISS tracking tool based on the output from the spreadsheet that we will generate on Dropbox using the following command:

```
$ sudo nano iss_track1.py
```

14. From our Github repo, download the code for this recipe with this command:

```
$ git clone https://github.com/HudsonWerks/space-satellite.git
```

15. Browse the new directory and open up the following tile:

```
$ cd space-satellite
$ sudo nano iss_track1.py
```

Take a look at the opened code. It piggybacks on the wonderful Open-Notify API developed by rocket maker and satellite wonk, Nathan Bergey, and is nicely commented and broken down into clear sections, including a call to an API, the visual map projection code, the color values for the map, the coordinates that we want to track, and the timing for the data updates.

16. If you are running headless, we will use a method here that you may not be familiar with, called *X-session*. This is basically an SSH remote session that can run X-commands and load graphical windows within your regular SSH terminal. So, on your desktop client box, open up another terminal window, this time with the following:

```
$ ssh -X debian@<ip-address_here>
```

17. Run the Python script:

```
$ sudo python iss_track1.py
```

You may encounter the following error:

```
File "/usr/lib/python2.7/lib-tk/Tkinter.py", line 1712, in __
init__
self.tk = _tkinter.create(screenName, baseName, className,
interactive, wantobjects, useTk, sync, use)
tkinter.TclError: no display name and no $DISPLAY environment
variable
```

If so, here is how you can fix it:

```
$ sudo xauth add `xauth list`
```

If all goes as expected, your screen output (over the X-session terminal) will look similar to this:

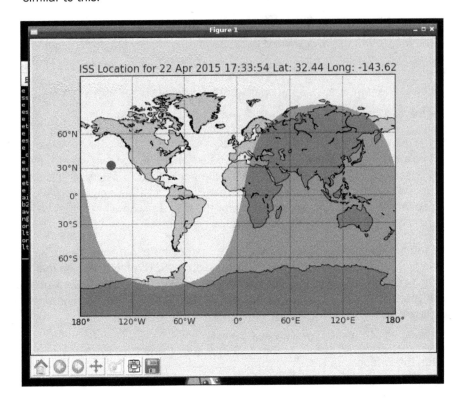

The blue dot shows the current location of the ISS with its coordinates updated every minute.

18. Quit the script by pressing *Ctrl + C*.

There's more...

High definition camera views from the ISS can be found at:

- http://eol.jsc.nasa.gov/ForFun/HDEV/
- http://columbuseye.uni-bonn.de/

Tracking using RTL-SDR

One of the more exciting add-ons to our BBB satellite and object tracking recipes is an extremely low-cost USB dongle called RTL-SDR. RTL is short for Realtek RTL2832U controller and tuner chipset, which is inside this dongle and can be purchased for around USD $20.00.

Besides being cheap, the best part of the story is SDR, which stands for **Software Defined Radio**. SDR is kind of what it sounds similar to: instead of using hardware components, such as amps, mixers, filters, and modulators, it is radio with its key functions driven by software.

SDR can receive signals over a very wide band of frequencies (for example, from 50 to 2500 MHz) without actually requiring specialized hardware. Using various software modules, SDR also performs different radio protocols. The result is that this software—in conjunction with an RTL dongle—now replaces what used to be a wide variety of specialized radio components.

For radio enthusiasts (including old school ham radio operators) and hackers alike, the flexibility of SDR is compelling; you can now transmit and monitor anything across a vast radio spectrum from cordless phones to Bluetooth devices, microwave ovens, car alarms, video devices, ZigBee, airplanes, and even satellites.

The RTL-SDR dongle

See also

SDR is a large topic and we will only explore a handful of recipes using it. You can learn more about its applications at the principal source for all things related to RTL-SDR at http://www.rtl-sdr.com/about-rtl-sdr/.

Because of its many uses, certain applications of SDR and similar radio scanners may be illegal in some countries. Before proceeding with any of the following recipes, ensure that you will not encounter any restrictions on usage at https://en.wikipedia.org/wiki/Scanner_%28radio%29#Legislation.

Airplane tracking with RTL-SDR

Before diving into some of the more challenging and arcane "upper atmosphere" options to use RTL-SDR, we will do a recipe that's a little easier and more down to Earth, namely tracking planes.

This recipe is derived from a variety of sources, including David Scheltema's tutorial on Make Magazine (`http://makezine.com/projects/tracking-planes-with-rtl-sdr/`), which is a Debian variation on an RPi version. It also comes via the posts of David Taylor of Edinburgh, Scotland (`satsignal.eu/raspberry-pi/dump1090.html`) and Drew Fustini of Chicago, Illinois (`element14.com/community/community/designcenter/single-board-computers/blog/2014/04/07/sdr-and-sbc-cheap-thrills-with-radio-waves`) for Angstrom on the BBB. Additionally, Adafruit has a lesson for the RPi, which either borrows from or is inspired by the references mentioned before. All of these miss some steps, however, to make it fly on the current BeagleBone Black Debian distros, be it Wheezy or Jessie.

Getting ready

Here are the materials needed:

- The RTL-SDR dongle.
- An antenna—You could spend hundreds of dollars on this part of your kit. However, there are numerous low-cost and plenty powerful antennas that will get you a good signal for all of our recipes. Here, we use a Diamond antenna (`http://www.aesham.com/glass/magnet/diamond-antenna-mr-75s/`), and it only costs USD $38.00.
- An antenna adapter—If you use an antenna other than the small one that often comes with the dongle, such as the one mentioned before, you will need to buy a separate adapter. Don't worry! They're cheap, too, and ours was only about USD $6.00 (`http://amzn.to/1WoB7Lq`).
- Powered USB.
- Ethernet or Wi-Fi connectivity.

How to do it...

Perform the following steps:

1. Attach the antenna to the RTL-SDR dongle via the USML adapter.
2. Power your BBB via a 5V power supply, plug the SDR dongle directly into the USB port, and connect via Ethernet.

3. Always ensure that your packages are up to date; let's upgrade them here using the following command:

```
$ sudo apt-get update && sudo apt-get upgrade
```

4. Check that the dongle is recognized with this command:

```
$ lsusb
```

The output should look similar to this, with the Realtek SDR dongle appearing:

```
Bus 001 Device 002: ID 0bda:2838 Realtek Semiconductor Corp.
RTL2838 DVB-T
Bus 001 Device 001: ID 1d6b:0002 Linux Foundation 2.0 root hub
Bus 002 Device 001: ID 1d6b:0002 Linux Foundation 2.0 root hub
```

5. Log in as root with this command:

```
# sudo -i
```

6. As we will create a stripped-down firmware toolset for RTL-SDR here, we need to compile software from source files. We first need to install cmake, a tool that we came across in an earlier chapter. As a reminder, cmake is an alternative method to build packages and can be installed as follows:

```
# apt-get install cmake
```

7. Then, install the USB library for RTL-SDR, as follows:

```
# apt-get install libusb-1.0-0-dev
```

8. Next, we will grab the RTL-SDR library and configure and compile it with make. The last command here will take a few minutes to complete:

```
# git clone git://git.osmocom.org/rtl-sdr.git
# cd rtl-sdr
# cmake ./ -DINSTALL_UDEV_RULES=ON
# make
```

9. Now, install it with the following command:

```
# make install
```

10. Head back up to the root directory, where we need to bring the aircraft scanner-specific package on board. This requires another series of downloading, setting up, and installing ingredients, which goes as follows:

```
# cd
# git clone https://github.com/antirez/dump1090.git
# cd dump1090
# make
```

11. Configure the path for the shared libraries:

```
# echo "/usr/local/lib/" >> /etc/ld.so.conf
```

12. Let's run a test, ensuring that we are in the `dump1090` directory:

```
# cd /home/debian/dump1090
# ./dump1090
```

If your RTL dongle/scanner is operating as it should, the command will begin quickly dumping any nearby aircraft to standard output. If you use the small antenna that came with your dongle, its range will be very limited. Press *Ctrl + C* to interrupt the command.

13. The last step is to put this galloping data in an easier-to-read format. In the terminal window, paste the following command:

```
$ ./dump1090 --interactive --net --net-http-port 8081
```

This last command and its options tell `dump1090` to begin outputting data in a more viewable form. One version of this output is immediately visible in your terminal window, with the data refreshed continuously and sorted into tidy columns by flight number, altitude, speed of aircraft, latitude, and so on.

Even more interesting is the `--net-http-port 8081` option, which sends the data via HTTP to a specified port—in this case, the 8081 port. With this option enabled, we can open a browser and access a web page with some JavaScript, and the Google Map API is available as part of the installed package.

14. So, open a browser and paste the following address into the window using one of the following:

```
http://beaglebone.local:8081/
http://192.168.7.2:8081/
http://your_bbb_ip:8081/
```

You will immediately see a Google Map along with a sidebar window showing a rollup of the data. Move the map around until it is positioned at your current location, and you should see plane icons appearing. Clicking on an icon pulls this particular flight's data into the frame.

Watch the icons closely to see what kind of general range your receiver and antenna are getting before the aircraft disappears from the screen.

15. To quit the program, type *Ctrl + C* in the BBB's terminal window.

There's more...

▶ Check out the Raspberry Pi version of RTL-SDR used as a portable SDR scanner at `https://learn.adafruit.com/freq-show-raspberry-pi-rtl-sdr-scanner?view=all`.

▶ Public Lab has a wonderful write up describing how plane tracking using RTL-SDR yielded information about FBI's surveillance aircraft at `http://publiclab.org/notes/ajawitz/06-11-2015/raspberry-pi-as-marine-traffic-radar`.

Satellite tracking using GPredict and RTL-SDR

SatNOGS is an open source initiative to build a network of ground stations around the world to track satellites. Thousands of **low Earth orbit** (**LEO**) satellites are its principal focus. Its goal is to provide a toolset and tech stack (hardware and software) that is low cost and easy to build.

The project supports VHF and UHF bands for satellite reception with the default configuration. Its software automatically tracks, receives, and records satellites as they pass overhead while automatically scheduling observations and recording them to an online database shared among other participating ground observers.

For the purpose of simplicity, we will not cover how to build the whole hardware part of the system, which includes a high gain antenna, tracking motors, and a standard RTL-SDR dongle as a receiver. In our recipes, we will only use the dongle and a low-cost antenna. You are welcome to get more ambitious with the hardware. More details are at the SatNogs website (`https://satnogs.org/`).

Setting up the software stack requires two pieces: a satellite tracker and a ground station.

Satellite tracker

For the tracking software, they suggest one of two packages: either GPredict, a popular and venerable open source solution for satellite tracking and orbit prediction, or a custom open source client that the SatNogs team built in Python. The latter is more robust and interoperates more easily with the antenna and rotor mechanism. However, since we will not illustrate the build out of the rotor and the hardware parts of the system, we will do a recipe around GPredict.

Ground Station

On the ground station side, you could again use GPredict, which includes this kind of functionality. However, in our recipe we will build the SatNogs Network custom client as it lets us taste some new coding flavors. Once installed, the tool gives operators an efficient way to both plan their observations and combine their tracking data with multiple ground stations around the world.

GPredict

SatNogs suggests two tools for satellite tracking: their own custom package and GPredict. We will only look at how to use GPredict as this package is more widely used and can serve as a jumping off point for satellite tracking beyond just the SatNogs initiative.

Gpredict is a real-time satellite tracking and orbit prediction application that can track an unlimited number of satellites and display the data in tables and numerous graphical views. The application actually exists for more than just Linux distributions; it includes the Windows and Mac OS X versions. However, unlike the commercial OS versions, we will build a recipe set on our open source microcomputer that gives us greater flexibility on several fronts, such as the following:

- **Dedicated device**: A BBB SatNogs platform gives you the ability to create a dedicated satellite tracking device in lieu of turning over your desktop or laptop exclusively to satellite tracking.

- **Optimal placement**: The position of your ground station's antenna is critical as it impacts the quality of your data and experience. Creating a device that can be enclosed, protected, and positioned in a location optimized for better satellite tracking is a better long-term strategy than leaving your laptop on the roof of a building.

- **Custom alerts and signals**: A device that can deliver a custom signal indicating when the satellites are approaching opens up numerous possibilities for physical computing, IoT-enablement, and a more indelible user experience.

Getting ready

The following are the materials needed:

- An RTL-SDR dongle.

- An antenna—For the recommended low-cost antenna that we are using, see the Diamond antenna in the prior recipe on plane tracking (`http://www.aesham.com/glass/magnet/diamond-antenna-mr-75s/`). Attach the antenna to the RTL-SDR dongle via the uSML adapter.

- An antenna adapter—If you use an antenna other than the small one that often comes with the dongle, such as the one mentioned before, you will need to buy a separate adapter. Don't worry! They're cheap too, and ours was only about USD $6.00 (`http://amzn.to/1WoB7Lq`).

- Powered USB.

- Ethernet or Wi-Fi connectivity.

How to do it...

Here are the steps that you need to perform:

1. Install package dependencies through the following commands:

   ```
   $ sudo apt-get install automake build-essential make
   $ sudo apt-get install intltool libgoocanvas-dev
   $ sudo apt-get install libgtk2.0-dev libcurl4-openssl-dev
   ```

2. Grab the source file and untar it as follows:

   ```
   $ wget http://downloads.sourceforge.net/project/gpredict/
   Gpredict/1.3/gpredict-1.3.tar.gz
   $ tar -zxvf gpredict-x.y.z.tar.gz
   ```

3. Navigate to the new directory created with this command:

   ```
   $ cd gpredict-1.x
   ```

4. Run the usual steps to compile and install, as follows:

   ```
   $ sudo ./autogen.sh
   $ sudo ./configure
   $ sudo make && sudo make install
   ```

 We recommend downloading the GPredict manual at `http://sourceforge.net/projects/gpredict/files/Gpredict/1.3/gpredict-user-manual-1.3.pdf/download`.

5. Once you've got GPredict installed, you will want to use its graphical interface as it enjoys a robust GUI and is easier to operate than the command line. If you don't have an external monitor connected to your BBB, power down and then attach it. Alternatively, just continue headless and run GPredict via vncserver:

    ```
    $ vncserver
    ```

6. Open up GPredict. Then, update the **two-line element** (**TLE**) files. TLE is a format originated by NASA to display Keplerian elements. Commonly called Keps, these are sets of numbers allowing satellite tracking programs to calculate a satellite's position in space while giving us specific information about its orbit at a specific moment. Keps must be updated, however, which is easy to do in the **Update** menu.

> Here is an example of a Keplerian element for the International Space Station:
>
> 6 May, 2004
>
> ISS
>
> 1 25544U 98067A   04127.92349537 .00017095 00000-0 14786-3 0 7232
>
> 2 25544 51.6276 176.0525 0011067 106.0444 249.6038
>
> 15.69246258311835

7. GPredict uses the term "module" for what you use as your dataset of the satellites you want to track. So, create one by navigating to **File** | **Create New Module** | **MODULE NAME** | **.XX**.

8. From the little down arrow button in the upper-right corner of the screen, select **Clone**. This will create a clone of the module that you will customize and configure for this recipe.

9. Next, go to **Configure** | **Ground Station +** and give yours a name. Mine is NYC because that's where I live.

10. Determine your location, either using a preset value from the **Select** option or by filling in the **Latitude** and **Longitude** fields. I've done the latter to get a more precise location. Various websites can provide you with GPS coordinates. I used http://mygeoposition.com/ as it includes elevation as a variable.

11. Now, we want to choose our satellites. Although there are countless "birds" up there in the heavens, for simplicity's sake, we will stick with our touchstone, the ISS. If you cloned the module as described in the preceding steps, you will only need to remove the nonISS satellites as the ISS is already in the list. However, you may also choose from the more than 1200 satellites listed in the GPredict database.

12. Once you make your selection, the main window will begin populating the data with the ISS's position. There are numerous options to customize the views of your modules, which you can learn from the very thorough user manual.

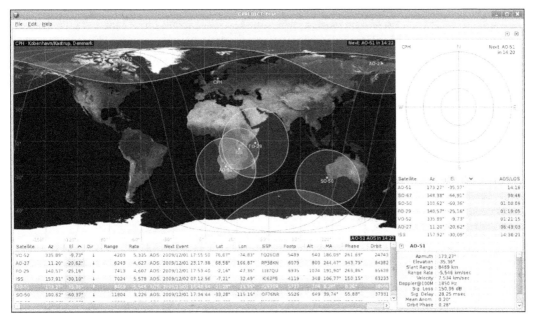

The Gpredict user interface

What a beautiful view you've got on your BBB!

There's more...

▶ To learn more about TLEs, the venerable Radio Amateur Satellite Organization, aka AMSAT, explains it well at `http://www.amsat.org/amsat-new/tools/keps_tutorial.php`.

▶ Other amateur and educational satellite tracking projects can be found at `http://funcube.org.uk/`.

Satellite tracking using the SatNogs Network client / ground station and RTL-SDR

In the previous recipe, we compiled and installed the part that actually tracks the satellite. Now, we need to add the piece of the system that allows us to manage the potential flood of data, share it with others, and have them share their data back with us.

Note that this has been tested successfully on Debian Wheezy (3.8) and Debian Jessie (13.4).

Getting ready

The materials needed are as follows:

- An RTL-SDR dongle.
- An antenna—for the recommended low-cost antenna that we are using, refer to the Diamond Antenna in the prior recipe on plane tracking (http://www.aesham.com/glass/magnet/diamond-antenna-mr-75s/).
- An antenna adapter—if you use an antenna other than the small one that often comes with the dongle, such as the one mentioned before, you will need to buy a separate adapter. Don't worry! They're cheap too, and ours was only about USD $6.00 (http://amzn.to/1WoB7Lq). Attach the antenna to the RTL-SDR dongle via the uSML adapter.
- Powered USB.
- Ethernet or Wi-Fi connectivity.

How to do it...

Here are the steps you need to perform:

1. Check that `pip` is installed and the package management system used to install and manage packages is written in Python through the following command:

   ```
   $ pip list
   ```

   As Python 2.7.9 and later versions (on the Python2 series) and Python 3.4 and later versions include `pip` by default, you may have pip already. If not, you can install it this way:

2. Download `get-pip.py` at https://bootstrap.pypa.io/get-pip.py.

3. Then, run the following:

   ```
   $ sudo python get-pip.py
   ```

4. Install package dependencies via the following command:

```
$ sudo pip install virtualenvwrapper
```

 virtualenv is a tool designated to address the problem of dealing with packages' dependencies while maintaining different versions for different projects. For example, if you work on two Python Django websites, one that uses Django 1.2 and another 0.96, there is no way to keep both versions if you install them into the standard `/usr/lib/python2/site-packages`. virtualenv creates two isolated environments.

`vitualenvwrapper` takes virtualenv a step further by providing commands that can be invoked from the terminal window.

5. So that your program knows where to find `virtualenvwrapper`, modify your bash profile with the following command:

```
$ sudo nano ~/.bashrc
```

6. At the end of the open file, append it with the following:

```
export WORKON_HOME=$HOME/.virtualenvs
source /usr/local/bin/virtualenvwrapper.sh
```

7. Reload the bash script with the following command:

```
$ sudo source ~/.bashrc
```

8. Time to install the dependencies. Use the following commands:

```
$ sudo apt-get install libxml2-dev libxslt1-dev python-dev
$ sudo pip install django
$ sudo pip install django-dotenv
```

9. Now, it's time to get the custom package created by the SatNogs team. First, we will clone the source code from the repository as follows:

```
$ git clone https://github.com/satnogs/satnogs-network.git
```

10. Set up the virtual environment. On the first run, you should create it and link it to your project path. The following commands will do this:

```
$ cd satnogs-network
$ mkvirtualenv satnogs-network -a .
```

(Note the . symbol at the end of the command, and don't use `sudo`.)

11. Set your environmental variables as follows:

```
(satnogs-network)debian@beaglebone:~/satnogs-network$ cp .env-dist
.env
```

 Take note that you are now in a virtual directory (satnogs-network)
debian@beaglebone:~/satnogs-network$

12. Activate your python virtual environment with the following command:

```
$ workon satnogs-network
```

13. Install the local development requirements as follows:

```
$ pip install -r requirements/dev.txt
```

This step may take a while and consume most of your BBB's resources as it downloads, compiles, and installs the development platform to share your SatNog tracking data.

14. Create and set up the database with the following command:

```
$ sudo ./manage.py migrate
```

15. We are nearly there now. Create a superuser using this command:

```
$ ./manage.py createsuperuser
```

Follow the prompts to input a username, e-mail address, and password.

16. Next, we will add some demo data into the database so that there is something to look at the end of the road as follows:

```
$ ./manage.py initialize
```

17. Whew! Time to run the server. Use the following command:

```
$ sudo ./manage.py runserver your_ip_address_here:8000
```

If you experience problems getting the browser to resolve an address, shut down the server (by pressing *Ctrl + C*), and rerun the command with the following network address:

```
$ sudo ./manage.py runserver 0.0.0.0:8000
```

The address, 0.0.0.0, allows you to reach the server from any machine in your network.

18. And now the last stop: open up a browser on your desktop machine to the IP address and the port you used in the previous step. The SatNogs Network web-based GUI should open with a variety of functions for starting a satellite tracking project.

    You can sign up as a Ground Station operator by first confirming your user credentials. Look in the terminal window for the following output, which contains a verification link:

    User <NAME> at example.com has given this as an email address.

    To confirm this is correct, go to http://your_ip_address_here:8000/accounts/confirm-email/generated_string_here/

19. Once you've validated your email address, you can add a Ground station on the SatNog Network (`https://network-dev.satnogs.org/`) similar to the ones in the following screenshot:

Now, the next time you reboot or shut down the server and the `virtualenv` environment and want to run SatNogs again, just jump right to the following three main steps, and you will be off to the races:

```
$ cd satnogs-network
$ workon satnogs-network
$ sudo ./manage.py runserver your_ip_address:8000
```

Adding other interfaces – ISS tracking and text to speech

It's time to make the dog talk. Or, at least, make BeagleBone Black a little more verbal. Here, we will show you the ingredients to have the board tell us—instead of showing us—when the International Space Station is getting close.

Getting ready

The materials needed are:

- A USB Audio dongle—We will use an inexpensive, low-profile version (`http://bit.ly/1KxQatr`), though any USB version is fine
- An audio speaker with a mini jack that plugs into the audio dongle
- A USB-powered hub
- A 5V power supply
- An Internet connection, Ethernet or Wi-Fi

Power up your BBB via the 5V supply, open a terminal window on your client box, then SSH into the board.

How to do it...

There are five parts to this recipe:

- Audio setup and testing
- Installing Text to Speech (TTS) and testing
- Python coding to calculate the ISS's current distance from you
- Bash scripting
- Doing a `cron` job to automatically run all of these

Part I: Audio Setup and testing

Perform the following steps:

1. Although you may have some of these tools on board your BBB already, we should check to make sure. The following commands will be useful:

   ```
   $ sudo apt-get update
   $ sudo apt-get install alsa-base alsa-utils
   $ sudo apt-get install mplayer
   ```

2. Check that the system sees your audio dongle with this command:

```
$ lsusb
Bus 001 Device 002: ID 1a40:0201 Terminus Technology Inc. FE 2.1
7-port Hub
Bus 001 Device 001: ID 1d6b:0002 Linux Foundation 2.0 root hub
Bus 002 Device 001: ID 1d6b:0002 Linux Foundation 2.0 root hub
Bus 001 Device 003: ID 0d8c:013c C-Media Electronics, Inc. CM108
Audio Controller
```

3. Take a look at which audio devices are available through the following command:

```
$ aplay -l



**** List of PLAYBACK Hardware Devices ****
card 0: Black [TI BeagleBone Black], device 0: HDMI hdmi-hifi-0 []
   Subdevices: 0/2
   Subdevice #0: subdevice #0


card 1: Device [USB PnP Sound Device], device 1: USB Audio [USB
Audio]
   Subdevices: 1/2
   Subdevice #1: subdevice #1
```

4. On the BBB, ALSA gives preference to the HDMI port's audio channel, which we need to change to the USB sound dongle. First, we have to disable the HDMI audio output with this command:

```
$ sudo nano /boot/uEnv.txt
```

Edit the following line:

```
##Disable HDMI
#cape_disable=capemgr.disable_partno=BB-BONELT-HDMI,BB-BONELT-
HDMIN
```

After editing, the preceding line should look similar to this:

```
##Disable HDMI
cape_disable=capemgr.disable_partno=BB-BONELT-HDMI,BB-BONELT-HDMIN
```

5. Save the open file (by pressing *Ctrl + O*) and then enter and exit `nano` (by pressing *Ctrl + X*).

6. Next, we will modify the ALSA configuration file so that it recognizes our audio dongle as the default device:

```
$ sudo nano /etc/modprobe.d/alsa-base.conf
```

7. Duplicate the following line:

```
# Keep snd-usb-audio from being loaded as first soundcard
options snd-usb-audio index=-2
```

8. Then, comment out one of the lines and change -2 to 0 in the uncommented line:

```
# Keep snd-usb-audio from being loaded as first soundcard
#options snd-usb-audio index=-2
options snd-usb-audio index=0
```

9. Save the open file (by pressing *Ctrl + O*) and then enter and exit `nano` (by pressing *Ctrl + X*).

10. Reboot your BBB with this line:

```
$ sudo reboot
```

11. Verify that the HDMI audio is no longer present and that only the USB dongle appears by pasting this command:

```
$ aplay -l^s
**** List of PLAYBACK Hardware Devices ****
card 0: Device [USB PnP Sound Device], device 0: USB Audio [USB Audio]
Subdevices: 1/1
Subdevice #0: subdevice #0
```

12. Confirm that it loaded properly and is available to ALSA with this command:

```
$ cat /proc/asound/cards
 0 [Device         ]: USB-Audio - USB PnP Sound Device
         C-Media Electronics Inc. USB PnP Sound Device at usb-musb-hdrc.1.auto-1.5, full
```

13. Open up `alsamixer` so that we can tweak the volume settings. You should see your sound dongle as the default device in the upper-left corner of the GUI:

```
$ alsamixer
```

Choose the **Speaker** option and use the up arrow to increase the volume:

The Alsamixer window

14. Close the window with the *Esc* key.

15. Do a simple test to check audio output with the following command:

```
$ aplay /usr/share/sounds/alsa/Front_Center.wav -D
sysdefault:CARD=0
```

You should hear the nice lady say in English "Front. Center."

Whew! Not exactly Plug and Play, but that's open source for you....

Part II: Installing TTS

Let's move along to making the BBB speak using the text-to-speech (TTS) engine, SVOX Pico. Although there are other TTS options available, such as E-Speak, Festival, and Google Voice (referenced at the end of this recipe), Pico's quality is better than most and does not require a cloud connection:

1. As it is not available in the Debian repos for ARM devices, we need to install SVOX Pico from source. First, however, we need to ensure that we have all dependencies with these commands:

```
$ sudo apt-get update
$ sudo apt-get install automake libtool libpopt-dev
```

2. Now, we can install the source files using these commands. It is not too lengthy an install; it takes perhaps around five minutes to complete:

```
$ git clone -b upstream+patches git://git.debian.org/collab-maint/
svox.git svox-pico
$ cd svox-pico
$ cd pico
$ automake
$ sudo automake
$ ./autogen.sh
$ ./configure
$ sudo make all
$ sudo make install
$ sudo ldconfig
```

3. Run a sample text to speech test using two different audio playback tools, `mplayer`, which we just installed, or `aplay`, which is already on our system:

```
$ pico2wave -w test.wav "This is Ground Control" | mplayer -ao
alsa:device=hw=0 test.wav
```

Take note of the various settings and options needed to run the package properly. Pico2wave uses wav files, so we will first use the -w option and then the filename that we will create. This will be followed by the actual text that will be recorded and spoken. The last options are those to choose a playback tool (in this case, `mplayer`), set the right device, and then call the filename just recorded.

Alternatively, we can use another audio package: `aplay`. Although it is not as full featured as `mplay`, it is easier to use as it requires fewer settings. Run the following command for this:

```
$ pico2wave -w test.wav "This is Ground Control" && aplay test.wav
```

Regardless of the player you use, you should get a female speaker saying This is Ground Control in the English language out of your speaker. You can change the output, of course, including the speaker's language, as long as it is English (UK or US), German, Italian, French, or Spanish.

Part III: Python coding to calculate the ISS's current distance from your location

Next, we will use some Python code to track the International Space Station.

1. If you did the earlier recipe in this book with GPredict to track the ISS, you would already have the repo downloaded. If not, get it from our GitHub repo and then browse the directory as follows:

    ```
    $ git clone https://github.com/HudsonWerks/space-satellite.git
    ```

    ```
    $ cd space-satellite
    ```

2. Let's take a look at what the code does. You can open it up in a nano editor window by running this command:

    ```
    $ sudo nano ISS_current_distance.py
    ```

    Alternatively, you can copy and paste the code into a new Cloud9 file.

    For simplicity's sake, we will use a different set of code to track the ISS than we did an earlier recipe in this chapter. Here, we do not want to run an X-session as in the previous example; instead, we want to focus on an alternative user interface. However, a good exercise would be to combine the two pieces of code into one so that you can exploit both TTS and a graphical rendering of the ISS location in the same script.

    The code is heavily commented and pared down to only output the current distance from the latitude and longitude coordinates you set and stop once the task is completed. . In fact, before moving on, you must input your home latitude and longitude coordinates in the designated code blocks in order for the script to run:

    ```
    home_lat = HOME_LATITUDE
    ```

    ```
    home_long = HOME_LONGITUDE
    ```

3. After inputting your coordinates, save the modified code then run it:

    ```
    $ sudo python ISS_current_distance.py
    ```

    You should see a multidecimal number showing the current kilometer distance from your coordinates (your number will vary, naturally):

    ```
    3631.37279398
    ```

The output is a little underwhelming, isn't it? However, this is by design; it does not keep updating the number as we run the script according to specified intervals, and we want the TTS engine to capture a snapshot in real time of the ISS's location relative to where you are.

Part IV: Creating a bash script

To create a more interesting experience, we will have a bash script run the Python code, stamp the time, and tell us all about it via the TTS engine:

1. Open up a `nano` editor window and create a new file, as follows:

   ```
   $ sudo nano timeTTS-ISS.sh
   ```

2. Copy and paste the following bash code in the open window:

   ```
   #!/bin/bash

   # Create a variable that will run the Python script
   ISS=$(sudo python /home/debian/ISS-current-distance.py)


   # Create a variable that will grab the current UTC time, combine
   it with the output from the Python script, and include the text
   that we want the TTS engine to speak
   NOW=$(date +"Ground Control time is %M minutes past %l %p U T C
   with current distance to the International Space Station $ISS
   miles")


   echo $NOW


   # Run the TTS against the variable we created, and then play it
   back
   pico2wave -w GroundControlTime-ISS.wav "$NOW"
   aplay GroundControlTime-ISS.wav
   ```

   The comments are pretty self-explanatory; two variables are created: one to run the Python file and the other to do a current timestamp. After this, combine the variables together into a TTS audio file that is played back.

    Be careful not to truncate code that you copy and paste either in or out of a `nano` window.

3. Make the file executable with the following command:

   ```
   $ sudo chmod +x timeTTS-ISS.sh
   ```

Part V: Setting up a cron job

We want to automate the use of the bash and python scripts so that we can get continuous readings and feedback without having to manually start them:

1. Set up a `cron` job so that the script will run on a schedule. We have not done this for several chapters, so here is what we will do:

    ```
    $ sudo crontab -e
    ```

2. Copy and paste the following line at the bottom of the open window:

    ```
    */30 * * * * sudo bash /home/debian/timeTTS-ISS.sh
    ```

    This will run our script at 30-minute intervals. Change `30` to `1` in order to test it right away.

We've done it! A talking BeagleBone Black that captures dynamically generated tracking data and tells us when the International Space Station gets within striking distance!

There's more...

Text to Speech

> ►   The TTS options on Rpi, most of which can be ported to the BBB, can be found at `http://elinux.org/RPi_Text_to_Speech_(Speech_Synthesis)`.

> ►   E-Speak—For install and setup instructions, refer to `http://hudsonwerks.com/beaglebone-black-recipes/voice-recognition-tts/`.

> ►   Festival—This is a quick and easy option, commonly used on Rpi, with various tutorials available.

> ►   Google Voice—This is a great reference for higher quality voices and variety. However, the engine is cloud-based, so you need continuous internet access to use it. Additionally, Google will often throttle usage from scripts by pinging the service, so you may encounter difficulties using it.

Voice recognition

The other leg of a voice user interface is voice recognition, which is beyond the scope of this book. However, several tutorials are out there for both the BBB and the RPi that can take you down the path of voice-actuated device control.

Take a look at the Jasper project through the following links:

- `http://blog.oscarliang.net/raspberry-pi-voice-recognition-works-like-siri/`

- `http://jasperproject.github.io/documentation/installation/`

- `https://teslafly.wordpress.com/2014/09/22/installing-jasper-on-the-beaglebone-black/`

Blogger and technologist Steve Hickson has also made great strides in getting voice recognition on board the RPi at `http://stevenhickson.blogspot.com/`.

Other space-related Projects

A variety of other projects using the BeagleBone Black for space-related purposes are underway. Here are a few:

- NASA's ice rovers and the BeagleBone Black: NASA's Jet Propulsion Lab is using the BBB in an early prototype for a rover that could be used on Jupiter's icy moon, Europa. Being tested in icy conditions in Alaska, the rover actually crawls on the under side of the ice as if it's on the ground (`https://youtu.be/sY5WQG3-3mo`). Here is a close-up of BeagleBone Black inside the ice rover:

Credit: NASA/JPL.

Here, you can see an ice rover about to descend underneath the ice.

Credit: NASA/JPL.

Here is the BBB-powered rover crawling under the ice.

Credit: NASA/JPL.

- ▶ **BeagleSat**: This is an excellent **Google Summer of Code** (**GSOC**) project developed by Niko Visnjic. The objective of this work-in-progress is to send a BBB-driven sensor payload into space aboard a CubeSat, the small form factor satellite payload specification (`http://nvisnjic.com/beaglesat/`). Code for the project is also available on Github at `https://github.com/nvisnjic/BeagleSat`.

- ▶ NASA's CubeQuest challenge: For more information, refer to `http://www.nasa.gov/cubequest/details/`.

Index

A

Adafruit I/O
  URL 277
**Advanced Linux Sound Architecture
    (ALSA) 172**
airplane tracking
  RTL-SDR used 292-295
alternative script
  writing, Python used 90
AMSAT
  URL 299
antenna
  URL 296
application
  debugging remotely, from Eclipse 127-143
  debugging remotely, from GDB
    server 127-143
apt-get
  used, for installing packages 46-48
Audio Cape Rev. B 168
autotools
  arcana, URL 120
  toolset, URL 120
  utility programs 119

B

basic shell script 114, 115
Beacons
  about 262
  BBB, setting up 265-267
  simple IoT test environment, setting up 264
  smartphone, setting up 264
  URL 268

BeagleBone Black (BBB)
  about 2-4
  audio, bringing on 214, 215
  boot up 2-4
  controlling, SSH used 48, 49
  controlling, Virtual Network Computing (VNC)
    used 50-52
  display 5
  power requisites 5
  prerequisites 2
  System Reference Manual, URL 84
  URL 284
BeagleRT 211
BeagleSat
  URL 314
Bluetooth Classic
  installation troubleshooting, URL 268
  versus BTLE discussion, URL 268
Bluetooth Low Energy (BLE)
  about 261
  classic Bluetooth 261
  key elements 261
BoneScript
  about 62
  URL 68
boot time
  optimizing 145
BTLE documentation
  URL 268
Bubble app
  URL 268
button press function
  about 91-93
  using 90

C

D

Thank you for buying
BeagleBone Black Cookbook

About Packt Publishing

Packt, pronounced 'packed', published its first book, *Mastering phpMyAdmin for Effective MySQL Management*, in April 2004, and subsequently continued to specialize in publishing highly focused books on specific technologies and solutions.

Our books and publications share the experiences of your fellow IT professionals in adapting and customizing today's systems, applications, and frameworks. Our solution-based books give you the knowledge and power to customize the software and technologies you're using to get the job done. Packt books are more specific and less general than the IT books you have seen in the past. Our unique business model allows us to bring you more focused information, giving you more of what you need to know, and less of what you don't.

Packt is a modern yet unique publishing company that focuses on producing quality, cutting-edge books for communities of developers, administrators, and newbies alike. For more information, please visit our website at www.packtpub.com.

About Packt Open Source

In 2010, Packt launched two new brands, Packt Open Source and Packt Enterprise, in order to continue its focus on specialization. This book is part of the Packt open source brand, home to books published on software built around open source licenses, and offering information to anybody from advanced developers to budding web designers. The Open Source brand also runs Packt's open source Royalty Scheme, by which Packt gives a royalty to each open source project about whose software a book is sold.

Writing for Packt

We welcome all inquiries from people who are interested in authoring. Book proposals should be sent to author@packtpub.com. If your book idea is still at an early stage and you would like to discuss it first before writing a formal book proposal, then please contact us; one of our commissioning editors will get in touch with you.

We're not just looking for published authors; if you have strong technical skills but no writing experience, our experienced editors can help you develop a writing career, or simply get some additional reward for your expertise.

BeagleBone for Secret Agents

ISBN: 978-1-78398-604-0   Paperback: 162 pages

Browse anonymously, communicate secretly, and create custom security solutions with open source software, the BeagleBone Black, and cryptographic hardware

1. Interface with cryptographic hardware to add security to your embedded project, securing you from external threats.

2. Use and build applications with trusted anonymity and security software like Tor and GPG to defend your privacy and confidentiality.

3. Work with low level I/O on BeagleBone Black like I2C, GPIO, and serial interfaces to create custom hardware applications.

BeagleBone Home Automation

ISBN: 978-1-78328-573-0   Paperback: 178 pages

Live your sophisticated dream with home automation using BeagleBone

1. Practical approach to home automation using BeagleBone; starting from the very basics of GPIO control and progressing up to building a complete home automation solution.

2. Covers the operating principles of a range of useful environment sensors, including their programming and integration to the server application.

3. Easy-to-follow approach with electronics schematics, wiring diagrams, and controller code all broken down into manageable and easy-to-understand sections.

Please check **www.PacktPub.com** for information on our titles

BeagleBone Robotic Projects

ISBN: 978-1-78355-932-9   Paperback: 244 pages

Create complex and exciting robotic projects with the BeagleBone Black

1. Get to grips with robotic systems.

2. Communicate with your robot and teach it to detect and respond to its environment.

3. Develop walking, rolling, swimming, and flying robots.

Building a Home Security System with BeagleBone

ISBN: 978-1-78355-960-2   Paperback: 120 pages

Build your own high-tech alarm system at a fraction of the cost

1. Build your own state-of-the-art security system.

2. Monitor your system from anywhere you can receive e-mail.

3. Add control of other systems such as sprinklers and gates.

4. Save thousands on monitoring and rental fees.

Please check **www.PacktPub.com** for information on our titles

www.ingramcontent.com/pod-product-compliance
Lightning Source LLC
LaVergne TN
LVHW081332050326
832903LV00024B/1131